Marilyn Monroe

ALSO BY MICHELLE VOGEL
AND FROM MCFARLAND

Lupe Vélez: The Life and Career of Hollywood's "Mexican Spitfire" (2012)

Marjorie Main: The Life and Films of Hollywood's "Ma Kettle" (2011 [2006])

Gene Tierney: A Biography (2011 [2005])

Olive Borden: The Life and Films of Hollywood's "Joy Girl" (2010)

Olive Thomas: The Life and Death of a Silent Film Beauty (2007)

Children of Hollywood: Accounts of Growing Up as the Sons and Daughters of Stars (2005)

Marilyn Monroe
Her Films, Her Life

MICHELLE VOGEL
Foreword by GEORGE CHAKIRIS

McFarland & Company, Inc., Publishers
Jefferson, North Carolina

LIBRARY OF CONGRESS CATALOGUING-IN-PUBLICATION DATA

Vogel, Michelle, 1972–
Marilyn Monroe : her films, her life / Michelle Vogel ;
foreword by George Chakiris.
p.   cm.
Includes bibliographical references and index.

ISBN 978-0-7864-7086-0 (softcover : acid free paper) ∞
ISBN 978-1-4766-1359-8 (ebook)

1. Monroe, Marilyn, 1926–1962.   2. Motion picture actors
and actresses—United States—Biography.   I. Title.
PN2287.M69V64 2014   791.4302'8092—dc23   [B]   2014007859

BRITISH LIBRARY CATALOGUING DATA ARE AVAILABLE

© 2014 Michelle Vogel. All rights reserved

*No part of this book may be reproduced or transmitted in any form
or by any means, electronic or mechanical, including photocopying
or recording, or by any information storage and retrieval system,
without permission in writing from the publisher.*

On the cover: Marilyn Monroe in the 1953 film *Gentlemen Prefer Blondes*
(Twentieth Century–Fox Film Corporation/Photofest)

*No part of this book may be reproduced or transmitted in any form
or by any means, electronic or mechanical, including photocopying
or recording, or by any information storage and retrieval system,
without permission in writing from the publisher.*

Printed in the United States of America

*McFarland & Company, Inc., Publishers
Box 611, Jefferson, North Carolina 28640
www.mcfarlandpub.com*

Acknowledgments

Many thanks to Christelle Montagner, Luke Yankee, Bill Cappello, Bill Doyle, Paul Green, G.D. Hamann, Gregg Nystrom, James Robert Parish, Kristine Krueger, Greg Schreiner, Ned Comstock, Marian Collier Neuman, Scott Fortner, Jeff Stafford, Elisa Jordan, Michelle Morgan, George Bailey, Laura Petersen Balogh, Christoper Riordan, Angela Allen, Mary Mallory, Jonathon Auxier and Lois Smith.

As always, special thanks to my inner circle: My husband, Matt, our son, Ryan, my parents, Pam and Bob, and my cousin-in-law and friend, Jill, for *always* supporting me and encouraging me in my writing decisions, no matter what.

And to George Chakiris for his willingness to share his Marilyn Monroe memories throughout the book, including the foreword. I'm truly honored that our names share the cover.

Thank you to the following institutions: AMPAS (Margaret Herrick Library), University of Southern California (USC, Cinema-Television Library, Warner Bros. Archive) and the University of California (UCLA, Los Angeles), National Library of Australia.

Table of Contents

Acknowledgments
v

Foreword by George Chakiris
1

Preface
3

Introduction
7

The Travilla Effect
21

Filmography
29

Extra Parts ... and Missed Opportunities
179

Bibliography
197

Index
203

Marilyn's type dates as far back as I can remember. I'm not saying it isn't good. But she is a prototype of all the platinum blonds, curvy bundles and frothy frippery that the screen has ever seen.

—Alfred Hitchcock, *Stars and Stripes*, July 24, 1954

Foreword
by George Chakiris

Michelle Vogel gives wonderful insight into Marilyn Monroe's personal life while connecting her life to the films she made. This book makes us feel present, engaged and involved.

I was privileged to appear as a chorus dancer in two films with Marilyn Monroe, *Gentlemen Prefer Blondes* and *There's No Business Like Show Business*. She was a serious and dedicated artist. There was something special about the way she worked that made me reflect on the experience long after it was over. She captured my imagination.

Marilyn Monroe was so beautifully creative in her performance as Lorelei Lee in *Gentlemen Prefer Blondes* that people still seem unable to separate the performer from the performance. That's the type of artist Marilyn Monroe was. She felt a strong obligation to her audience, and in turn, the audience connected strongly to her. She treasured and honored that connection. She kept her audience in mind at all times. We know now that she was more than able to please her audience, and still remain true to herself. She knew (better than anyone else) exactly who Marilyn Monroe was ... and exactly who Norma Jeane was too. She was aware of the person she became, the person she used to be, the artist, the expectations of her fans and her place in the grand scheme of things. She had a great instinct and a keen, intelligent view of her work and career. She was very brave. Any advice and direction had to be true to her values and work ethic. She had great integrity.

Our personal experiences often influence our work, especially in creative fields such as acting, singing, and dancing. That self-expression can be very freeing. When I see Marilyn Monroe on the screen I always care very much about her, and the characters she played. The artist on the screen is someone I respect and admire.

As time has passed, we have continued to be fascinated by her. She deserves that fascination, that admiration, that respect. She definitely earned it. She had style—in spades. To this day, I admire her talent, her musical gifts and her work as an actress and entertainer.

When much that surrounds her might weather, she remains fresh, beautiful, uplifting to watch ... again and again. Some fifty years after her death, Marilyn Monroe is always contemporary—always now!

George Chakiris is a singer, dancer and actor with an international career in film, television and theater. In 1962, he won an Academy Award (Best Supporting Actor) and a Golden Globe award for his role as Bernardo, leader of the Sharks gang in West Side Story.

Preface

"Marilyn Monroe was a terrible actress!"

It's a statement I've heard many times, and generally it stems from ignorance rather than any solid foundation for those harsh words. After I inquire further, the clueless naysayer usually confesses to seeing only one, maybe two Marilyn Monroe films—sometimes *none at all*. Discrediting her entire body of work, especially based on such limited knowledge, is ludicrous. Yet it's an all too common occurrence.

This book was written around the fiftieth anniversary of Marilyn Monroe's passing. While I've endeavored to give readers a thorough study of her film career, an aspect of her life that is too often underappreciated and overlooked, it would be remiss of me to discount the mysterious and disturbing circumstances associated with her death. The following pages will deal with her tragic end. I'll then take you all the way back to the very beginning—her harrowing childhood and teenage years as a young wife, successful model and popular World War II pinup and cover girl.

Hundreds of books have been published about the many facets of Monroe's life, but her natural talent as an actress and all-around performer is too often dismissed as a footnote, weaved into an amalgamation of complex emotional and physical maladies, powerful men who used and abused her and, of course, her untimely end that to this day is shrouded in mystery.

Insecure, self-conscious and filled with anxieties because of her traumatic past, Monroe was damaged goods. For much of her young life, she was passed around like a stray dog, given shelter and fed for a while, then hustled along to the next home … and the next. From a very early age, she learned that she was a disposable commodity. Though she knew it, she never got used to it and she never got over it. Even at the height of her fame, both professionally and personally, she often felt disposable and was often treated as such. Some things never changed.

From her earliest days in Hollywood, Monroe diligently studied the craft of acting and she continued to do so throughout the course of her career. Her desire to constantly better herself enabled her to attain monumental success. She had a strong work ethic and a love of learning (she was an avid reader), yet her obsessive need for perfection caused many imperfections to surface. Her inability to believe in the quality of her own performances made her appear lax and unprofessional on set. That is, when she got to set.

She was tardy when she was a starlet and nothing changed when she became a bonafide movie star. Everyone worked on "Marilyn time." But there was no diva-like behavior associated with her lateness or inability to remember her lines. In reality, her innate shyness often caused her to be physically sick before a scene. Locked in her dressing room, Monroe, the sexiest woman in the world, an icon in the making, was riddled with angst, literally throwing up at the thought of having to perform, and at the same time, getting a reputation for being an unprofessional train wreck who disrespected her colleagues and her studio. Nothing was further from the truth. Her burgeoning "reputation" in the industry served to worsen her insecurities. It was a vicious cycle. As her star power increased, the pressure to perform and the pressure of the success or failure of the film riding on *her* performance caused her to put off the inevitable: stepping in front of the camera. She was contracted to do a film and the film was budgeted for dollars and days, but her fear of failure paralyzed her.

After her firing on *Something's Got to Give*, an August 12, 1962, article in the Louisiana paper the *Advocate* included a harsh quote from an unnamed director who had previously worked with her. "She simply doesn't belong in the business," he said. "Most of her ills are psychosomatic. They originate out of her basic insecurity, her nagging, ever-present self-doubt, the feeling that she has in her heart and mind that as an actress she's a fraud." The *Advocate* published the article soon after Monroe's death but the director quotes her in the present tense, so obviously he made those comments while she was still alive, probably sometime in the rocky few weeks between her firing and rehiring on the film.

Monroe truly believed that her days off were justified. That she was too sick to work. That she *couldn't* work. Upon her return to a set, she would often write notes of apology and pass them out to the cast and crew members, begging for their forgiveness and pleading with them to believe that she was "really sick" and unable to work. These late arrivals and no-shows were frequent, and even when she *was* "really sick," few believed her. She was the girl who cried wolf. When pills and booze were incorporated to help her sleep and to pep her back up again, it was nothing more than doctor-prescribed self-destruction.

Monroe's drug use *wasn't* recreational. The pills she took were prescribed to either alleviate or control a medical condition, and she was often plagued with multiple issues at once. Throughout her life, Monroe was treated for insomnia, severe respiratory infections, anxiety and depression and the chronic pain associated with the gynecological condition known as endometriosis, the latter being the likeliest reason (along with her drug and alcohol intake) for her multiple miscarriages. Since many of these conditions were treated at the same time, Monroe was consuming a cocktail of drugs (often washed down with alcohol) on a daily basis—for years.

It's no secret that disturbing memories of early abandonment, as well as childhood mental and sexual abuse, left her with emotional scars that ran deep. Her success as an actress did nothing to heal her wounds; in fact, it only served to open them a little further. It's clear that Monroe's past affected her in a myriad of ways, but the frequent focus on the negatives, most of which I'll touch on, do nothing more than label her as a lifelong victim.

Monroe achieved a level of fame during her lifetime (and beyond) that few people in *history* have equaled, or will *ever* equal. It wasn't by accident, it had little to do with luck and it certainly wasn't because she was a victim. Yet, in death, it's incredibly sad, and somewhat ironic, that she appears to have finally been deserving of the label so often given her. With all the evidence stacked up, it appears that she *was* most likely a victim ... a victim of murder.

Twenty years after Monroe's death, Los Angeles County District Attorney John Van de Kamp concluded a four-month inquiry that was sparked by a Los Angeles private detective's claims that Monroe was murdered by "a dissident faction of the CIA" or a similar group. Van de Kamp came to the conclusion that no evidence was found to warrant a criminal investigation. Within his 29-page report, he said, "Miss Monroe's murder would have required a massive, in-place conspiracy covering all the principals at the death scene…[including] the actual killer or killers; the chief medical examiner-coroner, the autopsy surgeon to whom the case was fortuitously assigned and most all of the police officers assigned to the case as well as their superiors in the LAPD" ("DA Rules Out Murder Plot in Marilyn Monroe").

No matter how many investigations and inquiries into her death arise, each conclusion is merely an opinion. The truth remains a mystery, and that's part of the reason why, to this day, her death remains an enigma.

As the book's title suggests, its main focus is Monroe's film career. As well as a cast and crew list, technical specifications, production and promotional details and a synopsis for each production, there will be coverage of events in her personal life during the making of each movie. Monroe's professional and personal lives were very much intertwined, and what happened on-screen was directly affected by what was happening off-screen. While her personal highs and lows will be included, this book is essentially a "go-to guide" for readers wanting to learn more about her films and the drama that often occurred behind the scenes.

Though her transformation from Norma Jeane to Marilyn was worlds apart, in both phases of her life, nothing ever came easy.

Introduction

Five decades have passed since that historic August 5, 1962, morning, when at thirty-six years old, the most famous woman in the world was found lying naked in her bed, face down with one hand outstretched and clutching her bedside telephone. Her last desperate call for help had come too late. She had taken her last breath. Marilyn Monroe was dead.

"Acute barbiturate poisoning, ingestion of overdose" resulting from a "probable suicide" was the conclusion by coroner Thomas Noguchi. However, the conspiracy theories surrounding her death have ranged from accidental overdose to cold-blooded murder. With all the evidence stacked up, suicide is the most unlikely conclusion, but the conspiracy theories and the list of suspects involved reads like a real-life game of Clue.

Accidental overdose: not by Monroe herself, but a miscommunication between her doctors Ralph Greenson (psychiatrist) and Hyman Engelberg (internist) saw them both prescribing large doses of medication at the same time, without the other's knowledge. On August 4, 1962, Dr. Greenson had a six-hour therapy session with Monroe. It's long been suggested that he was unaware that she had been taking Nembutal throughout the day, but given the fact that he was with her for much of that day, it's inconceivable to think that he could be that oblivious to her actions. In the evening, the chloral hydrate enema that in all likelihood was administered by her housekeeper Eunice Murray, at the direction of Dr. Greenson, proved fatal. An accidental overdose due to medical misconduct is an entirely believable scenario.

Murder: Mafia don Sam Giancana, Teamsters boss Jimmy Hoffa and a government agency (the CIA and/or FBI) have all been suggested as possible murder suspects (Monroe's home was said to have been wiretapped). John and Robert Kennedy have been implicated in the most controversial and high-profile unsolved murder case of all time. Monroe had affairs with both men, knew too much and had made several threats to reveal information that would affect, if not destroy, their political careers. Whether any of these individuals were involved, either directly or indirectly, in Monroe's death is still up for debate, and after all these years, it most probably always will be. However, what is known is that the Kennedy brothers had broken all ties with Monroe. She was a scorned woman. She felt used … and she wanted revenge.

In the days prior to her death, Monroe had foolishly threatened the Kennedy brothers by telling them she was going to call a press conference to "reveal all" and expose their "secrets." A decade after Monroe's death, Eunice Murray admitted that actor Peter Lawford, brother-in-law of John and Robert Kennedy (Lawford was married to their sister, Pat), was at Monroe's home prior to her death, but he wasn't alone. Robert Kennedy accompanied him. Murray said that Kennedy and Monroe had "heated words" before he finally left (www.mysterioustimes.net).

Just hours after they left, Monroe's body was found. Robert flew out of Los Angeles County and Lawford returned to Monroe's house before police were notified of her death to do some "tidying up" and to remove any evidence of a relationship that Monroe and the Kennedy brothers had. It was a well-thought-out plan and the number of people involved was mind-blowing. Many of the witnesses have since died. Their often-told, ever-changing stories gelled well enough together so as not to indict anyone, but not well enough to allay suspicion.

In a mid–1950s diary entry, Monroe mentioned "a feeling of violence I've had lately, about being afraid of Peter [Lawford], he might harm me, poison me, etc. why—strange look in his eyes—strange behavior." She said she feels "uneasy at different times with him," and that she believes him to be "homosexual," even concluding that, "Peter wants to be a woman—and would like to be me—I think" (*Vanity Fair*, November 2010).

It's been suggested that the delay in notifying police of Monroe's death was to give Robert Kennedy enough time to fly far enough away to avoid implication. According to Lawford's ex-wife Deborah Gould (they were married for two months), Kennedy chartered a helicopter to San Francisco that night and Lawford went to Monroe's house to clean up the mess (Summers, p. 471).

In the meantime, while Monroe's body still lay in her bedroom, housekeeper Murray packed her bags, called an interior decorator to fix the broken window in Monroe's room and had both the washer and dryer running in the service porch that was located just off the kitchen. Murray told Sgt. Jack Clemmons that the window in Monroe's room was broken (from the outside) to gain access because her bedroom door was supposedly locked. A fine story, except the glass from the broken window lay on the ground outside, a clear indication that the window was broken from the *inside*. The evidence debunks Murray's version of events. And it was only the beginning. Her version of events changed often.

Without doubt, Monroe had gotten in way too deep with a variety of *very* powerful people. The type of people who had the means and the motive to get rid of her *if* she posed a threat. And, whenever she felt wronged or betrayed, as she certainly did with both Kennedy brothers, she made threats. Monroe made several phone calls on the night of her death, yet her phone records inexplicably vanished into thin air, thus protecting the identities of the people she called (and associated with), fueling the conspiracy-theory fire. Her infamous red diary, which had detailed accounts of everything she did, and with whom, also disappeared. Despite large monetary offers for its return, it has never resurfaced. Within those pages certain private conversations were supposedly noted in detail, including those she had with Robert Kennedy about CIA plans to poison Cuban dictator Fidel Castro, with gangster Sam Giancana's help. She also detailed the government's investigation into union leader Jimmy Hoffa's Mafia links. When Robert Kennedy told her which mobsters they were going after, Monroe passed the information on to Frank Sinatra, who has long been suspected of strong Mafia ties ("Joe DiMaggio Died Convinced JFK Had Monroe Killed," February 11, 2003). Further supporting this fact, Monroe's little white dog was named "Maf," a tongue-in-cheek reference to Sinatra's Mafia connections. Following Monroe's death, "Maf" was adopted by Sinatra's secretary, Gloria Lovell. He was hit and killed by a car soon after.

Despite Monroe's perilous link to the Mafia world, DiMaggio's son Joe Jr. said his father staunchly believed the Kennedys killed her. DiMaggio also thought it was conceivable that both JFK and Bobby Kennedy were victims of orchestrated mob killings. Following each of the Kennedy brothers' deaths, while the rest of the world mourned, DiMaggio told his son that they got what they deserved. DiMaggio's hatred for the Kennedys ran deep, so on September 18, 1965, many wondered what would happen when DiMaggio and Robert Kennedy came face-to-face at Yankee Stadium for a Mickey Mantle tribute. The tense moment was recounted in *DiMaggio: Setting the Record Straight* (Engelberg and Schneider, p. 282, 283).

Kennedy was among those on the field when DiMaggio was introduced. Joe strode from the dugout, shook hands with the others on the field, and walked past Bobby as if he weren't there. It was a snub witnessed by a huge audience, both at the stadium and on television.

> Decades later, when DiMaggio was invited to appear at a charity event at the Kennedy Center in Washington, he only agreed to accept the invite if he was assured that no Kennedy would be there. When he was asked why he would bar family members who had never harmed him, he said, "It's in their blood, and what they did to me will never be forgotten. They murdered the one person I loved."

Monroe suffered from frequent mood swings, recurring anxiety, paranoia and depression, as well as chronic insomnia throughout her adult life. She was surrounded by enablers and she had become addicted to potent barbiturates (doctor-prescribed) that she would often mix with alcohol in an effort to get to sleep. Additionally, she would immerse herself in lengthy, emotionally draining psychoanalysis sessions, sometimes twice a day, with Dr. Greenson, an attempt on her part to talk everything out and better understand her current state of being.

Whenever her moods faltered, she feared that, like family members on her mother's side, she was going insane. The very thought of a genetic pre-disposition to mental illness was an ingrained paranoia that often heightened her nervous state, sending her into even deeper depression. As Monroe got older and her insomnia got worse, more pills were the answer—or so she thought. The increased drug intake affected her work ethic and often left her with slurred speech and an inability to stay on schedule.

The one consistency throughout her working life was that she was always late. It was a habit that irked her colleagues, infuriated her directors and caused productions to run over schedule and budget. To be fair, there were many times when her absences were understandable. Various illnesses (including multiple pregnancies that ended in miscarriages, some that were never publicly reported) prevented her from working, but her tardiness was frequently due to excessive pill and alcohol consumption. Chronic anxiety attacks would prevent her from being able to turn "Marilyn Monroe" on for the cameras. And on these days, she just wouldn't show up at all. Despite her reputation for being "one" with the camera, Monroe was often paralyzed with fear at the thought of walking onto a film set and performing. She often insisted on closed sets and she was unable to act if someone off-camera was in her line of sight. The side effects of her excessive drug and alcohol abuse left her unable to remember the simplest of lines.

At her worst, she needed as many as fifty takes. At her best, she could nail a lengthy scene in a single take. The inconsistencies were *that* extreme. But as nerve-wracked as Monroe's colleagues were after shooting a film with her, they were able to walk away and eventually recover from the experience. For Monroe, those extreme inconsistencies, on multiple levels, were her life. There was no walking away. No recovery. Sleep was her one escape, and even that was hard to come by.

Purposefully or not, Monroe had overdosed several times throughout her life, but at the time of her death, she had been rehired by Fox (at a much higher salary and with her choice of director) to finish *Something's Got to Give* (1962). She had recently moved into a new home, and she had several social engagements and promising film roles lined up. By all reports, she was in good spirits and looking forward to the future. It was entirely possible that she could have taken her own life, but not probable.

The facts: There was no glass in her bedroom and no running water in the nearby bathroom (her home was in the middle of an extensive renovation and the water was turned off) for Monroe to take the fifty-something pills that was suggested in the autopsy report. There were *no* pills in her digestive tract or stomach and there were no needle marks. Nothing appeared to have been injected, or so the autopsy report states. Yet another discrepancy arises here. Monroe had been getting frequent "vitamin shots" (the last of which was administered on August 3) from Dr. Engelberg. There *had* to be needle marks on her body somewhere. Additionally, the so-called "vitamin shots" caused Monroe to act and appear "high." Clearly, the frequent injections contained something far more potent than vitamins (Spoto, p. 626).

With the erroneous medical observation that no evidence of needle marks were present on Monroe's body, that meant the Nembutal and Chloral Hydrate had to have been administered anally. A self-administered overdose via an enema? Not likely.

Despite there being no evidence of pills in Monroe's system, "oral ingestion" was still the final conclusion. Oral ingestion of fifty-plus pills by a woman who was known to have trouble swallowing pills *with* water, and there was no accessible water available to her? Monroe had 4.5 milligrams percentage of Pentobarbital (Nembutal) and 8.0 milligrams percentage of Chloral Hydrate in her bloodstream. Her liver had 13 milligrams percentage of Pentobarbital. These levels are high enough to indicate that an overdose via injection occurred.

It also appeared as though Monroe's body had been moved (her back was marked and bruised, indicating that she had either fallen onto her back, or perhaps rigorous CPR was given to her on the floor) and the death scene staged to look like a suicide. The evidence in relation to Monroe's death and the hours leading up to it, and afterwards, points to anything but suicide. Based on signs of lividity, her actual time of death was estimated to be between 10 and 10:30 p.m. on the evening of August 4, 1962. From the time her body was discovered, it took over four hours for police to be called to Monroe's home. Why?

At approximately 4 a.m. on August 5, Sgt. Jack Clemmons of the Los Angeles Police Department was the first officer on the scene. Interviewed repeatedly over the years, he adamantly stated that he believed that "somebody murdered her. It was an out-and-out case of murder!" (Slatzer, p. 240).

However, the cover-up was firmly in place before he arrived at Monroe's home in those early morning hours. Despite evidence suggesting otherwise, the "suicide" ruling had been decided upon before Clemmons even walked in the door.

Over the years, there have been many unanswered questions. Disappearing evidence, doctored records, missing lab samples, conflicting accounts of her last day from those who knew her, the list goes on and on. Then, there were the two high-profile murders that occurred soon after: the assassination of President John F. Kennedy on November 22, 1963, a little over a year after Monroe's death, and the assassination of his brother, Senator Robert F. Kennedy, on June 6, 1968. Within a six-year period, Marilyn Monroe and the Kennedy brothers were all dead.

Coincidence? Probably not.

Not satisfied with the "probable suicide" conclusion, Deputy Coroner Lionel Grandison said that despite his strong misgivings, he was forced to sign Monroe's death certificate under protest. In 1978, he revealed that there were numerous bruises on Monroe's body that weren't listed on the autopsy report, suggesting a violent struggle prior to her death. He also claimed that one or more necrophiles employed at the county morgue had sexually violated Monroe's corpse before it was released for burial (Aggrawal, p. 16).

Additionally, tissue samples from the kidney, stomach, liver and intestines, sent to the lab by Dr. Noguchi for further testing, all very conveniently went missing. Grandison said:

> The whole thing was organized to hide the truth. An original autopsy file vanished, a scrawled note that Marilyn Monroe wrote and which did not speak of suicide also vanished, and so did [Sgt. Clemmons's] police report. I was told to sign the official report—or I'd find myself in a position I couldn't get out of [www.trivia-library.com].

While her controversial death has elevated her mystique to a whole other level, Monroe's universal appeal as a model, actress, singer, dancer, sex symbol and Hollywood icon is far greater than she could have ever imagined. Until her groundbreaking contract renewal following the formation of Marilyn Monroe Productions, without doubt, Monroe was one of the worst paid actresses in Hollywood history. Yet ironically, in death, she has become one of Hollywood's most prolific moneymakers. Fifty years on, there's no sign of the value of her likeness and image taking a nosedive. In 2011, *Forbes*' richest dead celebrity list listed Monroe as the third highest money earner for that year. At $27 million, she came in behind Michael Jackson and Elvis Presley.

* * *

After the end of their nine-month marriage, Monroe and DiMaggio were close; DiMaggio was Monroe's savior during many difficult times. During the last years of her life, she realized he was the man she was meant to be with—forever. Some say they were heading for a second shot at marriage and were even engaged at the time of Monroe's death. Actress Jane Russell, her co-star in *Gentlemen Prefer Blondes* (1953), confirmed this: "Right before [Monroe] died, she was planning to marry Joe DiMaggio, her second husband, again, and she had a new movie contract. So I don't think she killed herself. Someone did it for her. There were dirty tricks somewhere." When reporter Wendy Leigh asked if Russell was suggesting that Jack and Bobby Kennedy were possibly the main suspects, she nodded darkly, saying, "Soon after Marilyn died, I met Bobby Kennedy and he looked at me as if to say: 'I am your enemy'" (Leigh, "Jane Russell: My Friend Marilyn Did Not Kill Herself").

On the day she married DiMaggio, Monroe made a bizarre request: If she were to die before him, she asked that DiMaggio leave flowers on her grave every week. Despite their tumultuous relationship and subsequent divorce, DiMaggio kept that wedding day promise, not forever, but for twenty years (until September 1, 1982). At an estimated cost of between

$500 and $850 per year, he ensured that six red roses were delivered twice a week to his ex-wife's crypt in the Corridor of Memories at Westwood Memorial Park in Los Angeles.

When told of Marilyn's death, her mother Gladys showed no emotion, for she had no memory of Norma Jeane, or of the movie star that she had become. Due to the mental incapacity of Monroe's mother, the simplest of chores was impossible for her to undertake, so planning her iconic daughter's funeral arrangements was out of the question. A few years following her daughter's death, Gladys was released from institutional care and was well enough to work at a nursing home. She moved to Florida to be closer to her last living child, Berniece Miracle, and she died on March 11, 1984, of heart failure. She was eighty-two years old.

Monroe's half-sister Berniece agreed that DiMaggio would be the right person to identify the body and take charge of funeral arrangements. Despite their short-lived marriage, DiMaggio was a mainstay in Monroe's life. He was trusted to carry out Monroe's final wishes in a loving and respectful way. Monroe's long-time business manager Inez Melson helped DiMaggio compile the list of funeral attendees. And there weren't many. Though thousands would have come, if allowed, only thirty-one people were invited to the private service. In doing so, DiMaggio and Melson prevented Monroe's final exit from turning into the Hollywood circus it inevitably would have become.

Monroe's first husband, Jim Dougherty, at the time a member of the Los Angeles Police Department, was working on the day of her funeral and didn't attend. Her third husband, Arthur Miller, declined the invitation. Dean Martin, who stood his ground and staunchly supported Monroe during the *Something's Got to Give* dispute (even though his agent admitted his stance was self-serving), wasn't invited. Despite the snub, he showed up to pay his respects anyway. He was turned away at the gate, as were Frank Sinatra, Peter Lawford, Sammy Davis, Jr., and others.

The police presence was strong and DiMaggio gave strict instructions not to admit anyone who wasn't invited, no matter how famous they were. DiMaggio believed that many of these "Hollywood types" and hangers-on had somehow morally played a part in Monroe's fatal downfall and he hated them for it.

Lying in an open bronze casket that was lined with champagne satin, Monroe was dressed in a green Pucci dress and her neck was adorned with her favorite chiffon scarf. The invasive autopsy had caused such damage to her scalp, it was decided that she should wear a platinum blonde wig, the one she wore in *The Misfits*. With a heavy heart, her longtime makeup artist and friend Allan "Whitey" Snyder did her makeup for the very last time. He later admitted it took an entire flask of gin to get him through the traumatic experience. Doing Monroe's post-mortem makeup was a promise he jokingly made to her years before; Monroe playfully reminded him of it when gifting him with a gold money clip that carried the inscription, "Whitey Dear, While I'm still warm, Marilyn." Like DiMaggio, Snyder was a man of his word, a devoted friend and confidante. As difficult as it was for him, he kept his promise, making her beautiful for one last time—for all eternity.

DiMaggio refused to leave Monroe's side for the entire night before her funeral. Kneeling beside her casket throughout their final night together, he was determined not to leave her until he had to, only doing so the following morning to shower and change into his dark blue suit for the funeral service. DiMaggio's son (Monroe's stepson) Joe Jr. wore his Marine uniform. Both men solemnly walked side by side behind the hearse.

Following the 1 p.m. service at the Westwood Village Mortuary Chapel in Westwood Memorial Cemetery on August 8, 1962, DiMaggio, weeping uncontrollably, leaned over Monroe's body, placed a posy of pink teacup roses in her hands, kissed her for the very last time and tearfully mumbled, "I love you, I love you, I love you" (Cramer, p. 419).

Monroe had requested that Judy Garland's "Somewhere Over the Rainbow" be played at her funeral service, and DiMaggio made sure it was. Her acting coach Lee Strasberg read a touching five-minute eulogy. He ended with:

> I cannot say goodbye. Marilyn never liked goodbyes, but in that peculiar way she had of turning things around so that they face reality—I will say au revoir. For the country to which she has gone, we must all someday visit.

Ironically, the day of her funeral was the same day that many believed DiMaggio and Monroe had chosen to remarry. DiMaggio mourned her loss for the rest of his life. He never remarried.

From Norma Jeane to Marilyn, Monroe almost had a dual existence, two lives in one that were split somewhere down the middle. The same could be said for DiMaggio. "The Yankee Clipper" was a legend in his own right. His high-profile baseball career with the New York Yankees, and later his role as "Mr. Marilyn Monroe," gave him two diverse life chapters. Joe DiMaggio passed away from lung cancer at age 84 on March 8, 1999. Almost four decades following Monroe's death, he took solace in his own imminent passing for one reason: According to his lawyer, DiMaggio's last words were, "I'll finally get to see Marilyn" (Engelberg, Schneider, p. 239).

In a 1987 TV interview, actor Tom Ewell confessed that of all the people in the world that he would have liked to have seen Monroe stay with, it was Joe DiMaggio. "Joe was a wonderful man," he said. "She loved him and he loved her." During the filming of *The Seven Year Itch* (1955), their smash hit film together, and afterward, Ewell also admitted *his* love for her. Agreeing with the interviewer's assessment of Monroe being "an incredible creature," Ewell concluded, "And she had a lousy shot at life."

Monroe's death is just part of the complex puzzle that makes up the story of her life. No matter how popular she became, she carried an inherent sense of sorrow, a soulful sadness, ingrained so deep that no amount of public adoration would heal her. At her peak, she was loved and wanted by the world; yet as a child, she was shuttled from one foster family to the next. The identity of her father was a mystery, and her mother was insane and institutionalized for years at a time. Despite the eventual worship of millions, her biological family, the people who were supposed to love her, no matter what—didn't. Or couldn't. The love and veneration of a world of strangers never made up for that loss.

Monroe married three times, and each union ended in divorce. Monroe's marriage to Joe DiMaggio is considered her second, but it's been alleged that she was married to author Robert Slatzer (1927–2005) for a few days during October of 1952. A quickie wedding in Mexico was supposedly followed by an annulment ordered by Twentieth Century–Fox production chief Darryl F. Zanuck, who insisted that the image of his star would be compromised if she was thought of as a married woman. Supposedly, all documents proving the union were destroyed. Many Monroe biographers doubt Slatzer's claim that he was briefly Mr. Monroe.

A history of gynecological problems and multiple miscarriages robbed her of her own children, but she remained in close contact with her stepchildren. Joe DiMaggio, Jr., was one

Joe DiMaggio's New York Yankees career was already a couple of years behind him by the time he married Marilyn on January 14, 1954. By then he was used to his own intense fame, but phase two of his life was so embroiled in being "Mr. Marilyn Monroe" that his explosive temper, intense jealousy and hatred of Hollywood and its "show business types" ensured their marriage would end before they ever had a chance to celebrate their first wedding anniversary. Despite the post-divorce years, DiMaggio became one of Monroe's most loyal supporters (Library of Congress).

of the last people to speak with her, telephoning her on the evening of August 4, 1962, a few hours before her death; he called to inform her of his broken engagement. Isadore Miller, father of Arthur Miller, adored his one time daughter-in-law. They remained close and she continued to call him "Dad" even following her divorce. He even accompanied her to JFK's Presidential Birthday Gala on May 19, 1962. She often wrote to Miller's children when they were away at summer camp. Playful, funny, informative letters, sometimes written in the voice of one of the various pets she owned, were solid proof that she was a faithful and dedicated woman, capable of real love and desperate for a family, no matter how it came to be. On the other hand, she could also be incredibly fickle. It wasn't beyond her to cut people off without an explanation.

* * *

On June 1, 1926, Norma Jeane Mortenson was born in the Los Angeles General Hospital's charity ward to an attractive Hollywood film cutter, Gladys Baker Mortenson. She was baptized Norma Jeane Baker. Her mother's mental illness (a combination of post-partum depression and paranoid schizophrenia) necessitated lengthy stays in psychiatric institutions. The kidnapping of Gladys' first two children, a son and a daughter, by her abusive, alcoholic ex-husband Jasper Baker did nothing to help her state of mind.

On June 13, just twelve days after her birth, Norma Jeane was put into the care of a deeply religious couple, Ida and Albert Wayne Bolender, neighbors of her maternal grandmother Della. Albert was a postman and Ida devoted her time to taking care of the various foster children who came to them. Ida was a strong-minded woman, a strict but fair mother figure. Albert had a softer side and took such a shine to Norma Jeane, he considered her his daughter. The Bolenders lived comfortably on a small property located in Hawthorne, California. Gladys paid the couple about $25 per month to take care of Norma Jeane and she was in their care for about seven years.

In June 1933, just after Gladys was released from her latest long-term hospital stay she collected her daughter. But, for Norma Jeane, the Bolenders represented home. Though Gladys visited her daughter when she could, she was quiet and distant. The Bolenders were the only "family" she knew, and now this strange woman (who sometimes visited), her mother, appeared from nowhere and told her to pack up her things and come with her. Norma Jeane did as she was told but the incident was catastrophic for the entire household. Thinking they too would be ripped from the security of the Bolender household, the other children living in the home hid in the bedroom closets. The Bolenders were inconsolable. They had dearly wanted to adopt Norma Jeane, just as they had legally adopted a baby boy, Lester, the son of a seventeen-year-old. Ida would often lovingly refer to Lester and Norma Jeane as "the twins" because they looked so much like biological siblings and were almost exactly the same age. Now, the entire family was being ripped apart. Other foster siblings during Norma Jeane's stay were Mumsey, Alvina, Noel and Nancy. Norma Jeane's years with the Bolenders were the closest she ever came to a functional family environment.

While many accounts of Norma Jeane's childhood paint an extremely grim picture of poverty and misery, the hard times only came *after* leaving the Bolenders' care. With them she had love, stability, and food on the table. There were other children to play with, nice clothes, music lessons and plenty of pets. Her favorite was a loyal dog "Tippy," gifted to her by her foster father, Albert. The little black and white dog was Norma Jeane's shadow, following her everywhere, even to school. Norma Jeane was brokenhearted when a neighbor of the Bolenders shot the dog for rolling around in his garden.

Within months of collecting Norma Jeane from the Bolenders, Gladys was back in the hospital. Norma Jeane never returned to the Bolenders' care. Her legal guardian was now

Grace McKee Goddard, her mother's best friend. Like the Bolenders, Grace loved Norma Jeane, but unlike the Bolenders, her living environment was less than ideal and there was little stability there. The yo-yo of foster families that followed would do permanent damage to Norma Jeane and ingrain a deep fear of abandonment along with insecurities that would last a lifetime.

Following her release from the hospital, Gladys turned to Christian Science for solace. She spent hours studying the religion, paying little mind to her daughter, essentially becoming a religious fanatic. Ironically, throughout her life, Gladys was a woman who spent much of her time as a medical patient, yet she would often dress in a nurse's uniform, preach the teachings of Christian Science and insist on healing people's afflictions without the use of medicine.

Not surprising, Gladys was too fragile to exist in the outside world, let alone take care of a child. With the Bolenders gone and her mother once again institutionalized, Grace McKee Goddard would also abandon Norma Jeane. In the late summer of 1935, Grace took a frightened Norma Jeane through the front doors of the Los Angeles Orphans' Home. Her mother Gladys had already been declared "legally insane" and the state considered Norma Jeane a half-orphan because her only known parent was institutionalized. As cruel as it seemed, Grace was following the letter of the law in order to become Norma Jeane's legal guardian. The state of California required a child to reside full time in an orphanage for at least six months to a year, for evaluation. Then, if the paperwork filed was approved, Grace could take her back home with her. At least that was the plan.

Norma Jeane's orphanage file described her as "healthy and normal, with good appetite and uniform sleep. She seems happy, doesn't complain and even says she loves her classroom." By 1937, the year of her release, Norma Jeane's behavior and demeanor had changed dramatically. One assessment stated, "If she is not approached in a patient way, she looks terrified. I recommend to place her in a protective family." A February 20, 1937, assessment stated, "Sometimes she seems anxious and dull ... and then she begins to stutter. [She] is also prone to coughing fits and frequent colds... [I]f she is not treated with much patience and constantly reassured, she is prey to panic attacks..." On June 7, 1937, shortly after Norma Jeane's eleventh birthday, Grace took her back into her care. Once again, it was a temporary situation, for Grace's new husband "Doc" set his sights on Norma Jeane, making passes at her whenever he had too much to drink. Though her orphanage stay was less than ideal, Mrs. Dewey, the head of the institution, had a soft spot for Norma Jeane. In 1947, a decade after she'd left, her file was proudly updated: Mrs. Dewey wrote, "Norma Jeane Baker wins a certain success in cinema and promises to become a star. She is so beautiful and has taken an actress [*sic*] name—Marilyn Monroe."

* * *

When Norma Jeane was a year old she was almost deliberately smothered to death by Della Monroe—her grandmother! On August 4, 1927, soon after the attempted strangulation, Della was admitted to the Norwalk State Hospital. On August 23, she had a fatal heart attack during a rage attack. She was fifty-one years old. Myocarditis (inflammation of the heart) was her official cause of death. Her death certificate also states that she had contributory manic-depressive psychosis, an acute symptom that may well have come from her severe heart condition, thus causing a lack of oxygen to the brain, mirroring the same symptoms of a pre-disposed mental disorder (www.cursumperficio.net).

Della's husband, Norma Jeane's maternal grandfather Otis, lived out his final days in a mental institution. However, his insanity wasn't due to a genetic disposition to mental illness; he had contracted syphilis of the brain, known as Neurosyphilis (not sexually transmitted) from the unhygienic living conditions in Mexico, where he lived and worked. He was only forty-three years old when he died.

Norma Jeane's maternal great-grandfather, Tilford Hogan, hung himself from a barn beam when he was eighty-two years old; his ailing health and financial troubles were too much to bear. Her maternal uncle, Marion Otis Monroe (her mother's brother), was diagnosed with paranoid schizophrenia; the same illness that her mother was also said to have inherited. Married with three children, Marion left his home for work on November 20, 1929, telling his wife Olive that he'd be home by five for dinner. He never returned. The police and the Missing Persons Bureau weren't able to find him. The Shayer Detective Service in Los Angeles conducted a three-year search and also came up with nothing. He was never heard from again. A decade after his disappearance, he was declared legally dead.

Norma Jeane's mother's family had been mentally unstable for generations; and Norma Jeane was entirely convinced that she was genetically inclined to follow in their footsteps.

When Norma Jeane was about eight, she was sexually molested by a boarder in a foster home. Her abuser reportedly paid her to keep his crime a secret. While Norma Jeane eventually had the courage to tell her foster mother about the abuse, the woman (some reports suggest it was her mother) responded by slapping her face and refusing to believe her. As previously mentioned, shortly after Norma Jeane's release from the orphanage in 1937, Grace Goddard's husband "Doc" made several drunken advances toward her, and in 1938, her thirteen-year old cousin Jack Monroe raped her, while she was living with his grandmother, Ida Martin.

Through no fault of her own, Norma Jeane had been moved frequently from one foster home to the next and several of these moves were due to her being the victim of both mental and sexual abuse. Her removal from the situation further inflicted the belief that she was to blame, that she had somehow brought the abuse upon herself.

From time to time, whenever Gladys was released from the hospital, she attempted to reclaim her daughter. Unfortunately, her mental state always declined to the point of her being readmitted in worse condition than she was previously. When this happened, Norma Jeane was once again left with no one to love her and nowhere to go. Norma Jeane watched her hysterical mother being carried away to one mental hospital after another. They were images that never left her.

The negative reaction to Norma Jeane's account of being sexual abused, along with the abuse itself, together with her harrowing abandonment at the orphanage when she was nine years old, caused her to develop a chronic stutter. While she eventually conquered her speech impediment, the lasting effects of childhood rejection and neglect, night terrors, a fear of sleeping and the horrors of repeated molestations were demons that haunted Norma Jeane throughout her adult life. Had she stayed within the loving confines of the Bolender home, there's no doubt her life would have turned out differently.

While Norma Jeane's birth certificate names Gladys's second husband Martin Edward Mortensen as her father, many reliable sources concur that her father was C. Stanley Gifford, a supervisor at Consolidated Film Industries, where Gladys worked. Gladys hoped her pregnancy would hook Gifford into marrying her, but upon hearing of her impending motherhood, Gifford wanted nothing more to do with Gladys, or his child. Gladys was a soon-to-be divorcee *and* pregnant with an illegitimate child. In those days, society cruelly labeled divorced women as bad wives who couldn't keep their husbands, and unmarried mothers were as low and immoral as a common thief. Gladys fell into both categories.

Though Gifford's family members have long denied that he was Norma Jeane's father, Mortensen (the correct spelling, though his name was wrongly spelled "Mortenson" on Norma Jeane's birth certificate) had left Gladys months before Norma Jeane was even conceived. Gifford was in a relationship with Gladys during the time she became pregnant, and unless she cheated on him, he was definitely Norma Jeane's father.

It's not surprising that fantasy played a large role in Norma Jeane's young life. Her mother once told her that a photo of a man (probably Gifford) resembling Clark Gable was an image of her father. So she pretended that Gable *was* her father. Unlike her own father, she knew where she could see Gable—any time. He was often in a new film down at the movie theater. The movies were her escape. Whenever she had the opportunity to visit a darkened theater to watch her favorite actors in their latest Hollywood productions, she did.

By 1938, when Norma Jeane was 12, Grace Goddard placed her with yet another relative; this time it was her aunt, Ana Lower. Of all the homes Norma Jeane had been in, Aunt Ana's was the most secure. Ana was in her sixties, divorced and with no children of her own. Norma Jeane welcomed the religious comfort and security that came with Aunt Ana's Christian Science views. Norma Jeane lived with Aunt Ana for a few years, and then Ana's serious heart condition prevented her from staying any longer. Once again, Norma Jeane went back into the care of Grace Goddard.

In early 1942, with the country in the midst of the Second World War, Norma Jeane was now a teenager. With no one to financially support her (and no means of self-support), she was faced with yet another stint in the orphanage. A couple of weeks after her sixteenth birthday, she made a decision to prevent that from ever happening again. At the suggestion of Grace Goddard, she dropped out of high school and on June 19, 1942, married twenty-one-year-old Jim Dougherty, the handsome son of the Goddards' neighbors. Ana Lower made Norma Jeane's wedding gown. Norma Jeane and Jim had been dating exclusively for months. They look genuinely happy in their wedding photos.

At the time of their marriage, Dougherty had a steady job at an aircraft factory. In 1944, he joined the United States Merchant Marine, and he was shipped overseas the year after that. Norma Jeane moved in with her mother-in-law Ethel and got a job as a parachute inspector at the Radioplane Company, a defense plant in Van Nuys, California. Later she sprayed down the planes (in the "doper-brush" room) with a noxious varnish, a task that was less than desirable. By all accounts, she was a conscientious worker, quiet, polite and generally well-liked by her colleagues. Working a 60-hour week, her salary (minimum wage) was twenty dollars.

Some time during 1945, Army photographer David Conover toured the plant and photographed many of the women at work. He was assigned to showcase the various tasks they were doing to aid in the war effort. Along with her female counterparts, Norma Jeane was photographed in her work clothes with a spray can and a propeller in her hand. Despite the unusual props and unflattering attire, Conover instantly noticed her model potential. Norma Jeane's first photo shoot was for *Yank* magazine and she landed on the cover.

Norma Jeane left Radioplane and set her sights on a modeling career. On August 2, 1945, she signed a contract with Emmeline Snively of the Blue Book Modeling Agency. Though she was a natural in front of the camera, when she was offered modeling classes, she jumped at the opportunity to better herself. The fee was deducted from her first modeling jobs. At this point, the gradual transformation from her curly, natural brown hair color to auburn to honey blonde, and eventually platinum blonde began. She was only nineteen years old but Norma Jeane was well on her way to becoming Marilyn Monroe. Conover's discovery was the beginning of a whole new career and a path that would inevitably lead to a lucrative modeling career ... and a divorce.

Much to her mother-in-law's dismay, Norma Jeane soon became one of Blue Book's most popular models. Appearing on dozens of magazine covers, she quickly developed a type of celebrity status. Though he was still stationed overseas, Jim Dougherty made it quite clear that no wife of his would be posing in front of a camera. He wanted a housewife, not a cover girl. But Norma Jeane had come too far and had worked too hard to give up now. In order to move forward, she knew she had to go back. When Norma Jeane moved out of her mother-in-law's house, once again Ana Lower was her savior. Norma Jeane soon relocated, albeit briefly, to Nevada. In order to obtain a "quickie" divorce, the plaintiff must be a resident of that state. Norma Jeane technically complied with the law and filed a Nevada address for four months, but most of that time she was living and working as a model in Los Angeles.

On July 5, 1946, while her husband was still overseas, Norma Jeane officially filed papers to end her marriage. On September 13, a heartbroken Jim Dougherty was legally divorced from his beautiful young wife. A week before the divorce was finalized on September 5, 1946, *Daily Variety* announced that Jane Ball and Norma Jeane Dougherty had been signed to new contracts at Twentieth Century–Fox. Despite years of hardship and against all odds, for the first time in her life, Norma Jeane Dougherty was an independent, self-made, self-sufficient woman.

While fantasies and dreams had helped get her through her difficult childhood and teen years, the icon that she would become and the image that she would represent to millions of people throughout her film career, and for decades beyond her own lifetime, was incomprehensible—even to her.

The Travilla Effect

Marilyn Monroe started her professional association with leading Hollywood costume designer William Travilla (or Travilla as he was known and credited in the industry) in two 1952 productions, *Don't Bother to Knock* and *Monkey Business*. Travilla was Oscar-nominated for his work on two other Monroe films, *There's No Business Like Show Business* (1954) and *Bus Stop* (1956). For 1963's *The Stripper*, a film that Monroe turned down, he was honored with yet another nomination. Before his working relationship with Marilyn Monroe began, Travilla won an Academy Award for his work on the 1948 Technicolor feature *Adventures of Don Juan*, starring Errol Flynn.

Monroe and Travilla collaborated on eight films, including some of her biggest hits: *Don't Bother to Knock* (1952), *Monkey Business* (1952), *Gentlemen Prefer Blondes* (1953), *How to Marry a Millionaire* (1953), *There's No Business Like Show Business* (1954), *River of No Return* (1954), *The Seven Year Itch* (1955), and *Bus Stop* (1956).

At 5' 5½" and 118 pounds and with "va-va-voom" measurements of 35–22–35, whether she was donning Hollywood's finest designs or posing in her birthday suit, Marilyn Monroe was the perfect model. Fox once proved this notion, releasing the tongue-in-cheek shot (published in 1952 in *Stare* magazine) of her wearing a fringed Idaho potato sack. And yes, she *still* looked good. Monroe's voluptuous figure was often poured into her costumes, but take an in-person look at any one of her surviving film dresses, or the *Bus Stop* leotard, and you might be surprised how tiny they are. Though she's widely known for her voluptuous figure, the majority of her iconic film-worn-wardrobe was no bigger than a U.S. women's size eight. That said, pills, booze, illness and pregnancy all caused her weight to fluctuate. There were times when she was quite lean (especially apparent in her last, unfinished film, *Something's Got to Give*); she was much heavier during the latter part of *Some Like It Hot* (1959) because she was newly pregnant; her weight fluctuated the most during her marriage to Arthur Miller.

Travilla dressed Monroe off-screen too. Before she accepted her Hollywood's "Fastest Rising Star of 1952" award from *Photoplay* magazine at the Beverly Hills Hotel in 1953, Travilla helped sew her into the sheer gold lamé gown (the pleated skirt was created out of a single circle of fabric) that she had briefly worn onscreen in *Gentlemen Prefer Blondes*. The dress had no zipper. The only way in was to be sewn in. The only way out was to be cut out!

Travilla initially told Monroe that it was a costume, not a dress, and that it was "too sexy and flashy" for real life. "The gown," he said, "was designed for a quick scene to accent Marilyn's hip wiggling. When she decided to wear the dress to a Hollywood banquet, I said

Marilyn Monroe proved that she could look good in anything ... even a potato sack!

The Travilla-designed "pink dress" for Marilyn Monroe's "Diamonds Are a Girl's Best Friend" number in *Gentlemen Prefer Blondes* (1953) wasn't the original choice of costume, but after Monroe's nude calendar scandal, the risqué, jewel-encrusted showgirl bodysuit that Travilla had originally designed was nixed by the studio.

to her, 'You're a little idiot. That dress can't be worn anywhere except in front of a camera. I won't allow it out of the studio'" (*The Kingsport Times,* August 18, 1961).

Not taking no for an answer, Monroe went over his head and straight to Darryl Zanuck, who agreed to release the dress for her to wear to the awards ceremony. She promised Travilla that she'd walk like a lady. Despite her promise, Marilyn and "the dress" caused a sensation. Travilla said, "When she walked around the tables into the banquet, the roof practically caved in" (*The Kingsport Times,* August 18, 1961). Not surprisingly, she was front page news the following day. Joan Crawford was at the dinner and her harsh criticism of Monroe's choice of bold attire was printed in newspapers across the country the following day: "[Monroe] should be told that the public likes provocative feminine personalities, but it also likes to know that underneath it all the actresses are ladies…" (Quirk and Schoell, p. 166).

Off camera, Monroe was simplistic with her clothing and jewelry choices. Diamonds did nothing for her, but she adored shoes.

During the 1950s, the strict Hollywood Production Code was still in place. And Marilyn Monroe kept them very busy, with the eyes of the censors often focusing on her curves, and more importantly, if those curves were appropriately covered.

While the "Diamonds Are a Girl's Best Friend" dress is an iconic part of movie history, initially, Travilla had something entirely different in mind. He originally designed a $4,000 showgirl-esque fishnet bodysuit, adorned in jewels and with a suggestively placed jewel-encrusted chandelier type adornment at Monroe's crotch. The costume was completed with a floor-length velvet and diamond tail. It was a look that was almost the exact opposite of the strapless pink gown that we now associate with the song and Monroe's performance. It was a look the studio approved, that is, until the controversy surrounding Monroe's infamous nude calendar surfaced in 1952. The photo entitled "A New Wrinkle" was the original calendar shot. The more widely known "Golden Dreams" pose was released only *after* Monroe's identity was revealed. Fox was not about to let Monroe parade around in costumes that implied nudity and supported *that* calendar. Travilla was told to tone things down and design something that was less provocative. The result was the pink dress.

Travilla was a master at his work, an artist. Meticulously folding the pink fabric into the shape of Monroe's body, hugging every curve in just the right places, he put an envelope with a hidden zip in the center of the dress and six cotton-covered poppers held it in place on the side. The massive butterfly bow was stiffened and stuffed with ostrich feathers and horsehair, and to keep it from drooping, it was secured on each side with thread that can only be seen if you look very carefully on a closeup still shot. The bodice was extensively boned to keep Monroe's breasts from popping out the top (Finnigan, "Dressing Marilyn Monroe").

The studio went into damage control over the nude calendar scandal by initially denying the photos were of their star. Zanuck told Monroe that if the public found out that she had posed for the calendar, her career could be finished. But Monroe refused to lie about the photo and the studio relented. It was risky, but on March 13, 1952, during filming on *Monkey Business,* she bravely went ahead and released a statement. Admitting the photo session was something she did as a last resort three years earlier because she was out of work and desperately needed the money, she explained that photographer Tom Kelley had repeatedly asked her to pose nude for him but she had declined every time. However, when she lost her film contract, the bills were mounting up and she had no way of paying them. Monroe said that she picked up the phone and told Kelley that she'd do it, but only on one condition:

Opposite: Designed by Travilla, this showgirl costume was deemed too risqué for Monroe's "Diamond Are a Girl's Best Friend" number in *Gentlemen Prefer Blondes* (1953). It was eventually replaced by the strapless "pink dress" and matching glove ensemble that is now so synonymous with the performance. It was a still-sexy, but lady-like contrast to Travilla's original provocative vision.

that Kelley's wife Natalie be present at all times. It was Natalie who draped the simple red velvet backdrop for Monroe to pose upon. In a half-hearted bid to hide her identity, Monroe signed Kelley's release "Mona Monroe."

> Tom didn't think anyone would recognize me. My hair was long then. But when the picture came out, everybody knew me. I'd never have done it if I'd known things would happen in Hollywood so fast for me... I was told I should deny I'd posed... But I'd rather be honest about it ["Sweatergirl Marilyn Monroe Admits 'Arty' Calendar Pose," *Stars and Stripes*].

In prudish 1950s America, where actors were told to toe the line or else, with morals clauses written into their studio contracts, somehow Monroe was able to bypass the boundaries, break the rules, and *still* endear herself to the public. An honest confession that could have easily turned into career suicide became a publicity move for the ages. The raw vulnerability that Monroe willingly let the public see was something that few, if any, Hollywood stars would dare display, and it worked in her favor.

Gentlemen Prefer Blondes wasn't released until over a year after Monroe admitted the nude woman in the calendar was her. While the calendar showed Monroe completely naked, a costume implying nudity still showed less than Monroe had shown in that now infamous 1949 nude session for Kelley. Ironically, Monroe's decision to bare all was a situation that she was forced into following Fox's refusal to renew her film contract. At the time, Monroe's car had been impounded. She had no work, no money and the rent was due. Following the two-hour shoot (twenty-four shots were taken, but only two were produced), Kelley paid Monroe exactly the amount needed to get her car back: $50.

Kelley didn't fare much better. He sold the rights to the two photos for $900, and the Western Lithograph Company created the calendar and made millions of copies, earning millions of dollars in the process. By the mid-fifties, sales tallies for the Golden Dreams calendar totaled eight million copies.

Additionally, *Playboy* founder Hugh Hefner used Monroe's image from the Kelley photo shoot in the first issue of *Playboy* magazine. At a cover price of 50 cents, the first issue was released in December of 1953—and sold almost 54,000 copies. Now a prime collectible, a mint condition copy of that issue with Monroe as the centerfold can fetch upwards of $5,000 at auction (*Playboy Magazine Price Guide Checklist, 1996*). Though Monroe and Kelley received a diminutive financial reward from the photo session, their names are forever connected because of it and their careers were springboarded to another level as a result of the publicity and overwhelming public reaction.

Travilla's iconic ivory halter-neck dress with the billowing pleated skirt, commonly referred to as the "subway dress" and specially designed for Monroe for *The Seven Year Itch* (1955), was purchased for $200 by actress and Hollywood costume collector Debbie Reynolds in 1974. It took Reynolds several decades, but she amassed one of the largest, most impressive personal collections of movie memorabilia in the world. For various reasons, her lifelong dream to open a Hollywood museum went unrealized. In 2011, the "subway dress" sold at auction for $5.6 million (including $1 million in fees), amid 600 other costumes and pieces of Hollywood memorabilia. Additionally, Monroe's figure-hugging red-sequined dress from *Gentlemen Prefer Blondes* was auctioned. Despite a pre-sale estimate of $200,000 to $300,000, it sold for a staggering $1.2 million.

The Monroe and Travilla team served to showcase Hollywood glamor at its finest. He—

the artist. She—the canvas for his creations. As the years roll by, and when or *if* a Travilla-Monroe design reappears on the collectible market for resale, newspapers will scurry to report the auction details and wealthy collectors from around the world will feverishly bid into the millions for a dress designed by Travilla and worn by Monroe. Aside from Dorothy's ruby slippers from *The Wizard of Oz* (1939), there is no greater prize for a collector than a screen-worn Marilyn Monroe costume, even more so if it's a Travilla design. Travilla's impact in creating "the look" that made Marilyn Monroe the film and fashion icon that she's become is unquestionable.

A week before Monroe's death, William Travilla was dining with a friend at a restaurant when he spotted a very thin woman with no makeup sitting across the room. Travilla's friend said she looked like Marilyn Monroe. "She wishes!" said Travilla. Then he heard that unmistakable laugh. It *was* her. He left his table and went over to say hello, but the man who played an integral part in creating the Marilyn Monroe look was met with a blank stare. She had no idea who he was. She was sitting with Peter Lawford and his wife, and a woman he didn't recognize. The silence was unbearable, and then all of a sudden she said, "Billy!" Travilla left the restaurant broken-hearted. He later admitted he felt like writing her a nasty letter; after all they'd been through, he was gutted by her failure to recognize him. She died a few days later. "I'm so glad I didn't write that letter," he said (Riese and Hitchens, p. 520).

William Travilla successfully continued his career beyond Marilyn Monroe, making his mark in television (most notably for *Dallas* and *Knots Landing*) and earning multiple Emmy nominations (including two wins) for his work. He died on November 2, 1990, of lung cancer. He was seventy years old.

Filmography

Dangerous Years
(1947)

Marilyn Monroe appeared as Evie, the waitress. Sol M. Wurtzel Productions and Twentieth Century–Fox. 62 minutes. *Director:* Arthur Pierson. *Producer:* Sol M. Wurtzel. *Writer:* Arnold Belgard. *Original Music:* Ralph Stanley (aka Raoul Kraushaar). *Cinematography:* Benjamin H. Kline. *Production Dates:* July 15 to July 31, 1947. *Release Date:* December 7, 1947. *Genre:* Drama. Black and White. *Other Cast:* William Halop (Danny Jones), Scotty Beckett (Willy Miller), Richard Gaines (Edgar Burns), Ann E. Todd (Doris Martin), Jerome Cowan (Weston), Anabel Shaw (Connie Burns), Darryl Hickman (Leo Emerson), Dickie Moore (Gene Spooner), Harry Harvey, Jr. (Phil Kenny).

Emmeline Snively of the Blue Book Modeling Agency strongly advised Norma Jeane to sign a contract with National Concert Artists Corporation to help guide her into a film career. On the morning of July 17, 1946, Norma Jeane's agent Helen Ainsworth (and soon-to-be agent Harry Lipton) arranged a meeting for their new client at Twentieth Century–Fox studios. After nervously reading several lines from Judy Holliday's *Winged Victory* (1944), actor turned Fox casting director Ben Lyon was impressed enough to arrange for Norma Jeane's first screen test two days later. The test took place on the set of the newest Betty Grable feature, *Mother Wore Tights*, and she was signed to her first film contract on August 26, 1946. Since she was not yet twenty-one, Grace McKee Goddard co-signed the contract. The standard six-month agreement would earn her $75 per week. Before the contract expired, the studio could option her for a further six months with a $25 rise in salary for each six-month renewal, up to two years. Though Howard Hughes of RKO was said to have noticed Norma Jeane on the cover of a magazine shortly before her screen test with Fox, his studio wasn't quick enough to sign her.

On July 7, 1946, Hughes had crashed his prototype aircraft into the home of actress Rosemary DeCamp. Hospitalized with broken ribs and second and third degree burns, from his sickbed, Hughes was in no condition to actively pursue his interest in Norma Jeane. Though rumors have long swirled that Norma Jeane did indeed make a screen test for RKO, no proof of any such test has come to light.

Signed to her first studio contract, Norma Jeane Dougherty needed a new name—a Hollywood name. While her divorce from first husband Jim Dougherty was imminent, Lyon wasn't satisfied with using his name (or Mortenson or Baker) professionally. Her given name Norma Jeane wasn't suitable either. Lyon originally came up with the name Carole Lind, a

Monroe had a small part as Evie the waitress in *Dangerous Years* (1947).

homage to Carole Lombard and Jenny Lind, the Swedish opera singer, but it still didn't feel like the right fit. Norma Jeane suggested Monroe as a last name, taken from her mother Gladys Baker's maiden name. Jeane Monroe was a consideration for awhile, but Lyon still didn't like it. Variations of the name Jeane were all too common and it didn't have the right flow with Monroe. Lyon then suggested Marilyn, taken from the legendary stage actress (and also Lyon's ex-fiancée) Marilyn Miller. And there it was—Marilyn Monroe was born. Ironically, years later, following her marriage to playwright Arthur Miller, Marilyn Miller would become Monroe's legal name. The name Marilyn Monroe wasn't legal until papers were filed in 1956. Even after her marriage to Joe DiMaggio, Monroe's legal name was Norma Jeane DiMaggio.

Monroe's initial few months as a contract player were dedicated to learning her craft. Along with the other newly signed players, she was given singing, dancing and acting classes. She paced the studio lot in an attempt to soak up everything possible about the art of moviemaking, befriending anyone who was kind enough to teach her what they knew. Makeup artist Allan "Whitey" Snyder became one of her first true Hollywood friends. Snyder did her makeup for her screen test and he worked with her throughout her career, becoming her personal makeup man. He was with her to the very end—literally. The hardest job of his life was keeping his emotions in check so that he could do Monroe's makeup for the very last time—for her funeral. Hollywood relationships so often develop and disintegrate with the blink of an eye, but Monroe and Snyder remained close and loyal to the very end.

Initially, there was no film work on offer for Monroe and until there was, her presence wasn't contractually required. But her enthusiasm never waned and she thought it only right to show up for work, even if there was no work to be had. Though film work would eventually come, Fox utilized her modeling experience and used her extensively for studio publicity shots. Her $75-a-week salary (part of which she would regularly send to her mother Gladys) was guaranteed, whether she worked or not.

On January 30, 1947, a series of photos of Monroe appeared in the *Los Angeles Times*. They showed her playing and reading with a toddler girl, as well as taking care of what looks like infant twins. The article described Monroe as an orphaned eighteen-year-old (she was twenty) baby-sitter who was spotted by a talent scout and signed to a studio contract. Her biography was that neat and sweet. There was no mention of Monroe's marriage and divorce to Jim Dougherty or anything about her mentally ill mother. They were kept hidden.

In February 1947, Monroe's contract was renewed for another six months and the studio sent her to drama classes at the Actors Laboratory. To her delight, she was eventually used as an extra in several films that required crowd scenes. Though *Dangerous Years* was filmed after *Scudda-Hoo! Scudda-Hay!*, it was the first of the two films released. It was a bit part with only a few lines, but at least it was something, and she did get noticed. Though she ended up playing a waitress, studio records show that she was initially cast as a secretary.

Working in a teenage hangout called "The Gopher Hole," Monroe's character Evie is used to the all-too-frequent cheesy pick-up lines from the young male customers, and she knows how to handle them. We see Evie walk to the counter and order, "Six more all-day sundaes."

Gene (Dickie Moore) walks in with a friend and says, "Hey look! There's Evie." He approaches her with an enthusiastic, "Hi, Evie!"

She cuts him down with, "Hi, small change."

In a desperate attempt to get her attention, Gene says, "Wait! I've got money tonight! Am I going to see you later?"

"If I'm not too tired," says an uninterested Evie.

"But, Evie, I thought we had a date!" Gene says.

"Look, this tray weighs a ton." She then turns and walks away.

While Monroe's part was fleeting, she still made an impression on audiences. But Twentieth Century–Fox didn't see enough promise in her performance to keep her around. On August 25, 1947, not long after filming on *Dangerous Years* was complete, the studio dropped her contract. Her final studio paycheck, dated August 31, 1947, was for $104.13.

Soon after she was dropped from her Fox contract, Monroe responded to a *Los Angeles Times* ad and attended an open casting call for a role in the stage production of the Hollywood spoof, *Glamour Preferred*. She was given the second lead, a role she shared with actress Jane Weeks. They played the same part on alternating nights, and it was Monroe's first time in a stage play in front of a paying audience. Opening at the Bliss-Hayden Miniature Theatre in Beverly Hills on October 12, 1947, *Glamour Preferred* closed on November 2. In the late summer of 1948, Monroe graced the small stage of the Bliss-Hayden Miniature Theatre again, this time co-starring in a production of *Stage Door*. Though she dabbled in the theater early on, it was a medium that required faultless execution when it came to lines and timing. It wasn't for her.

Scudda Hoo! Scudda Hay! (1948)

Marilyn Monroe appears as Betty. In a church scene, she's seen briefly in the background (wearing a pale blue pinafore and a white blouse). As she descends the church steps, she smiles and says, "Hi, Rad!" to June Haver's character. Haver responds, "Hi, Betty." Monroe is also in a canoe scene. Twentieth Century–Fox. 95 minutes. *Director:* F. Hugh Herbert. *Producer:* Walter Morosco. *Story:* George Agnew Chamberlain. *Screenplay:* F. Hugh Herbert. *Original Music:* Cyril Mockridge. *Cinematography:* Ernest Palmer. *Costume Design:* Bonnie Cashin. *Production Dates:* Late February to early May 1947. *Production Cost:* $1.685 million. *Domestic box office receipts:* $2 million. *Release Date:* March 11, 1948 (Iowa, Nebraska, Missouri and Kansas). *Genre:* Comedy-Drama-Romance. Technicolor. Other Cast—June Haver (Rad McGill), Lon McCallister (Daniel "Snug" Dominy), Walter Brennan (Tony Maule), Anne Revere (Judith Dominy), Natalie Wood (Eufraznee "Bean" McGill), Robert Karnes (Stretch Dominy), Henry Hull (Milt Dominy), Tom Tully (Robert "Roarer" McGill).

Marilyn Monroe's first speaking role came in *Scudda-Hoo! Scudda-Hay!* (1948). With her Fox contract dropped, money was tight and she relied on the generosity of newfound friends. Actor-singer John Carroll and his wife, MGM casting director Lucille Ryman, were extremely generous with their time and their money. The Hollywood power-couple was well known in the industry for offering guidance to up-and-coming actresses with exceptional talent—no strings attached. Following Monroe's contract cancellation with Fox, the Carrolls took her under their wing. They paid for her lessons at the Actor's Lab, gave her $100 a week and allowed her to stay in their apartment rent-free. During this time, Monroe was introduced to many of the important people in the industry.

Though Ryman was influential at MGM, Monroe's "look" was said to be unsuitable for the studio at the time. She continued with her modeling and acting classes and, with the constant encouragement of the Carrolls, she remained hopeful that someone would recognize her potential and give her the big break that she so desperately needed.

It didn't take long.

In February of 1948, Joseph Schenck, former president of United Artists and co-creator (in 1933 with Darryl F. Zanuck) of Twentieth Century Pictures (they merged with Fox Film Corporation in 1935), noticed Monroe at a party. Schenck was one of the most influential men in the film business and if anyone could help her, he could. With Schenck, there most certainly were strings attached. Intimate dinners followed their first meeting and Monroe accompanied him around town. Whether or not their relationship was sexual is up for debate. Schenck, former husband of actress Norma Talmadge, was a well-known womanizer in his day, but by 1948 he was almost seventy.

By March 9, 1948, Harry Cohn, head of Columbia (and a friend of Schenck), had agreed to give Monroe a six-month contract. Cohn was of the most temperamental and most despised moguls in Hollywood, but Monroe was once again signed to a film studio and she was thrilled. Just as her contract was due for renewal, Monroe would witness

Cohn's slimy, malevolent personality first hand. But for now, she was oblivious. Aside from a weekly wage, there were additional perks that came with being signed to Columbia. Very comfortable accommodations at the Bel Air Hotel were included in the deal, and the studio stylists set their sights on transforming and glamorizing her look. Monroe's still dark blonde hair was brought down to a platinum blonde tone—Jean Harlow blonde!

Incidentally, Monroe's "look" was carefully crafted and molded over the course of several years. But once that look was achieved, it would be carefully duplicated from that moment on. In her online article "Marilyn Monroe: The Star with Marbles in Her Bra," reporter Hannah Betts of *The Telegraph* (March 13, 2012) wrote that Monroe's makeup artist Allan "Whitey" Snyder had revealed that it was during the preparation of *Niagara* (1953) that the Marilyn Monroe look, as we know it, was fully realized. In order to attain the pert-nippled look at all times, Monroe insisted that small marbles or buttons be sewn into her bras or dress bodices. Despite being born and raised in the California sun, she stayed out of it, for the sole reason that a pale complexion insured that she was "blonde all over" (*The Daily Register*, August 5, 1952). She was so radically luminous, her skin radiated an alabaster tone, like a porcelain doll. A March 1961 issue of *Esquire* magazine ran an article by A.T. McIntyre which began by posing a question:

> What is Marilyn Monroe really like? She is like nothing human you have ever seen or dreamed, and nothing on the screen can prepare you for her. It is not special lighting which brings out Monroe and leaves her supporting actors to fade into the woodwork—she is astonishingly white, so radically pale that in her presence you can look at others about as easily as you can explore the darkness around the moon.

Scudda Hoo! Scudda Hay! **(1948) marked Monroe's first film appearance (though not the first released). Here she is in a canoe scene with an unidentified starlet. In another scene, wearing a blue pinafore and a white blouse, she descends the steps of a church following services. She smiles and greets June Haver's character with "Hi, Rad!"**

Monroe would slather her face with layers of Vaseline, hormone cream and Nivea to give her skin a luminous glow under the studio lights. In finishing, a light smear of Laszlo foundation would be topped off with powder by Anita of Denmark. Her features were meticulously shaded and shaped and her lips were coated with five shades of lipstick. Different colors gave the appearance of a plumper pout. Darker red on the outer corners, lighter reds in the middle, topped off with gloss to give the sensuous wet look. Then there was the signature beauty spot, an augmented facial mole that was flesh-toned; Monroe insisted on it being darkened to avoid the natural appearance of a skin-colored bump on her face. From film to film, the darkened mole came and went; and it sometimes moved from one place to another. It wasn't unusual for Monroe's intricate makeup job to take an hour and a half. She had the natural foundation to work with but she was still a manufactured creation, carefully crafted to fit a "look," a look that to this day is copied and emulated the world over, but never equaled.

Monroe's introduction to Columbia's drama coach, the volatile, German-born Natasha Lytess, was the start of a long, tumultuous, co-dependent and extremely needy relationship that few people understood. Though Monroe's Columbia contract was paying her $125 per week, more than she had ever earned to date, the ever-generous Carrolls insisted she keep her paycheck for other expenses. They continued to fund her acting lessons, which now consisted of private tuition, away from the studio, with Lytess as her teacher. In 1950, Lytess resigned from her position at Columbia to become Monroe's acting coach on an exclusive basis. Their unlikely partnership would last until the mid-fifties.

Less than a week after signing her Columbia contract, Monroe received word that her beloved aunt Ana Lower had died on March 14, 1948. Most of her past she was glad to leave there, but Aunt Ana was an exception. Pre–"Marilyn Monroe," she was one of the few solid foundations in Norma Jeane's unsettled life. Though she had been in poor health for many years, Aunt Ana was always available, welcoming and supportive. Hers was a home that Monroe could always go back to, and she did—often. Now she was gone.

At the time of *Scudda Hoo! Scudda Hay!*'s production, Marilyn Monroe was just another unknown starlet appearing in her very first film. In the world of Hollywood trivia, the film goes down in history because it was Marilyn Monroe's first film and her first speaking part to be filmed. *Dangerous Years* was shot later and released first.

To coincide with the farm theme of the film, *Scudda Hoo! Scudda Hay!* had its world premiere on March 11, 1948, in two hundred cities in the Midwest states of Iowa, Nebraska, Missouri and Kansas (*The Oelwein Daily Register,* March 1, 1948). It was the first of two productions featuring both June Haver and Monroe. The second was *Love Nest* (1951).

Ladies of the Chorus
(1949)

Marilyn Monroe appeared as Peggy Martin. Columbia Pictures. 60 minutes. *Director:* Phil Karlson. *Producer:* Harry A. Romm. *Story:* Harry Sauber. *Screenplay:* Harry Sauber and Joseph Carole. *Original Music:* Allan Roberts and Lester Lee. *Cinematography:* Frank Redman. *Musical Supervisor:* Fred Karger. *Production Dates:* April 22 to May 3, 1948. *Release Date:* December 30, 1948. Re-released on November 1, 1952, with new titles placing Monroe's name above the title. *Genre:* Musical. Black and White. *Other Cast:* Adele Jergens (Mae Martin), Rand Brooks (Randy Carroll), Nana Bryant (Mrs. Adele Carroll), Eddie Garr (Billy Mackay), Steven Geray (Salisbury), The Bobby True Trio (Musicians). Soundtrack—"Anyone Can Tell I Love You" and "Every Baby Needs a Da Da Daddy": Written by Lester Lee and Allan Roberts. Sung by Marilyn Monroe. "I'm So Crazy for You": Written by Lester Lee and Allan Roberts. Sung and Danced by Adele Jergens (Virginia Rees dubbing). "The Ladies of the Chorus": Written by Lester Lee and Allan Roberts. Sung by Marilyn Monroe and Adele Jergens (Virginia Rees dubbing). "You're Never Too Old": Written by Lester Lee and Allan Roberts. Sung by Nana Bryant. *Tagline:* A FRONT-ROW VIEW OF THE BURLESQUE WORLD!

Shot in just eleven days, *Ladies of the Chorus* was Monroe's first starring role. Musical supervisor Fred Karger was assigned to teach Monroe her two songs for the film, "Anyone Can Tell I Love You" and "Every Baby Needs a Da-Da-Daddy." (Monroe's performance of "Every Baby Needs a Da Da Daddy" was later cut into the war film *Okinawa*.) It didn't take long for Karger and Monroe's working relationship to get personal—and serious. Karger introduced her to his family, including his young daughter from his marriage to soon-to-be-ex-wife Patti Sacks. At thirty-two, Karger was ten years Monroe's senior. She was young and fell easily in love. He was smitten too, but he never considered Monroe "wife material."

Shortly before filming began on *Ladies of the Chorus,* Monroe had moved from the Carrolls' apartment to the Studio Club, accommodation that specifically catered to young Hollywood starlets. But Monroe concocted a plan to entrench herself into Karger's life, and pull at his heartstrings, by telling him that she was staying in a rundown apartment block instead. Karger was so appalled that he insisted that she move in with his mother, Anne. Her plan had worked, or so she initially thought.

Everyone who knew Karger's mother called her Nana and she would soon become another mother figure in Monroe's life. The two women adored each other. Karger's sister, Mary, would also develop a close relationship with Monroe. Though Fred's extended family truly loved Monroe, he was extremely critical of her, often putting her down by telling her that she was uneducated, not good enough and too emotional. He was always looking to change her in one way or another: her clothes, her personality, her looks. He suggested she visit an orthodontist to straighten her slightly protruding teeth and, in the hope that she would become his wife, Monroe dutifully did as he asked. He wasn't the first man to fall in love with her and then want to change her, and he wouldn't be the last. While Monroe was still living with the Kargers, the Studio Club called Columbia to ask about her whereabouts. That was when Karger realized he'd been had. He instantly broke off their relationship, also telling her that he didn't think she was good enough to be his daughter's stepmother. Though Karger and Monroe's relationship soured, a split that devastated her for several years, Monroe maintained a close relationship with his mother throughout her Hollywood career and they were in contact right up until Monroe's death. Both she and Mary were invited by Joe DiMaggio to Marilyn's private funeral. Fred Karger went on to marry and divorce actress Jane Wyman—twice. He died on the 17th anniversary of Marilyn Monroe's death, August 5, 1979. He was sixty-three.

The opening song sees Monroe front and center with a bevy of beauties singing the title song, "The Ladies of the Chorus." Peggy (Marilyn Monroe) is a young burlesque chorus girl who sings alongside her loving, yet overprotective mother Mae (Adele Jergens).

Adele Jergens (left), less than ten years Monroe's senior, played the part of her mother in *Ladies of the Chorus* (1948). Though Monroe got good reviews for her performance, Columbia decided not to renew her contract. The reason for the decision was clear: Monroe had refused to spend a weekend aboard the yacht of studio head Harry Cohn.

Her mother doesn't allow Peggy to date and Peggy is fed up with being treated like a child. When Bubbles (Marjorie Hoshelle) calls Mae a "gray-haired old hag," Peggy physically attacks her. As a result of the fight, the insufferable star of the show walks out but Peggy takes her place and fills her slot to perfection and becomes the new darling of burlesque. Finally emerging from her mother's shadow, she revives the flagging show and wins the heart of Randy (Rand Brooks), a wealthy man who sends her orchids every night following her performance. While her daughter falls head over heels in love, Mae is concerned that a well-to-do fella and a burlesque dancer are a rotten combination, and she speaks from experience. Mae's husband (Peggy's father) also came from a wealthy family and fell for Mae, the sexy burlesque dancer. While she initially resisted his constant proposals because of their class differences, she eventually married him and left her burlesque career behind her ... or that's what she thought. When her husband's family and friends found out that she was a burlesque dancer, they were horrified. The marriage was annulled and Mae went back to the theater, but not as the star. Now she was one of the ladies of the chorus ... and an expectant mother.

Mae insists her daughter's marriage won't work, just like hers didn't. Mae advises Randy to tell his mother (Nana Bryant) about Peggy and about her career. If she accepts her for who she is completely, Mae will then give her consent for him to marry her daughter.

Randy tells his mother about Peggy, but he gets cold feet when she asks which prominent family she comes from. He decides not to tell her the whole story, at least not until she meets with Peggy and her mother.

An elegant engagement party is thrown for the happy couple. Mae's friend, the burlesque comedian Billy (Eddie Garr), shows up to celebrate. Peggy loves Billy and considers him an avuncular figure. Meanwhile, Billy has carried a torch for Mae for years. During the party, while Peggy is happily dancing with her fiancé, one of the band members recognizes her as "the burlesque queen" and asks her to sing a song. Humiliated, Peggy knows Randy's mother will be furious and she runs upstairs to her room. Thinking the worst, Peggy and her mother pack to leave, but to everyone's surprise, Randy's society-driven mother tells Peggy that if she and her son love each other, that's all there is to it. With the help of Billy on piano, Randy's mother returns to the party and sings a raunchy song in front of her snobby friends. She then reveals that she was once a lady of the chorus herself. Later, when Mae asks her what shows she appeared in, it's revealed that it was all a ruse, cooked up between Billy and herself to help Peggy gain acceptance into their stuck-up social circle. Peggy and Randy kiss, and, after years of waiting, Billy kisses Mae too.

Monroe was almost twenty-two at the time of filming. Adele Jergens, who played her mother, was only nine years Monroe's senior. Critics favorably reviewed Monroe's performance. She was given her first opportunity to sing and dance on screen, and additionally, she would receive her first screen kiss, courtesy of Rand Brooks. The pressbook for *Ladies of the Chorus* touted Monroe's performance as "amazingly reminiscent of Jean Harlow."

With Monroe's Columbia contract approaching its renewal date, Harry Cohn was said to be unimpressed with Monroe's acting ability and thought she looked "too heavy" in *Ladies of the Chorus*. Monroe had a different story to tell. She claimed that Cohn invited her to spend a weekend with him aboard his yacht (Leaming, p. 16). Knowing what that invitation meant, Monroe refused. Cohn was a man known for his vindictive personality and explosive temper; to say he was disliked within the industry would be an understatement. Cohn had

Monroe's future in his hands and he wanted to see how far she'd be willing to go in order to get re-signed. Monroe's rejection certainly influenced his decision not to renew her contract.

On September 8, 1948, after just one film, Monroe and Columbia severed all ties. *Ladies of the Chorus* was her only appearance for the studio, but Columbia also used her photograph during several scenes of *Riders of the Whistling Pines* (1949), starring Gene Autry.

Love Happy
(1950)

Marilyn Monroe appeared as Grunion's Client. Artist Alliance, Inc. and United Artists. 83 minutes. Working titles: *Blonde Heaven, Blondes Up, Diamonds in the Basement, Hearts and Diamonds, Kleptomaniacs. Director:* David Miller. Producers: Lester Cowan, Mary Pickford (uncredited). *Screenplay:* Frank Tashlin and Mac Benoff. *Story:* Harpo Marx. *Original Music:* Ann Ronell. *Cinematography:* William C. Mellor. *Production Dates:* August to mid–September, 1948. *Release Date:* October 12, 1949. *Genre:* Comedy-Crime-Musical. Black and White. *Other Cast:* Groucho Marx (Detective Sam Grunion), Harpo Marx (Harpo), Chico Marx (Faustino), Ilona Massey (Madame Egelichi), Vera-Ellen (Maggie Phillips), Marion Hutton (Bunny Dolan), Raymond Burr (Alphonse Zoto), Melville Cooper (Throckmorton), Paul Valentine (Mike Johnson), Leon Belasco (Mr. Lyons), Eric Blore (Mackinaw), Bruce Gordon (Hannibal Zoto). *Tagline:* New Musical Girlesque!!!

Based on her walk, Groucho Marx chose Marilyn Monroe for her bit part out of a lineup of three girls. Each girl was asked to walk and when Monroe showcased her signature wiggle, there was no competition. She not only got the part, she shared feature billing with the Marx Brothers.

Love Happy is the last Marx Brothers feature film, and it's far from their best. Groucho Marx plays Sam Grunion, a private eye in search of the missing Royal Romanoff diamonds. As he narrates the story, he tells the audience about the case that baffled him for over a decade. Madame Egilichi (Ilona Massey) is the thief, but when Harpo intercepts the diamonds, which are hidden in a sardine can, it's the perfect set-up for the usual tried and true Marx Brothers shtick that is the foundation for the rest of the film. Bad guys chasing good guys, Harpo being captured and interrogated for three days by Madame Egilichi and her crooked cronies and refusing to speak ... because he *never* speaks, but what do they know? As usually, plenty of sight and sound gags are incorporated into the madcap story. Harpo ends up escaping with the diamonds and Groucho ends up married to Madame Egilichi.

Groucho was presented with three beautiful starlets for the walk-on part in *Love Happy*. He took less than five seconds to make his choice, saying, "There's only one, as far as I'm concerned. The blond." The girl was signed for the part. He said:

> For her scene she wore a dress cut so low that I couldn't remember the dialogue. Very soon other men throughout the world would be suffering similar fevers, for the girl was Marilyn Monroe [Kanfer, p. 324].

As per her contract, Monroe received $125 for her one day of work on *Love Happy*. She received an additional fee for a two-hour still photo shoot afterward, and $100 per week

Title card for *Love Happy* (1949).

(plus expenses) for a three-week cross-country promotional tour that left Hollywood on June 10. Monroe cut the tour short. Though it wasn't her first film role, she was still given an "Introducing Marilyn Monroe" credit and the role *did* introduce the world to her seductive walk.

There's a knock on the door of Grunion's Detective Agency and in sways Marilyn Monroe. Dressed in a floor-length strapless evening gown and carrying a fur stole, her entrance is all about "the walk" and Groucho's reaction to her.

> GROUCHO: "Is there anything I can do for you?" Then, turning to the camera, he addresses the audience, saying, "What a ridiculous statement!"
> Monroe drapes herself on him and says, "Mr. Grunion, I want you to help me."
> GROUCHO: "I have a little sand left, what seems to be the trouble?"
> Monroe then turns, sashays toward camera and seductively purrs, "Some men are following me."
> GROUCHO: "Really? I can't understand why!"

Her role was small, but producer Lester Cowan felt it was beneficial for the film to send Monroe on the promotional tour. In a February 8, 1949, letter to Groucho, Cowan wrote, "*Life* magazine has approved a cover on Marilyn Monroe and a story which assumes she has a bit in the picture. Immediately the cover appears, I have been planning to send her on a publicity tour to principal cities in advance of the film. Her immediate future is in our hands." Monroe visited New York City, Detroit, Cleveland, Chicago, Milwaukee and Illinois, but she grew tired of playing the role of the traveling billboard-bimbo and she returned home earlier than scheduled, much to Cowan's dismay.

Plagued with financial delays, *Love Happy* used product placement as an innovative way of funding the floundering production. Several advertising signs display the names of companies who paid to have their logos shown as part of the film's story. *Love Happy* wasn't the first film to feature a brand name product on screen, but it was the first feature film to be partially funded by corporate sponsorship. Kool cigarettes, Wheaties, General Electric, Fisk Tires, Baby Ruth candy bars, Bulova watches, and the flying red horse (the iconic symbol of Mobil gas) were all featured in Harpo's hilarious rooftop chase scene. However, in order to get higher advertising fees out of each company, Cowan guaranteed the participating companies ridiculously high audience numbers and box office receipts. The legal ramifications that followed got the production into a deeper financial mess than it was already in before the advertisers were brought aboard to save it!

The film was originally conceived by Harpo Marx as a solo vehicle for himself. Chico, a lifelong compulsive gambler, was deep in debt, and it wasn't the first time. Out of loyalty to Chico, Harpo wrote him into the story to help pay off his gambling debts. Without Groucho, no one was interested in backing the film at all. Though Groucho was doing radio and television work, he agreed to come back to support his brothers.

And there it was, the very last Marx Brothers film (as a threesome) was born. That said, it's not really a Marx Brothers film at all. In a strange twist, at no time do all three brothers appear on screen together. So, while the backers got their way and got all three brothers to appear, the film is still very much a Harpo film.

The Marx Brothers are without doubt one of the greatest comedy teams of all time, but it's all about teamwork, and the best part of a Marx Brothers film is when all three are on-screen and interacting. In *Love Happy*, it's as if there was a concerted effort to keep the boys apart, a long-running gag that builds anticipation and only serves to disappoint when the end credits roll and the audience realizes they've been had.

Mary Pickford produced the film, but she was so unhappy with the finished product that she demanded her name not appear in the credits. She wasn't the only one who was disappointed. During interviews, Groucho readily admitted to the film being terrible and both he and Harpo "forgot" to mention its existence in their memoirs.

Love Happy received a much-needed financial boost (over $100,000) when it was re-released in 1953. Despite Marilyn Monroe's appearance being a minute or so in length, *Love Happy* was re-released to capitalize on her current fame. Newly billed as a Marx Brothers co-star, her image was plastered all over the 1953 publicity material. The shameless marketing line, "The Picture That Discovered Marilyn Monroe" was splashed across ads and posters.

The Miami News (July 9, 1950):

> It's the old but ageless Marx Brothers formula of a bevy of bosomy babes, pantomime, whimsy, good music, and considerable ogling of the aforementioned femmes by the trio of zanies... Besides the inimitable talents of Harpo, Chico and Groucho, you'll also find sexy Ilona Massey, pert and pretty Vera-Ellen, curvaceous Marilyn Monroe, songstress Marion Hutton, dancer Paul Valentine, and the comic, continental violinist, Leon Belasco. They all add up to great entertainment.

A Ticket to Tomahawk (1950)

Marilyn Monroe appeared as Clara (uncredited). Her character is a member of Madame Adelaide's (Connie Gilchrist) dance troupe. She performs a group song ("Oh, What a Forward Young Man You Are") along with co-stars Marion Marshall, Joyce Mackenzie, Barbara Smith and Dan Dailey. Twentieth Century–Fox. 90 minutes. *Director:* Richard Sale. *Producer:* Robert Bassler. *Writers:* Mary Loos and Richard Sale. *Original Music:* Cyril Mockridge. *Cinematography:* Harry Jackson. *Costume Design:* René Hubert. *Production Dates:* August 15 to October 21, 1949. *Filming Locations:* Denver & Rio Grande Western Railroad, Durango, Colorado; Molas Lake, Silverton, Colorado; Rockwood, Colorado; Silverton, Colorado. *Production Cost:* $1.91 million. *Domestic Box Office Receipts:* $1.3 million. *Release Date:* April 18, 1950 (Denver, Colorado). *Alternate title:* The Sheriff's Daughter. *Genre:* Comedy-Musical-Western. Technicolor. *Other Cast:* Dan Dailey (Johnny Behind-the-Deuces), Anne Baxter (Kit Dodge Jr.), Rory Calhoun (Dakota), Walter Brennan (Terence Sweeny), Charles Kemper (Chuckity), Connie Gilchrist (Madame Adelaide), Arthur Hunnicutt (Sad Eyes), Will Wright (Dodge), Chief Yowlachie (Pawnee), Victor Sen Yung (Long Time).

Marilyn Monroe appears as Clara, one of the beautiful showgirls in the Madame Adelaide (Connie Gilchrist) dance troupe. The showgirls have a memorable song-and-dance number with Dan Dailey's character, Johnny-Behind-the-Deuces, and in one scene, where Johnny boards the train and waves goodbye to his wife and five daughters, it's no coincidence that the little girls' names are, "Connie, Barbara, Marion, Marilyn and Joyce." It was a witty nod to the real-life names of the showgirls, but few audience members picked up on the gag.

In Colorado, Fox decided to do some promotion in conjunction with a local hospital: The studio put together a baseball team to play the home team. All the locals attended, filling the bleachers to capacity. Monroe was on the team and she decided to give the crowd a show. She went up to bat, hit the ball and started running, but just before she got to first base her jeans "fell down," revealing her black lace undies. The crowd went crazy (Buskin, Richard. *Blonde Heat: The Sizzling Screen Career of Marilyn Monroe*, p. 45).

Anne Baxter stars in the first of three films with Monroe. The second, *All About Eve* (1950), was released in the same year. Lastly, they would both appear in the all-star cast of *O. Henry's Full House* (1952), but they shared no screen time. Though she was initially cast as Polly in *Niagara* (1953), Baxter was unhappy with her lack of screen time and she left the production soon after shooting began.

In 1951, the Writers Guild of America nominated husband-and-wife writing team Richard Sale and Mary Loos for Best Written American Western for *A Ticket to Tomahawk*. In February 1949, Fox bought their screenplay for $30,000. Some innovative exhibitors of the film noticed that theatergoers seemed confused by the film's title so they changed the title of the film themselves. When *A Ticket to Tomahawk* was renamed *The Sheriff's Daughter*, ticket sales increased dramatically. Fox informed of the successful experiment and they briefly considered doing the same, but since the film had already been released in most major cities, it was too late.

A wardrobe test shot of Monroe as Clara in *A Ticket to Tomahawk* (1950).

The Asphalt Jungle
(1950)

Marilyn Monroe appeared as Angela Phinlay. MGM. 112 minutes. *Director:* John Huston. *Producer:* Arthur Hornblow, Jr. *Writers:* Based on a 1949 novel by W. R. Burnett. *Screenplay:* Ben Maddow and John Huston. *Original Music:* Miklos Rozsa. *Cinematography:* Harold Rosson. *Production Dates:* October 21 to December 21, 1949. Opening scenes shot in Cincinnati, Ohio, and closing scenes shot in Lexington, Kentucky. *Release Date:* May 23, 1950. *Genre:* Crime-Drama. Black and White. *Other Cast:* Sterling Hayden (Dix Handley), Louis Calhern (Alonzo D. Emmerich), Jean Hagen (Doll Conovan), James Whitmore (Gus Minissi), Sam Jaffe (Doc Erwine Riedenschneider), John McIntire (Police Commissioner Hardy), Marc Lawrence (Cobby), Barry Kelley (Lt. Ditrich), Anthony Caruso (Louis Ciavelli), Teresa Celli (Maria Ciavelli). *Academy Awards:* Best Actor in a Supporting Role—Sam Jaffe (nominated); Best Cinematography, Black and White—Harold Rosson (nominated); Best Director—John Huston (nominated); Best Writing, Screenplay—Ben Maddow and John Huston (nominated). BAFTA Awards: Best Film from any Source (USA, nominated). Directors Guild of America (DGA Award): Outstanding Directorial Achievement in Motion Pictures—John Huston (nominated). Edgar Allan Poe Awards: Best Motion Picture—Ben Maddow (won). Golden Globes (USA): Best Cinematography, Black and White—Harold Rosson (nominated); Best Motion Picture Director—John Huston (nominated); Best Screenplay—John Huston and Ben Maddow (nominated). National Board of Review (USA): Best Director (NBR Award)—John Huston (won). Venice Film Festival: Best Actor (Volpi Cup)—Sam Jaffe (won). (Golden Lion)—John Huston (nominated). Writers Guild of America (USA): Best Written American Drama—Ben Maddow and John Huston (nominated). The Robert Meltzer Award—Ben Maddow and John Huston (nominated). And, in 2008, the Library of Congress (USA) deemed *The Asphalt Jungle* "culturally, historically, or aesthetically significant." It was selected for preservation in the National Film Registry (USA). *Tagline:* The City Under the City.

A film noir crime thriller directed by John Huston, *The Asphalt Jungle* was brilliantly adapted for the screen by Huston and Ben Maddow. Harold Rosson's artful cinematography makes each scene a visual treat. Starring a fine array of actors, the strength of the ensemble cast glues the gritty story together. All portray characters who have an individual depth.

A group of small-time crooks band-together to pull off a jewel heist worth half a million dollars. The plot proves that even the best-laid plans can fall apart, not because of incompetence in the planning, but because of fate and the moral shortcomings of the people involved.

The lead-up to the robbery introduces each character. The heist scene is tense, without the distraction of music to detract from the job at hand. The aftermath and climax pack a punch as each character is brought down by his own greed and frailties. Huston was a master at bringing realism to his films, even if that realism was hard to take. Here, he humanizes his hoodlums by telling the story from their side, thus evoking a genuine compassion from his audience for underground characters with faults and weaknesses. There isn't a weak link in the cast, and under his direction, they all shine. *The Asphalt Jungle* set the bar for all crime films, and all these years later, few come close to equaling its brilliance.

Marilyn Monroe plays a small role as the mistress of Alonzo D. Emmerich (Louis Calhern), a crooked lawyer who awaits his "take" in the jewel haul. While Monroe's status as a kept woman is evident, she refers to her much older lover as her Uncle Lon in order to get their relationship past the censors.

A seductive publicity pose for John Huston's *The Asphalt Jungle* (1950).

The Asphalt Jungle is gritty and drama-filled from start to finish. You'll find yourself rooting for the bad guys and you'll feel dirty doing it, but while the criminals appear to pull off the elaborate jewel heist without consequences, the Production Code would never allow it. As the film winds down post-heist, each of the characters that we've grown to forgive for their sins is struck down for their crimes. They all had their reasons, but the riveting conclusion sends a clear message: Crime *doesn't* pay.

The reviews were favorable, and by now, Marilyn Monroe had well and truly caught the attention of audiences and critics alike. Harold Heffernan of the *Dallas Morning News* (June 18, 1950) wrote, "Virtually unbilled and unidentified in a current movie, *Asphalt Jungle,* Marilyn's breathtaking appearance immediately piques fandom's curiosity and imagination. Not since the brief introduction of another tempestuous blond, Shelley Winters, three years ago in *A Double Life,* has a newcomer stirred so much interest."

In November 1970, Darryl Zanuck was interviewed by *Look* magazine. Over the years, he and Monroe had a tumultuous relationship. She always believed he thought of her as a cheap novelty act, never as a real actress. But eight years after her death, Zanuck remembered when Joseph Schenck arrived at his house with Marilyn Monroe on his arm.

> One day, a great friend of mine, Joseph M. Schenck, brought over to my home in Palm Springs this very beautiful girl who was also on the plump side. I didn't jump up and say, "Oh, this is a great star," or anything like that. Later on, Joe said, "If you can work her in some role or something, some, you know, supporting role, do so." I did, but I didn't think that I had found any gold mine. John Huston gave her a hell of a good role in *The Asphalt Jungle* [1950]. Jesus, she was good in it. I thought it must have been the magic of Huston because I didn't think she had all that in her. But then I put her in *All About Eve* [1950], and she was an overnight sensation.

Monroe received $350 per week for her role in *The Asphalt Jungle*. She worked on the film for three weeks.

Right Cross (1950)

Marilyn Monroe appeared as Dusky Ledue, sometimes spelled "Ledoux" (uncredited). MGM. 90 minutes. *Director:* John Sturges. *Producer:* Armand Deutsch. *Writer:* Charles Schnee. *Original Music:* David Raksin. *Cinematography:* Norbert Brodine. *Costume Design:* Helen Rose. *Production Dates:* January 25 to early March 1950. *Release Date:* October 6, 1950. *Genre:* Drama. Black and White. *Other Cast:* June Allyson (Pat O'Malley), Dick Powell (Rick Garvey), Ricardo Montalban (Johnny Monterez), Lionel Barrymore (Sean O'Malley), Teresa Celli (Marina Monterez), Barry Kelley (Allan Goff), Tom Powers (Tom Balford), Mimi Aguglia (Mom Monterez), Marianne Stewart (Audrey), John Gallaudet (Phil Tripp).

Monroe plays Dusky Ledue, the date of sports reporter Rick Garvey (Dick Powell). Though she goes uncredited in her role, her character name is mentioned within the short scene that she has with Powell. Their conversation goes as follows:

> POWELL: "We'll have spaghetti with mushroom sauce, nice green salad, garlic bread, big bottle of Burgundy. I know just the place."
> MONROE: "Where?"
> POWELL: "My apartment."

MONROE: "Right from left field."
POWELL: "Spaghetti *a la* Rick Garvey. Best ya ever flopped ya lips over. Make it myself."
MONROE: "Wellll..."
POWELL: "Now, if you're a good girl, I'll tell you the recipe."
MONROE: "I know the ingredients."

Interrupted by Ricardo Montalban's entrance, Powell introduces Monroe as Miss Ledue, they exchange brief hellos and Powell reluctantly leaves his date at the table. The entire scene runs about a minute.

Right Cross is a tug-at-the-heartstrings boxing drama with Montalban starring as Johnny Monterez, a chip-on-his-shoulder, insecure Mexican prizefighter who breaks away from his longtime promoter Sean O'Malley (Lionel Barrymore) for a big money fight set up by Allan Goff (Barry Kelley). Johnny knows his fighting career is on borrowed time because of a weakened right hand, a serious problem that he keeps to himself. His last shot at providing for his elderly trainer and his daughter Pat (June Allyson), who just happens to be Johnny's on-and-off girlfriend, is to accept the fight. As part of the fight deal, Goff has promised Johnny a post-retirement income through merchandising, which would ensure Johnny the financial security to propose to Pat. Though his motives are good, Johnny's promoter (and Pat's father) is unaware of the reasons behind his move to the Goff camp. He sees Johnny's departure as nothing but betrayal. Soon after, Sean O'Malley has a fatal heart attack and Pat blames Johnny for breaking her father's heart.

In Johnny's dressing room after he loses the fight, sports writer Rick, Johnny's best

Dick Powell tries to seduce Monroe in this brief nightclub scene from *Right Cross* (1950).

friend, who also happens to be in love with Pat, tells Johnny a few hard truths and Johnny begins to realize his world is crumbling around him. Out of frustration and anger, he punches Rick and his worst fear comes true: His right hand is injured and his boxing career is over—for good. Physically and emotionally wounded, Johnny retreats to his training camp but Pat and Rick follow to mend their relationships. With Rick's help, Johnny and Pat reconcile and she accepts his proposal of marriage.

Right Cross is a particularly interesting post-war sports-themed romance, mainly because of its subplot dealing with Mexican-American racial issues and an interracial romance between Montalban and Allyson. While Rick lusts after Pat throughout the film, in real life Powell and Allyson had been married for almost five years when filming on *Right Cross* began. They remained married until Powell's cancer-related death on January 2, 1963. He was fifty-eight years old.

John Mitchum, Robert Mitchum's younger brother, appeared in an uncredited role as a reporter, and silent-comedy clown Chester Conklin went uncredited as a waiter. *Right Cross* received good reviews for its overall entertainment value and cross-cultural romance theme. The boxing scenes were touted as "thrilling" and "convincing."

The Fireball
(1950)

Marilyn Monroe appeared as Polly. Thor Productions and Twentieth Century–Fox. 84 minutes. *Working Title:* Dark Challenge. *Director:* Tay Garnett. *Producer:* Bert E. Friedlob. *Screenplay:* Horace McCoy. *Story:* Tay Garnett and Horace McCoy. *Original Music:* Victor Young. *Cinematography:* Lester White. *Production Dates:* November 28, 1949 to January 1950. *Release Date:* October 7, 1950. *Genre:* Sport-Drama. Black and White. *Other Cast:* Mickey Rooney (Johnny Casar), Pat O'Brien (Father O'Hara), Beverly Tyler (Mary Reeves), Glenn Corbett (Mack Miller), James Brown (Allen), Ralph Dumke (Bruno Crystal), Milburn Stone (Jeff Davis), Bert Begley (Shilling).

The Fireball, a low-budget independent film, capitalized on the popularity of roller derby. Much like professional wrestling, roller derby wasn't just a sport, it had entertainment value too. Enthusiastic crowd participation and players with big mouths and created personas were commonplace.

Thirty-year-old Mickey Rooney starred as Johnny Casar, a runaway from Father O'Hara's (Pat O'Brien) orphanage. After getting a job in a restaurant, he attends a rollerbowl and meets Mary (Beverly Tyler), a champion skater. She teaches Johnny how to skate and as his skills increase, so does his ego. When Johnny proves himself against the champion, big-mouthed speedskater Mack Miller (Glenn Corbett), he's offered a spot with the Bears, a champion skating team. Later, when he's honored with the title Athlete of the Year, the increasing fame goes to his head and he begins to lose the respect of those closest to him. Monroe plays Polly, a well-dressed roller derby "groupie" of sorts. She has a few brief scenes and a couple of lines.

However, when Johnny is struck down with polio, Mary and Father O'Hara stick by him and nurse him back to health. Though Johnny recovers and returns to the rink, his ego is again inflated by the adulation of the cheering crowds. When Father O'Hara asks Johnny to help guide an up-and-coming skater, he refuses and it's evident that Johnny has returned to his old, selfish ways. While playing the game, Johnny recalls the love, loyalty and selflessness showed to him by Mary and Father O'Hara during his illness; he then softens his stance by helping the rookie skater to score. Johnny's grandstanding ways are finally a thing of the past: He becomes a team player, thus reaping the rewards, both on and off the rink.

Monroe wears a gray-bodiced sweater dress with black sleeves in this production. It can be seen again in the last scene of *All About Eve* (1950) and also in *Home Town Story* (1951). She also wore the dress in a 1950 screen test for *Cold Shoulder*, a film that was never made.

All About Eve (1950)

Marilyn Monroe appeared as Miss Caswell. Twentieth Century–Fox. 138 minutes. *Working Title:* Best Performance. *Writer-Director:* Joseph L. Mankiewicz. *Producer:* Darryl F. Zanuck. *Original Music:* Alfred Newman. *Cinematography:* Milton Krasner. *Costume Design:* Edith Head and Charles LeMaire. *Production Dates:* April 10 to June 7, 1950. *Production Cost:* $1.4 million. *Domestic Box Office Receipts:* $2.9 million; $4.2 million (worldwide). *Release Date:* October 13, 1950. *Genre:* Drama. Black and White. *Other Cast:* Bette Davis (Margo), Anne Baxter (Eve), George Sanders (Addison DeWitt), Celeste Holm (Karen), Gary Merrill (Bill Simpson), Hugh Marlowe (Lloyd Richards), Gregory Ratoff (Max Fabian), Barbara Bates (Phoebe), Thelma Ritter (Birdie). *Academy Awards:* Best Picture (won); Best Screenplay (won); Best Director (won); Best Supporting Actor (George Sanders—won); Best Sound Recording (Monroe personally presented the Oscar to Thomas Moulton—won); and Best Costume Design (Edith Head—won). Bette Davis and Anne Baxter were both nominated for Best Actress, marking the first time that two actresses were nominated for starring roles in the same film. They both lost to Judy Holliday (*Born Yesterday*). Celeste Holm and Thelma Ritter were nominated for Best Supporting Actress. They both lost to Josephine Hull (*Harvey*). Best Art Direction (nominated), Best Editing (nominated), Best Score (nominated), and Best Cinematography (nominated). *Tagline:* It's all about women—and their men!

Marilyn Monroe's salary was $500 a week on a one-week guarantee, from May 11 to June 7, 1950. The film's star Bette Davis had little time for the up-and-coming starlet who was scripted to appear as aspiring actress Miss Caswell, the token-blonde party date of acidic theater critic Addison DeWitt (George Sanders); Monroe was terrified of Davis and Davis reveled in her fear. "She made me feel so nervous," said Monroe. "She didn't talk to me at all, just sort of swept around the set, nose and cigarette in the air. She's a mean old broad" (Staggs, p. 94). Sanders' own opinion of Monroe was put in print in his 1960 autobiography *Memoirs of a Professional Cad*: "Marilyn struck me as a character in search of an author and I am delighted she found Mr. [Arthur] Miller eventually."

Bette Davis plays the role of Margo Channing, an aging, jaded Broadway star with many insecurities. When Eve Harrington attends the theater each night to watch Margo perform, as her most devoted fan, she meets her idol and becomes a central part of her life. Margo trusts Eve, but as the film progresses, the audience realizes that Eve isn't the innocent that she appears to be. Eve is an aspiring actress and she learns everything she can about

Anne Baxter, Bette Davis, Marilyn and George Sanders in a scene from *All About Eve* (1950).

Margo, feeding off her insecurities, gaining her trust, with the self-serving intention of taking her man and her career away from her.

All About Eve is a masterfully told story, a Hollywood classic worthy of its fourteen Oscar nominations, an Academy record only equaled in 1998 by James Cameron's epic *Titanic*. As of 2012, it still holds the record as the only film in Oscar history to nominate its four female stars (Davis and Baxter for Best Actress and Holm and Ritter for Best Supporting Actress). Writer-director Joseph L. Mankiewicz gives the audience a witty and sarcastic behind-the-scenes peek into the rivalry and backbiting that is commonplace in show business circles.

Home Town Story (1951)

Marilyn Monroe appeared as Iris Martin, the secretary. MGM. 61 minutes. Working *Title: The Headline Story*. *Director-Producer-Writer:* Arthur Pierson. *Original Music:* Louis Forbes. *Cinematography:* Lucien Andriot. *Production Dates:* Early 1950 at Hal Roach Studios. *Release Date:* May 18, 1951. *Genre:* Drama. Black and White. *Other Cast:* Jeffrey Lynn (Blake Washburn), Donald Crisp (John MacFarland), Marjorie Reynolds (Janice Hunt), Alan Hale, Jr. (Slim Haskins), Barbara Brown (Mrs. Washburn), Melinda Plowman (Katie Washburn), Renny McEvoy (Leo, the Taxi Driver), Glenn Tryon (Ken Kenlock).

Arthur Pierson, who wrote, directed and produced this film, had already worked with Marilyn on *Dangerous Years* (1947). She supplied her own wardrobe for her role of the secretary, Iris Martin. Once again, she chose the gray-bodiced sweater dress with the black sleeves. According to *Daily Variety* (April 1, 1951), the film cost somewhere between $150,000 and $200,000 to make.

Home Town Story is a propaganda tale (subsidized by General Motors) focused on the life of Blake Washburn (Jeffrey Lynn), a disillusioned state senator who returns to his home town and his patient fiancée of seven years, Janice (Marjorie Reynolds), after failing to be re-elected. Convinced that John MacFarland (Donald Crisp) hoodwinked the public into voting for him, Washburn sets his sights on working for "the people" in a different way, by taking a job as editor at his uncle's newspaper, the *Fairfax Herald*. At first, he's revenge-driven, determined to reveal that MacFarland's factory is dumping waste into the river. After some investigating, he finds they're above-board and eco-friendly.

Title card for *Home Town Story* (1951).

Washburn's bitterness at losing the election, and losing it to an honest man, spills over into his reporting. With daily headlines slamming the profits of big business in America, he gets his voice back and regains the respect of the people for revealing the truth about corporate greed.

Alan Hale Jr. gives a commendable performance as Slim Haskins, the good-natured reporter friend of Washburn who's smitten with Monroe's character. Playing the newspaper's sexy secretary Iris Martin, Monroe parades around the *Fairfax Herald* office in tight clothing. She has few lines and little to do other than that.

Washburn's much-younger sister Katie (Melinda Plowman) goes on a class trip and gets trapped in a collapsed mineshaft along with her new puppy. A bulldozer is brought in to clear the rocks from the opening and most of the principal cast members look on as the precarious rescue effort takes place. The child and puppy are rescued alive, but Katie is in critical condition. MacFarland steps in and offers his private plane as the fastest mode of transport to the hospital. Piloting the aircraft himself, MacFarland flies Katie and her family to the only facility equipped to perform the life-saving surgery. After several tense scenes in the hospital, Katie pulls through, not only because of MacFarland's generosity, but also because of the machinery produced by the big businesses that Washburn was so hellbent in trying to bring down.

Washburn's attitude dramatically changes. Now resolved to the fact that his political career is behind him, he writes a positive article about MacFarland and asks his fiancée if she'd like to be married to a guy who's happy to be editor of the *Fairfax Herald*.

There were over three decades between on-screen siblings Jeffrey Lynn and Melinda Plowman, and less than eight years between Jeffrey Lynn and his on-screen mother Barbara Brown. But despite the misguided casting choices, *Home Town Story* is a tight hour-long example of 1950s American propaganda that is designed to entertain *and* send a message. That said, without Marilyn Monroe in the cast, it's fair to say this film would get little to no mention today.

As Young as You Feel
(1951)

Marilyn Monroe appeared as Harriet, the secretary. Twentieth Century–Fox. 77 minutes. *Alternate Titles: Will You Love Me in December?* and *The Great American Hoax*. *Director:* Harmon Jones. *Producer:* Lamar Trotti. *Writers:* Paddy Chayefsky and Lamar Trotti. *Original Music:* Cyril Mockridge. *Cinematography:* Joe MacDonald. *Costume Design:* Renie. *Production Dates:* December 15, 1950 to late January 1951. *Release Date:* June 15, 1951. *Genre:* Comedy. Black and White. *Other Cast:* Monty Woolley (John R. Hodges), Thelma Ritter (Della Hodges), David Wayne (Joe Elliot), Jean Peters (Alice Hodges), Constance Bennett (Lucille McKinley), Allyn Joslyn (George Hodges), Albert Dekker (Mr. McKinley), Clinton Sundberg (Frank Erickson), Minor Watson (Harold P. Cleveland), Wally Brown (Horace Gallagher), Russ Tamblyn (Willie McKinley).

The production of *As Young as You Feel* was yet another bittersweet time for Marilyn Monroe. On December 10, 1950, shortly before filming began, she had once again signed with Twentieth Century–Fox. At $500 per week, it was her highest salary to date. *As Young as You Feel* was her first film under this new contract.

Marilyn poses in front of a billboard advertising her latest film, *As Young as You Feel* (1951).

In an April 1, 1951, interview with Louella O. Parsons, Monroe explained her return to Fox:

> I am naturally shy, and I was so frightened when I first started to act that the words would not come out of my mouth. I was so impossible that after I finished school on the 20th lot I was fired. I had never met Darryl Zanuck, so when I came back to 20th he sent for me. He said, "So you were fired? I didn't even know you were here."

Monroe told Zanuck that she *should* have been fired. Parsons' story continues, "[Monroe] said, 'I was so scared I couldn't do a thing. But now I have studied voice and I have worked very hard. I was also fired from Columbia after six months' ("Parsons, "Marilyn Monroe: From Orphanage to Stardom").

Director Elia Kazan and a good friend, playwright Arthur Miller, visited the set of *As Young as You Feel*. Miller was then unhappily married to Mary Slattery; in five years, he and Monroe would wed. It was during this production that Miller first set eyes on and witnessed "the walk" of his second wife, Marilyn Monroe. He and Kazan stood mesmerized as Monroe swayed her way across a nightclub floor in a black lace dress. While some suggest that one heel of her shoe was shaved down to create the hip-swinging sashay that she was renowned for, Miller insisted that her walk was natural. He claimed her bare footprints on the beach clearly showed that her heel would descend precisely before her last toe print, and it was this pattern that swung her hips into motion (Bigsby, "Marilyn Monroe and Arthur Miller: Extract from Christopher Bigsby's Biography").

Kazan, although married, was a notorious womanizer. Without blinking an eye, he embarked on a torrid affair with Monroe. Kazan and Miller were friends, colleagues and as close as brothers. He knew Miller's feelings for Monroe, but that didn't stop him. For the duration of her affair with Kazan, Monroe maintained contact with Miller, writing letters, reading his novels and keeping a photograph of him on her bedside table. The three would even be seen out together. It was as though Kazan was keeping Monroe warm for Miller's eventual takeover. While their relationship survived sharing the same woman, it didn't survive their respective testimonies (or non-testimony in Miller's case) before the House Un-American Activities Committee led by Senator Joseph McCarthy.

Miller strongly opposed the hearings. When he was called to testify, he refused to cooperate and "name names." As a result, in 1957, he was convicted of contempt of Congress. He appealed the conviction and it was overturned on August 7, 1958. It was a rocky period that threatened not only his career, but the career of Marilyn Monroe. Miller despised those in the industry who chose to protect themselves by naming peers with possible Communist leanings. Kazan was one of the "tattlers" and it would be a decade before the men would utter another word to each other. Even then, their once close relationship wasn't the same. By late 1947, Kazan had co-founded New York's Actors Studio, a place where Monroe first observed, then studied her craft. The Actors Studio taught Monroe total immersion acting, known as "Method." It's somewhat ironic that the Actors Lab building is a former Greek Orthodox Church, since many of the students look to the "Method" as an alternate form of religion. By May of 1955, Marilyn Monroe was one of its newest disciples.

As Young as You Feel is a family-based story that drives home the "live to work, work to live" motto in a whimsical 1950s tone. Its highlight is the usual solid performances from veteran character actors Thelma Ritter as Della, the matriarch of the Hodges family and Monty Woolley as Hodges, the aging but happily employed hand press printer at ACME Printing

Services. When Hodges' paycheck includes a termination notice, it isn't because of his poor work performance, it's because of his age. Not ready to give up work at sixty-five, and not ready to be forced to do so, Hodges takes a stroll in the park, sits on a bench and re-reads the termination notice that has turned his world upside down. It's then he notices a company name that is in no way associated with his work—Consolidated Motors. After finding out that ACME Printing Services is a subsidiary of Consolidated Motors, Hodges comes up with a plan to get his job back. He'll pose as Harold P. Cleveland, the president of Consolidated Motors. As Cleveland, he'll change company policy and return to his job.

Mr. McKinley (Albert Dekker) gets word of the impending arrival of the "big boss." A paranoid Mr. McKinley wonders why the head of so many companies would choose ACME, Printing Services to visit. With little time for conjecture, he instructs his workers and executives to look busy when the president of Consolidated Motors arrives.

Hodges arrives with his hair and whiskers darkened and serving as his only disguise. Joe (David Wayne), the fiancé of Hodges' granddaughter Alice (Jean Peters), is the only ACME employee who recognizes the old man. Following his tour of the printing plant, Hodges, posing as Cleveland, meets with Mr. McKinley and his board. Of course, the discussion brings to light the lack of mature workers on staff at ACME and Hodges expresses disappointment over this. Making every effort to please, Mr. McKinley instructs his glamorous secretary Harriet (Monroe) to draft a letter to former employees from the past year to announce that the forced retirement of ACME workers is no longer company policy and that no matter their age, so long as they were willing, their jobs would again be open to them. Hodges breathes a sigh of relief and assumes the sham is all but over. Hodges next speaks to the Chamber of Commerce on the topic of aging workers. When his speech gets a standing ovation, a photo of Hodges, posing as Cleveland, along with an article about his motivational appearance, is printed in the evening paper. Despite the publicity, no one but Joe sees the resemblance between the two men, not even his close-knit family. Meanwhile, Hodges has charmed and danced his way into the heart of the unhappily married Mrs. McKinley (Constance Bennett). After a night of dancing with Hodges, posing as Cleveland, she tells her neglectful husband that she wants a divorce. Even after his true identity is revealed, the enamored Mrs. McKinley leaves home with suitcase in hand and ends up at the Hodges' front door. Bewildered, yet flattered by her infatuation, Hodges convinces Mrs. McKinley that she still loves her husband.

Once the real Mr. Cleveland (Minor Watson) gets wind of the impersonation, he and the executives at Consolidated Motors must decide whether or not to prosecute or congratulate Hodges. Though his initial self-serving antics exploded beyond his control, his dignified representation of the company brought Consolidated Motors nothing but positive press, and higher stock prices.

When Cleveland meets Hodges, he understands the meaning behind his initial plan and even offers him a public relations position with the company in New York. Not wanting to leave his family, Hodges respectfully turns him down.

Despite Mrs. McKinley's reconciliation with her uptight husband, Mr. McKinley spontaneously fires Hodges for all the trouble he's caused. Cleveland laughs off McKinley's emotional outburst and assures Hodges his job at ACME will be restored immediately, and for as long as he wants it.

Though Monroe's image is prominently displayed on modern-day promotional material

As Young as You Feel (1951) 55

Marilyn is poolside with the man who dropped everything and everyone in a bid to catapult her to stardom, Hollywood power agent Johnny Hyde.

for the film, it's walking the "false advertising" line very closely. This is far from a "Marilyn Monroe film," and certainly not a starring role. As Mr. McKinley's beautiful, blonde secretary she has a few scenes here and there, but essentially she's really nothing more than eye-candy and her character goes nowhere. Her stilted tone of voice (a style of delivery that drama coach Natasha Lytess had taught her) is on prominent display in *As Young as You Feel*.

While Lytess initially developed the technique to help rid Monroe of her nervous stutter, the clipped emphasis when pronouncing her *d*s and her *t*s often sounds unnatural and forced. Likewise, the lowering of her top lip when speaking, together with the peculiar, quivering mouth movements, were all part of the Lytess "style." From her facial expressions to her diction to her walk, there was so much going on, so much for Monroe to think about when delivering her lines, that many of her early performances come across as wooden and overly controlled. She was better than that, and her standout performance in *Clash by Night* (1952) proves it: Though Monroe was still very much under the influence of Lytess, she goes totally against the inflexible formula taught her, and the results are better than ever. *Clash by Night* and *Something's Got to Give* (1962), though a decade apart, are the two best examples of Marilyn Monroe's natural speaking voice on film. In both performances, her mannerisms and delivery feel genuine and unaffected by the rigidity of stylized teaching.

Many of the characters featured throughout *As Young as You Feel* come and go during the last moments of the film, but Monroe isn't one of them. We leave her in Mr. McKinley's outer office: Open-mouthed and outraged, she slumps back onto her desk after her enraged boss tells her, "Go fry an egg!" The film carries on and ends without her. Her performance didn't go without notice, Bosley Crowther of the *New York Times* (August 3, 1951) writing, "Marilyn Monroe is superb as [Albert Dekker's] secretary."

On May 11, 1951, Hugh French and Charles Feldman at Famous Artists Agency renegotiated Monroe's Fox contract, extending it from six months to seven years and raising her salary to $500 per week on a guarantee, which meant she was paid if she was working or not. She would be placed in films at the studio's discretion, and Fox had the right to review and renew (or not) her contract yearly. If she remained at the studio for the duration of the contract, her second year salary would increase to $750 per week. The third year she'd receive $1,250 per week, the fourth year $1,500 per week, the fifth year $2,000 per week and the sixth year $2,500 per week. And by 1957, her last contractual year, her salary would increase to $3,500 per week. Though Monroe enjoyed the security of the long-term contract, her salary was still very low, and the contract was squarely in favor of the studio. Loanouts were at Fox's discretion, and even if she was loaned to another studio, she'd receive her basic fee and anything over would be studio profit. Performing on TV, radio, recordings or theatrical plays weren't permitted unless Fox approved. Her refusal to appear in a film allocated to her would result in a suspension without pay, with the suspension period added to the tail end of the contract.

Prior to this deal, Monroe's appearance at the Fox exhibitor's party turned heads and set tongues wagging. She arrived an hour and a half late in a black strapless cocktail dress; Fox president Spyros Skouras led her straight to his table. When excited exhibitors demanded to know what films the stunning blonde would be seen in, Fox knew they'd struck gold and they needed to secure her services long-term. While this story is often cited as the reason Monroe got her new contract, the reality was, the offer had already been submitted to William Morris several weeks earlier, but not yet signed. Monroe's clause to include Natasha Lytess and put her on salary was the reason for the delay. But following Monroe's "wow" entrance at the Fox exhibitor's party, the studio immediately agreed to her request.

A few years after this contract was signed, Monroe would go on strike in a bid to renegotiate her wages and regain control of her skyrocketing career. Taking on an entire studio and its powerful executives, and breaking the terms of a contract she fought so hard to get in the first place was a brave move. If it didn't work, it quite probably meant career suicide. But she stood her ground and was victorious. As a result, the original seven-year contract was never exercised full-term. Backtrack to the end of spring of 1951, the long-term contract offered by Fox single-handedly secured Monroe's place as a rising star. It came to be because of the persistence of one man: Johnny Hyde.

On December 18, 1950, shortly after filming began, Monroe's agent Johnny Hyde passed away. Having represented Rita Hayworth, Lana Turner, Betty Hutton and Mae West, just to name a few, Hyde was one of the most powerful agents in Hollywood. Though he was almost thirty-one years Monroe's senior, like most men who crossed her path, age wasn't a factor and he fell deeply in love with her. He was a diminutive man of average looks and declining health; his reputation was much bigger than the man himself. Soon after Hyde set his sights on Monroe, he left his wife Mozelle and moved out of the family home. He moved into a rented house on North Palm Drive and Monroe moved in with him shortly thereafter. At the time, Monroe had been living on and off with Lytess, but she also kept a room in her name at the Beverly Carlton Hotel.

Hyde transformed Monroe—literally. In early January of 1949, Hyde bought out Monroe's contract with her previous agent, Harry Lipton. Despite representing other clients, his new obsession allowed him no time to devote to any of them. He began a one-man campaign to make Marilyn a star, from her platinum blonde hair being regularly dyed to avoid any sign of darker regrowth, to her wardrobe choices, her makeup, even plastic surgery on her nose and chin. Once again, Monroe dutifully did as she was told. Sometime in 1950, Dr. Michael Gurdin inserted a collagen implant into Monroe's chin. He had already performed a "tip rhinoplasty" to reshape the end of her nose (he made it look less bulbous and more feminine). Unlike the radical plastic surgeries performed today, Monroe's subtle surgical molding enhanced her natural features without changing her into an unrecognizable version of her original self.

While both Hyde and Lytess had Monroe's best interests at heart, from the time of their very first meeting, they despised each other. However, Lytess didn't reserve all her hatred for Hyde; *any* man in Monroe's life was looked upon as a threat and treated poorly. In fact, most people who came into contact with Lytess loathed her. It took many years, but eventually, Monroe's eyes were opened to her inability to interact with *anyone* else on a civil level.

Lytess saw Monroe as a serious actress and she felt her "relationship" with Hyde would give her the reputation of a young starlet who used an older man to get where she needed to be. She was better than that. Both Lytess and Hyde truly believed in Monroe's abilities, but they had different ideas of where her career should go. When Monroe moved in with Hyde, Lytess felt that her work with her and her direction for her would unravel.

Though Monroe and Hyde became lovers, Monroe was always very open and honest about the extent of her feelings for him. Hyde accepted the relationship for what it was. Always holding out some hope that Monroe would someday agree to marry him, he worked tirelessly to please her, shower her with gifts, call in favors and advance her career by opening doors for her. He exposed her to people she would never dream of meeting and places that she would never dream of going without him on her arm. They were the oddest of couples.

In his 2009 book *Arthur Miller: 1915–1962*, Christopher Bigsby writes about a conversation that Lytess and Monroe had following Hyde's death. According to Lytess, Monroe said:

> I knew nobody could help me like Johnny Hyde… But I felt sorry for him, too, and he was crazy about me. I never lied to him, and I didn't think it wrong to let him love me the way I did. The sex meant so much to him but not to me.

Monroe undoubtedly loved Hyde for all that he had done for her, but she was never in love with him and she never pretended to be. Becoming his wife would have made her a very rich woman, but it also would have destroyed her career. Despite the fact that she refused his repeated proposals, Hyde remained devoted to Monroe in every way. After several heart attacks, Hyde was well aware that he was living on borrowed time. He had long intended to rewrite his will, and he went as far as informing his lawyers that he wanted to make Monroe a one-third beneficiary of his estate. Though the 55-year-old Hyde died before his final wishes were legally put down on paper, his influence had already more than provided for Monroe's financial future. Because of him, over the course of the next few years, she would provide for herself and become the movie star that Hyde always knew she'd become. He may have gotten her started, but it was now entirely up to her to keep the momentum going.

On his deathbed, Hyde insisted that Monroe stay in the house they shared. He asked for her constantly but his family did everything in their power to keep her out of his hospital room. Ironically, Hyde had organized the careers and arranged studio contracts for some of Hollywood's most iconic stars, yet personally, he had failed to legally secure Monroe's place in his life following his death. Hyde's estranged wife exercised her rights as his legal partner and she ordered her lawyer to evict Monroe immediately following her husband's death. Monroe was stripped of every possession that Hyde had ever given her. Grief-stricken, she went back to the home of Natasha Lytess.

Though Monroe and Lytess had quarreled often about Hyde's "interference," which is how Lytess viewed his actions, she took Monroe back in, allowed her to grieve and then remolded her into what she wanted her to be: a serious actress. With Hyde gone forever, Lytess reveled in the fact that she was once again in control of Monroe's life and career. Whether she admitted it or not, it was a career that Hyde had very much created. Though she remained under contract with the William Morris Agency for several years after Hyde's death, they refused to take her calls. Now that Hyde was dead, no one was interested in Johnny's girl.

There are two conflicting accounts of Monroe's appearance at Hyde's burial. Though his family had banned her, one story has her showing up and causing a scene by dramatically throwing herself across his coffin, screaming his name in her grief. The other story tells of her waiting in dignified silence for everyone to leave before sitting in the cemetery to mourn in silence. She then took a single white rose from a floral arrangement and pressed it within the pages of her Bible as a keepsake. As with many areas of Marilyn Monroe's personal life, varying versions of exaggerated extremes have been recounted over the years.

Monroe soon fell into a deep depression. Feeling guilty for the workload that Hyde had taken on to propel her career, she felt responsible for his death. Still crushed over her broken romance with Fred Karger and now brokenhearted by the death of her mentor Hyde, the pain was too much to bear.

One afternoon, Lytess returned home hours early, and found Monroe unconscious with undissolved pills still in her mouth. Lytess had no idea how many had been ingested, as Monroe was rushed to a hospital. During the course of her life, Monroe's various overdoses were either serious cries for help or serious cries for attention; none were serious attempts to kill herself.

As Young as You Feel was shot during this traumatic and unsettling period, a time of immense change and personal loss, but also a time of immense hope for a future that both she and Hyde had worked so hard to achieve.

A few months previous, Marilyn Monroe was in the best position of her career to date. Twentieth Century–Fox conference notes (from October 11, 1950) relating to the first draft continuity confirms Marilyn Monroe in the role of Harriet. Darryl Zanuck describes her character as

> McKinley's secretary ... one look at her and we just know there is monkey-business going on. She is constantly fixing her face, tweezing her eyebrows, brushing her hair. When McKinley speaks to her his gruffness disappears and he becomes lamb-gentle. They are probably having an affair. If not actually, then it won't be long now. Then the "President of General Motors" arrives and when Harriet sees him the wheels start going round in her head. If she can attract this one she'll brush McKinley off like a piece of lint.

For the first year of her long-term contract with Fox, Monroe earned $500 per week. At Monroe's insistence, Lytess got just as much. With her $500 salary per week from the studio, together with $250 a week from Monroe for their private sessions, the drama coach was in better financial shape than Marilyn was. Monroe's insistence on Lytess being with her on set at all times, along with her overbearing presence, infuriated many a director.

Whenever a director gave Monroe instructions on how to play out a scene, Lytess would turn to her and repeat his instructions, word for word. It was almost as if the director was speaking another language and it was up to Lytess to translate his direction to Monroe in terms she could better understand. Realistically, Lytess said nothing the director hadn't already said; Monroe just related to the original direction better if it came from Lytess's lips.

Following each take, the moment "Cut" was called, Monroe would look straight past the director to Lytess for her endorsement of her performance. A nod of her head or a specific hand signal was the difference between her approval and disapproval. The director's opinion of a scene was secondary to Lytess's viewpoint. If Lytess said, "Do it again," Monroe insisted on doing the scene again too. The director was then forced to reshoot, even if *he* felt the take was good enough to print. This pattern continued from film to film. In hindsight, Lytess should be credited as co-director of every Monroe film she supervised. The pattern of disrespecting the director's position and undermining *his* vision for *his* film caused constant conflict and many heated battles. It wasn't unusual for directors to banish Lytess from sets.

But the bans would never last long. Monroe would feign illness until Lytess returned and the situation was resolved. Coincidentally, Monroe would be well enough to return to work at the exact same time Lytess was reinstated. And, from that moment on, the director would learn to bite his tongue until filming was over. After all, if there was no Lytess, there was no Monroe, and if there was no Monroe, there was no film!

According to promotional flyers for *As Young as You Feel*, Monroe, "the azure-eyed, honey-tressed actress with the most provocative chassis to reach the screen since Jean Harlow, has five wardrobe changes—each a sweater of a different type ... described by the costuming department as: 1. Loose fitting. 2. Draping. 3. Clinging. 4. Tight. 5. Gee whizz!!!"

Love Nest
(1951)

Marilyn Monroe appeared as Roberta "Bobbie" Stevens. Twentieth Century–Fox. 84 minutes. *Alternate titles: The Reluctant Landlord* and *A WAC in His Life. Director:* Joseph Newman. *Producer:* Jules Buck. *Screenplay:* I.A.L. Diamond. Based on a novel by Scott Corbett. *Original Music:* Cyril Mockridge. *Cinematography:* Lloyd Ahern. *Costume Design:* Renie. *Production Dates:* April 19 to May 16, 1951. *Production Cost:* $765,000. *Release Date:* October 10, 1951. *Genre:* Comedy-Drama-Romance. Black and White. *Other Cast:* June Haver (Connie Scott), William Lundigan (Jim Scott), Frank Fay (Charles Kenneth Patterson), Jack Paar (Ed Forbes), Leatrice Joy (Eadie Gaynor), Henry Kulky (George Thompson).

Anne Baxter and Jeanne Crain were first penciled in for the role of Connie. *Love Nest* rounded out the careers of veteran stars Frank Fay, a vaudeville veteran, and Leatrice Joy, a silent era leading lady; they play a married couple in their late fifties.

In 1946, when Jim Scott (William Lundigan) returns from the war, he arrives at the address of a home, *his* home, that he's yet to see in person: The New York City apartment building (337 Gramercy Place) was bought by his industrious wife Connie (June Haver) in his absence. At a price tag of $22,000, the young couple have invested everything they have and are mortgaged to the eyeballs, but an exuberant Connie has grand plans of fixing the place up and making a living from the rental income on the apartments.

Though they own the building, the Scotts make do with the uncomfortable basement as their own living quarters and are at the beck and call of the quirky tenants. Many of their tenants are women in their twilight years, so when the very charming Charley Patterson (Frank Fay) moves in, the lonely ladies are enamored with his frequent compliments and gentlemanly ways. Charley takes a liking to Eadie Gaynor (Leatrice Joy), a widow with a teenage daughter. As Charley sets his sights on Eadie, Jim and Connie get suspicious of his too-charming ways, especially after a potential tenant thinks she recognizes him from Cincinnati. Though she calls him by a different name, she's sure her instincts are correct and she leaves the building upset, declining to take the apartment because of his presence.

An FBI man shows up to inquire about Charley's whereabouts, and Jim and Connie inform the agent that he's on a business trip—or so he said. While out to dinner at a local restaurant, Jim and Connie spot Charley dancing with another woman. When Charley announces that he's proposed to Eadie and that she's accepted, a protective Connie is worried that Eadie will not only become Charley's next wife, but also his next victim!

To add more fuel to the fire, the vacant apartment is eventually rented by one of Jim's Army buddies, Corporal Stevens. But when Roberta "Bobbie" Stevens (Marilyn) shows up, Connie is enraged that her husband of three years (two and a half of them spent in the Army) has been stationed overseas with the seductive blonde model and ex–WAC.

Monroe's character introduces another layer to the problems the couple have in the building that of course spill over into their otherwise happy marriage. While Jim recognizes Roberta is a knockout, he's been nothing but faithful to Connie and he does his best to put her jealousy to rest. Nothing's going to stop his single pal Ed (Jack Paar) from pursuing her, though. Courtesy of writer I.A.L. Diamond, Connie gets a chance to throw Roberta a few sarcastic barbs, many of which are laugh out loud funny

Jim tries to find time to resume his writing career, writing a magazine article or two to earn extra cash to pour into their money pit building. Between fixing pipes, dealing with a jealous wife, suspecting a tenant is a wanted man, and a building inspector who threatens to condemn the building if an $800 wiring problem isn't redone in two weeks, the couple's days as New York City landlords are less than harmonious.

Following Eadie and Charley's wedding, they return home to find a FOR SALE sign on the building. Disturbed by the news, Charley enquires about how much money it would take to straighten things out. Jim explains the wiring problem and without blinking an eye, Charley pulls out a wad of cash and gives him the money to fix it. Reluctant at first, Jim accepts on the condition that the money be an advance on rent. Though Connie is desperate to keep the building, she's reluctant to take money from Charley (she suspects he's a swindler). When a headline about a multi-named Casanova who romances elderly widows for their money appears on the front page of the newspaper, Connie believes the description fits Charley perfectly.

Monroe promotes her latest film, her bikini body *and* Coca-Cola in this promotional still for *Love Nest* (1951).

Jim and Connie confront Charley and he admits he's made a living out of charming elderly women out of the riches that their husbands have left behind. However, he swears that he truly loves Eadie and that he is content to live out his days as Eadie's devoted husband. With the law on his tail, Charley starts to pack a suitcase in order to skip town until the story dies down. Jim and Connie, while not condoning his actions, adore Eadie and have a soft spot for Charley, so when the police arrive, Jim shows him the back way out. Charley gets stuck on a nail in the fence and much to Eadie's dismay, he's arrested and taken into custody. She vows to wait for him to return to her after serving jail time for his crimes.

With Charley behind bars, Connie tells Jim they have to turn the $800 he gave them over to the police because it's stolen money. However, the police find Jim first: They arrive late at night, the officer saying that Charley told them about the $800. And Charley *also* told the police that the money was given over as a bribe, so that Jim would hide him. Horrified by the lie, Jim is thrown into the same cell as Charley and lays into him about his deception. Charley says he needed to speak with Jim about a business proposition, and the lie was the only way to get to him.

Charley has accepted an offer of $5,000 to tell his life story while he's still a hot commodity—but it was on the condition that Jim write the story for him. Charley offers Jim half the money for the writing job and tells him to give the other half to Eadie. Of course, the money would solve all of Jim and Connie's financial problems, allowing them to keep their building. It's a deal too good to pass up. Charley begins dictating his life to Jim in the cell, starting with his birth. Next we see Charley's story in a bookstore window, a best seller as told to Jim Scott. For a lifetime of crime, Charley serves a scant 18 months in jail, returns to his beloved Eadie and swears that he's now a one-woman man. Jim and Connie keep the apartment building, renovate it and even turn down a $35,000 offer to sell it. In the last scene, Jim and Connie help Eadie and Charley down the front stoop with a double baby carriage. In it are Eadie and Charley's twin babies. It is the silliest scene of the film, since the pair are old enough to be grandparents. The thought of Eadie giving birth at her age is ludicrous, but perhaps it was I.A.L. Diamond's sense of humor. After all, he couldn't possibly think an audience would believe her to be of reproductive age!

Monroe appears for about ten minutes in total, but she still makes her mark in a role that once again clearly places her in the eye candy category. In one scene, she appears in a bathing costume, and though it's tame compared to today's standards, at the time, it was controversial enough for it to be shot on a closed set. In another scene, she undresses in her apartment and takes a shower. We see her in a sexy lace slip, and stepping out of the shower wrapped in a towel—but again, the scenes are mild today.

During the production of *Love Nest*, Monroe enrolled in an adult program at the University of California. She took classes in art appreciation and literature, not for publicity purposes but for self-betterment. Taking extra-curricular classes away from her film career, studying art, literature, history, drama, etc., was something she did her entire life. Few people took her interest in learning seriously, offering one ulterior motive after another as to why a woman who looked the way she did would want, or need, to study anything seriously at all. On yet another level, few thought that a woman with her looks would even be capable of learning anything more than applying the right shade of lipstick. Her *Love Nest* co-star Jack Paar fell into these arrogantly moronic "dumb blonde" assumptions, claiming he never saw her read a page of the books that she would religiously carry around on set, which prompted him to cruelly conclude, "[B]eneath the façade of Marilyn there was only a frightened waitress in a diner" (McCann, p. 45).

Let's Make It Legal (1951)

Marilyn Monroe appeared as Joyce Mannering. Twentieth Century–Fox. 77 minutes. *Alternate Titles: Don't Call Me Mother* and *Grandma Was a Gold Digger*. *Director:* Richard Sale. *Producer:* Robert Bassler. Based on the story "My Mother-in-Law, Miriam" by Mortimer Braus. *Original Music:* Cyril Mockridge. *Cinematography:* Lucien Ballard. *Costume Design:* Renie and Charles LeMaire. *Production Dates:* Early May to early June 1951. *Production Cost:* $835,000. *Domestic Box Office Receipts:* $1.25 million. *Release Date:* October 31, 1951. *Genre:* Comedy-Drama-Romance. Black and White. *Other Cast:* Claudette Colbert (Miriam Halsworth), Macdonald Carey (Hugh Halsworth), Zachary Scott (Victor Macfarland), Barbara Bates (Barbara Denham), Robert Wagner (Jerry Denham), Baby Annabella (Joan Fisher). *Taglines:* It's 10 percent improper!; It's 40 percent illegal!; It's 100 percent hilarious!; See blonde Marilyn Monroe, Miss Cheesecake herself!

This is a romantic comedy with little for Marilyn Monroe to do but look pretty and lust after the wealthy Victor Macfarland (Zachary Scott), who only has eyes for the soon-to-be-divorced Miriam Halsworth (Claudette Colbert). Miriam's soon-to-be-ex-husband Hugh (Macdonald Carey) is a compulsive gambler, and this is the reason for the couple's split. Despite his wife's hostility, he's still in love with her and he frequently visits the family home to take care of his beloved rose garden.

Hugh dates the superficial, much younger Joyce (Marilyn Monroe) in an attempt to make his Miriam jealous, but Miriam is too infatuated with the charming Victor to notice. Now that he's back in town, she hopes for a second chance at love with him.

In the meantime, Miriam and Hugh's spoiled daughter Barbara (Barbara Bates) is married to Jerry (Robert Wagner). They have an infant daughter, Annabella (Joan Fisher), whom neither pay particular attention to. Much to Jerry's dismay, they reside in Miriam's home. While Barbara spends most of her time sleeping in and pouting about her parents' break up, Jerry is fed up with the living arrangements and with his mother-in-law doing all of the domestic duties. In fact, he complains about the situation and his wife for most of the film. Jerry constantly bickers with his wife about her lazy ways and Barbara constantly complains to both her parents about her intolerable husband.

Following Miriam's divorce from Hugh she gleefully accepts Victor's marriage proposal,

L to R: Macdonald Carey, Marilyn, Zachary Scott and Claudette Colbert collide on the dance floor in *Let's Make It Legal* (1951).

but after finding out that the reason he suddenly ran out on her twenty years previously was because he lost her in a bet to Hugh, she blames her ex-husband for ruining her life and threatens to destroy his precious rose garden as revenge. Hugh decides to intercede and dig out the roses before Miriam gets to them first. His son-in-law Jerry helps him, but their midnight plant raid backfires, and they get caught in the act by two patrolling police officers.

When Miriam and Barbara arrive at the police station to bail them out, the press get wind of Victor's fiancée getting into a tussle with her ex-husband and their photograph is printed in newspapers across the country. Victor is furious at the unwanted publicity. He and Miriam get into an argument over the phone and she breaks off their engagement.

As Miriam continues to fight with Hugh over winning her in a game of craps with Victor two decades earlier, Hugh produces the two dice that he used in the game and he asks Miriam to roll them. After rolling the same number a few times, she realizes that Hugh didn't risk losing her at all—he cheated to win her. The dice are loaded! While Hugh's weakness for gambling was the reason behind their marital split, when he tells her that he had to cheat Victor because the stakes were too high to risk losing her, the couple kiss and make up.

Barbara Bates and Robert Wagner are an insufferable pair who do nothing but whine and complain, and both of them do it badly throughout the entire film. *Let's Make It Legal* would have been better without their unnecessary subplot to detract from the overall story. Monroe has few lines and little to do but look pretty and play the blonde floozy to Macdonald Carey's character. She appears more hyper and her vocalizations are faster and far less controlled than later on in her career.

Let's Make It Legal wasn't the only time Robert Wagner worked with Marilyn Monroe. According to his 2008 memoir *Pieces of My Heart: A Life*, Monroe had filmed several screen tests with him. He wrote: "I think I was in the test that got her a contract at Fox. I adored her. At this point in her career she wasn't troublesome at all. She knew her lines cold, was terribly sweet and eager to please, and I loved her."

Later in her career, Monroe was notorious for forgetting her lines, but on this film, Wagner said, "[S]he wasn't the problem. I was." He revealed that it took him forty-nine takes to complete just one shot and it was a number he never forgot.

Reviewer Margaret Bean of *The Spokesman-Review* (November 14, 1951) wrote:

> It's only a fair picture, although Claudette Colbert, Macdonald Carey, Zachary Scott and a flashy blonde, Marilyn Monroe, do very well in trying to make the pot boil... Marilyn Monroe is given showcase treatment, which proves that she is one more gift to the bathing suit industry. No wonder she has been voted Miss Cheesecake of 1951.

Miss Cheesecake of the Year was the title awarded her by *Stars and Stripes* magazine in 1951, and the following year the same magazine made her Cheesecake Queen of 1952.

Clash by Night
(1952)

Marilyn Monroe appeared as Peggy. RKO Radio Pictures. 105 minutes. *Director:* Fritz Lang. *Producer:* Harriet Parsons. *Screenplay:* Alfred Hayes. Based on the play by Clifford Odets. *Original Music:* Roy Webb. *Cinematography:* Nicholas Musuraca. *Production Dates:* October 8 to early December 1951; additional scenes late January 1952. *Release Date:* June 16, 1952. *Genre:* Drama. Black and White. *Other Cast:* Barbara Stanwyck (Mae Doyle D'Amato), Paul Douglas (Jerry D'Amato), Robert Ryan (Earl Pfeiffer), J. Carrol Naish (Uncle Vince), Silvio Minciotti (Papa D'Amato), Keith Andes (Joe Doyle). *Tagline*: Livin' in my house! Lovin' another man! Is that what you call bein' honest? That's just givin' it a nice name!

For *Clash by Night*, Fox loaned Monroe to RKO. Though she was still very much under the influence of Natasha Lytess, her performance as Peggy is surprisingly unaffected and natural, even more of a surprise since this was the film that marked the first appearance of Natasha Lytess on the set. Lytess was a formidable presence and it was the beginning of a co-dependent relationship that did nothing to help Monroe's confidence as an actress, though ironically, Lytess was a "must have" motivational tool, always on the sidelines to coach her and give her the confidence she needed to perform. Without Lytess on set, Monroe refused to utter a word. As the years went by, Monroe's star power grew but her self-confidence waned. Lytess fed off Monroe's soul. She knew Monroe relied on her; the reliance got to the point where she not only needed her by her side to work, she needed her to function *period*. Everyone but Monroe could see that Lytess was a hindrance to her wellbeing, her career and the film productions as a whole, but it would be seven years before Monroe would see it for herself.

Marilyn Monroe and Keith Andes in a promotional clinch from *Clash by Night* (1952).

Clash by Night was released hot on the heels of the risky revelation that Marilyn was the girl in the 1949 Tom Kelley nude calendar. Naturally, the media attention then gravitated towards this unknown blonde who was suddenly the talk of the town, and her co-stars resented the attention. Paul Douglas said, "Why the hell don't these goddamn photographers ever take any pictures of us? It's only that goddamn blonde bitch!" (Riese and Hitchens, p. 93).

Of course, RKO honchos were thrilled with the additional publicity, but for them, Monroe was only a temporary blip on their radar. The timing of the calendar photo breaking made for a decent box office return that no amount of general publicity could have brought to the film otherwise, and RKO was not forced into damage control like Fox. It was a win-win situation.

Monroe was contracted to Fox. This was *her* mess, and that made it *their* mess too. Both Monroe and the studio knew that an explanation would have to come eventually.

Box office receipts for *Clash by Night* proved the public didn't really care. Obviously, seeing Monroe with her clothes off prompted audiences to flock to theaters to see her with her clothes on. And critics noticed her too, not just for her looks, but for her acting ability. Monroe's performance in *Clash by Night* is a standout; she demands every minute of the audience's attention when she's on screen. In some instances, she even manages to do the unthinkable: She makes Barbara Stanwyck look dull. Edwin Schallert of the *Los Angeles Times* (June 7, 1952) wrote:

> [Keith] Andes and Miss Monroe in a counterpointing romance to the main plot make a great deal of their scenes in a very natural way. Miss Monroe has ideas about glitter such as Miss Stanwyck once had. But Andes succeeds in winning out with her along sounder lines.

Directed by Fritz Lang and produced by Harriet Parsons (daughter of gossip columnist Louella O. Parsons), *Clash by Night* is a film noir–esque drama based in the fishing village of Monterey, California. When the cynical and ever-restless Mae Doyle (Stanwyck) returns home after a decade away, her brother Joe (Keith Andes) is less than happy about it. Joe's girlfriend Peggy (Marilyn Monroe), a sardine cannery worker, gives Mae the welcome her brother doesn't, and Mae moves into the family home. Impressed with her worldly ways, Peggy enjoys Mae's company and defends her actions throughout the film.

Mae begins a relationship with the ever-reliable Jerry (Douglas), a kind-hearted local fisherman. His projectionist best friend Earl (Robert Ryan) has little regard for women and is the town's bad boy. He also finds himself attracted to Mae, but before Earl can make his move, Jerry asks her to marry him. Though Mae insists she wouldn't make a good wife and that she'd eventually break his heart, Jerry is too lovestruck to see Mae's shortcomings. Despite the fact that she doesn't love Jerry, she accepts his proposal in the hope that she'd gain some much-needed stability in the union.

Mae gives birth to a baby girl, but she's soon fed up with the mundane duties of a housewife and mother, and she seeks the excitement of something new, beginning an affair with, Earl. When Jerry finds out about the affair via his uncle (J. Carrol Naish), he confronts his wife and friend. When Mae confesses to her infidelity, Jerry yells that they're both "animals" and flees the scene.

Jerry finds Earl and almost chokes him to death before Mae breaks the men up. Hellbent on leaving town, Mae returns home to collect her daughter, but she isn't there. Unfazed, Earl wants Mae to forget all about her daughter and leave with him anyway. At this point, Mae sees what type of man Earl is and realizes that her rightful place is with her husband and daughter after all.

Mae finds Jerry on his boat and begs him for forgiveness. He agrees to give their marriage another try, but admits he may find it hard to trust her again. She agrees to his terms and tells him she's a changed woman. Jerry then tells Mae that their baby daughter is okay and asleep on the bunk. Mae goes to her and for the first time, she takes solace in the family life she once was so desperate to run away from.

In 1965, Barbara Stanwyck spoke about her co-starring role with Monroe:

> She was awkward. She couldn't get out of her own way. She wasn't disciplined, and she was often late, and she drove Bob Ryan, Paul Douglas and myself out of our minds … but she didn't do it viciously, and there was a sort of magic about her which we all recognized at once. Her phobias, or whatever they were, came later; she seemed just a carefree kid, and she owned the world [Smith, p. 233].

Director Fritz Lang recognized Monroe's frailties early on. He also witnessed the birth of the media frenzy that would become a suffocation for the rest of her life. Swarms of journalists flocked to the set to speak with and photograph Monroe following the nude calendar revelation. No doubt it was an unwelcome distraction for both cast and crew. Unfortunately, the hostility towards Monroe stuck, even after the reporters and photographers left. Co-star Paul Douglas did nothing to hide his anger about the situation; he was often inebriated and abusive and he objected to Monroe's name being above the title. To make matters worse, various crew members echoed his bullying tactics. They snickered at her for fluffing lines, and in one scene where she tripped and fell down a set of stairs, their unbridled laughter couldn't be contained. With no one coming to her aid, Monroe picked herself up and continued with the scene. This early lack of confidence stuck with her throughout her entire career. She wasn't strong enough to brush it off as an actor's initiation into a tough business. She allowed the criticisms to chip away at her already fragile soul until even she believed herself unworthy of being there, on set—or anywhere at all.

"Poor Marilyn was a scared girl," said Lang. "[She was] scared of everything...[W]hen Marilyn missed her lines—which she did constantly—Barbara [Stanwyck] never said a word. I remember a particularly difficult scene between the two of them in which Barbara was hanging out some laundry and Marilyn had to say one or two lines. Although Marilyn missed her cue three or four times, all Barbara said was, 'Let's try it again'" (Lang and Grant, p. 118).

Natasha Lytess was a dramatic, bony, dark woman, dark in both appearance and personality. She was the polar opposite of Marilyn Monroe. When she spoke, the words came out like a machine gun firing—fast, with aggressive force. When it was time to shoot a scene she would stand quietly to the side; though silent, her presence loomed like a hovering black cloud threatening rain. A system of code signals (head shaking, forehead wrinkling, smiling, closing eyes) would be enough for Monroe to know if the take was acceptable or not. It was as if Lytess and Monroe were part of a secret club and they were the only two members. Lytess was unbearable. Monroe was unbearable. Together they were insufferable. Her influence on Monroe was more of a hindrance than a help and Lang refused to continue directing *Clash by Night* unless Lytess was removed from the set. "I cannot work with somebody else directing behind my back," was his outraged cry (Zoltow, Maurice, "The Mystery of Marilyn Monroe"). Lytess's ban was short-lived. It always was. Monroe needed her, and so everyone else tolerated her through clenched teeth for the good of the picture.

At first, Monroe was so completely enamored by Lytess's structured, European teaching style and "dedication," she genuinely believed that without her acting coach beside her, she couldn't act. However, it's clear that Lytess used Monroe's insecurities against her by pretending to give her the emotional tools and confidence to perform, while subliminally filling her with angst and apprehension about herself as an actress—and as a person. The manipulation didn't go unnoticed. Monroe later said, "There were days when I couldn't figure out why [Lytess] kept me on as a student because she made me feel so shallow and without talent" (Schwarz, p. 281). Years later, Monroe replaced Lytess with Paula Strasberg. She too became a crutch. As difficult as both acting coaches were, without either of them, there was no Marilyn Monroe.

We're Not Married!
(1952)

Marilyn Monroe appeared as Annabel Jones Norris. Twentieth Century–Fox. 86 minutes. *Director:* Edmund Goulding. *Producer:* Nunnally Johnson. *Screenplay:* Nunnally Johnson and Dwight Taylor. Story: Gina Kaus and Jay Dratler. *Original Music:* Cyril Mockridge. *Cinematography:* Leo Tover. *Costume Design:* Elois Jenssen. *Production Dates:* Early December 1951 to late January 1952. *Production Cost:* $1.17 million. *Domestic Box Office Receipts:* $2 million. *Release Date:* July 11, 1952. *Genre:* Comedy-Romance. Black and White. *Other Cast:* Ginger Rogers (Ramona Gladwyn), Fred

Marilyn Monroe in a wardrobe test shot as Annabel in *We're Not Married* (1952).

Allen (Steve Gladwyn), Victor Moore (Justice of the Peace Melvin Bush), David Wayne (Jeff Norris), Eve Arden (Katie Woodruff), Paul Douglas (Hector C. Woodruff), Eddie Bracken (Wilson Boswell "Willie" Reynolds), Mitzi Gaynor (Patricia "Patsy" Reynolds Fisher), Louis Calhern (Frederic C. "Freddie" Melrose), Zsa Zsa Gabor (Eve Melrose), James Gleason (Duffy), Paul Stewart (Attorney Stone), Jane Darwell (Mrs. Bush), Al Bridge (Detective Magnus).

We're Not Married is a film made up of individual installments, all connected by a common event. Each episode is dedicated to a married couple, all of whom were married just prior to or shortly after Christmas by a justice of the peace, "Melvyn Bush" (Victor Moore). He was unaware that his authority to perform marriages didn't come into play until January 1, and the mistake isn't caught until a couple of years later, when one of the six couples he married files for divorce. Only then do they discover that they were never legally married to begin with! The remaining handful of couples that Melvyn Bush prematurely "married" received letters from the governor to notify them that they were never legally wed; each couple uses the information in a different way.

Steve Gladwyn (Fred Allen) and his wife Ramona (Ginger Rogers) host a popular morning radio show, and while they get along famously on air, it's all a charade. Off-air they either ignore or insult each other. When Steve opens their "you're not married" letter, he relishes the fact that his miserable married life has come to an end. Ramona feels the same way. But their $5,000-per-week contract was signed as a married couple and their radio boss demands they legally marry as soon as possible, or lose their lucrative job. This sequence is by far the funniest of the five, and both Rogers and Allen were praised for their performances in several reviews—for example, *Variety*'s (July 25, 1952):

> Plenty of entertainment is provided, however, in several sequences, most notably that in which Ginger Rogers and Fred Allen portray Mr. and Mrs. Happiness team on radio. Episode is hilariously enacted as first at home they never speak, and in the station they constantly bicker... Miss Rogers and Allen are standouts, both contributing delicious delineations which pay off sharply in laughs.

The next episode features Marilyn Monroe as Annabel Jones Norris, a career-driven beauty queen (Monroe gets to showcase her figure in various bathing suits). After she wins the "Mrs. Mississippi" contest, her devoted husband Jeff (David Wayne) grows increasingly frustrated with his wife's absence. While he takes care of the house and their baby, she pursues the next big pageant: "Mrs. America." When their "you're not married" letter arrives, Jeff is thrilled to announce to Annabel and her manager Duffy (James Gleason) that all of their hard work has been undone because she's not legally married, thus making her ineligible to accept any "Mrs." title. Jeff assumes the news is going to deflate her enthusiasm and keep her home with him and their child, but he assumes wrong: "Annabel" is overjoyed that she's a single woman and now eligible to enter the "Miss Mississippi" contest instead. Before remarrying, Jeff watches his "soon-to-be-wife" win the title of "Miss Mississippi."

Eve Melrose (Zsa Zsa Gabor) plays a gold-digging wife who sets up her wealthy husband in order to get a divorce and then half his assets. While Frederic Melrose (Louis Calhern) is on a business trip, he answers the door to his hotel suite expecting it to be his wife, who had earlier pretended to plan on paying him a visit. Instead, a woman that he's never seen before walks in with a small case in hand and precedes to get undressed in the bedroom. As his questions go unanswered, Detective Magnus (Al Bridge) appears just in time to see the woman come out of the bedroom in her robe and smoking a cigarette. It's all Eve needs to begin divorce proceedings against the innocent Frederic.

Frederic is baffled by the events of the evening, until he learns that his scheming wife is filing for divorce because of his "infidelities." As Eve and her cocky attorney (Paul Stewart) arrive at his office to dissect Frederic's assets, he opens their "you're not married" letter and learns that his marriage to Eve is, and always has been, invalid! His soon-to-be-ex-wife is now entitled to not one cent!

When Hector (Paul Douglas) opens his "you're not married" letter, he briefly daydreams about what it would be like to be a single man again. He then snaps back to reality and decides, at least initially, not to tell his wife Katie (Eve Arden) about the letter. In fact, he burns it. Prior to receiving the letter, their marriage is shown to be staid and less than ideal, but they're both set in their ways and amicably comfortable with each other.

Willie Fisher (Eddie Bracken) is happily married to Patsy (Mitzi Gaynor), but as he's shipped off to war, she informs him that she's pregnant. As he tries to digest the news, he gets his "you're not married" letter and he worries that their child will now be called illegitimate; especially so if he gets killed in the war. Willie's sergeant tells him that the only solution is "not to get shot" and return home following the war to get legally married. Desperate to make things right, Willie goes AWOL and informs his wife that they have to get married again, and all before his ship sails that evening. All of the couples except Eve and Frederic remarry before the film ends.

The *New York Times* (November 25, 1951) wrote that *We're Not Married!* would include the stories of seven couples; however the final film only included five. The sixth would have been the couple that filed for divorce only to find out they were never married to begin with; yet another episode was written and Hope Emerson and Walter Brennan signed to star in it. According to *The Hollywood Reporter* (July 25, 1952), their episode was filmed; it's anyone's guess as to why it was eliminated.

An October 24, 1951, memo from Darryl Zanuck to producer-screenwriter Nunnally Johnson noted his concerns over the revelation that Jeff and Annabel had already become parents without being legally wed. Since the five couples "assumed" they were married, that was a good enough reason for the censors to allow the somewhat controversial plot. Despite an all-star cast, there's something amiss with *We're Not Married*! Reviews were generally favorable, but it now feels awfully dated.

Don't Bother to Knock (1952)

Marilyn Monroe appeared as Nell Forbes. Twentieth Century–Fox. 76 minutes. *Alternate Titles: Night Without Sleep* and *Mischief*. *Director:* Roy Baker. *Producer:* Julian Blaustein. *Screenplay:* Daniel Taradash. Based on the novel by Charlotte Armstrong. *Cinematography:* Lucien Ballard. *Costume Design:* Travilla. *Musical Direction:* Lionel Newman. *Production Dates:* December 3, 1951 to January 14, 1952. *Production Cost:* $555,000. *Domestic Box Office Receipts:* $1.5 million. *Release Date:* July 18, 1952. *Genre:* Drama-Thriller. Black and White. *Other Cast:* Richard Widmark (Jed Towers), Anne Bancroft (Lyn Lesley), Donna Corcoran (Bunny Jones), Jeanne Cagney (Rochelle), Lurene Tuttle (Ruth Jones), Elisha Cook, Jr. (Eddie Forbes), Jim Backus (Peter Jones), Verna Felton (Mrs. Ballew), Don Beddoe (Mr. Ballew), Willis Bouchey (Joe, the Bartender).

Title card for *Don't Bother to Knock* (1952).

Taglines: SHE'S DYNAMITE!; It Opens the Door on the Screen's Most Exciting New Personality—MARILYN MONROE.; You never met her type before...; ...a wicked sensation as the lonely girl in room 809!

Don't Bother to Knock was Marilyn Monroe's first dramatic role. But it was far more than that. Her character, Nell, is a mentally ill woman with delusional thoughts and the role called upon her to evoke her real-life fears of following in her mother's descent into mental illness.

The story takes place one very eventful night at New York's McKinley Hotel. Eddie (Elisha Cook Jr.) is a conscientious hotel elevator operator who introduces his niece Nell (Monroe) to hotel guests Ruth and Peter Jones (Lurene Tuttle and Jim Backus). The couple has a function to attend in the hotel's ballroom and Nell is given the job of babysitting their young daughter Bunny (Donna Corcoran).

At first glance, Nell appears to be a quiet, unassuming type, but when Bunny falls asleep, Nell dresses in Ruth's negligee and slippers, tries on her jewelry, spritzes herself with perfume and indulges in a box of chocolates. As Nell's demeanor changes, the audience begins to feel uneasy about the innocent little girl that has been left in the care of a woman who is not quite mentally right.

Jed (Richard Widmark) is an airline pilot with a sharp tongue and, according to his girlfriend Lyn Lesley (Anne Bancroft), he also lacks an understanding heart, which is her main reason for breaking up with him. Lyn is the hotel's lounge singer, and she's ended her relationship with Jed via a letter. Not one to let go easily, Jed confronts Lyn about their relationship, but she's made up her mind. Jed retreats to his room to ponder his broken romance. While there, he spots Nell in the window across from the courtyard, seductively dressed and all alone; his interest is piqued and he soon decides to phone her. While Nell is at first hesitant to speak to the strange man on the other end of the line, her interest is also piqued, and she begins to talk to Jed.

Nell's uncle interrupts the call when he stops by to see how she and Bunny are doing. Furious that Nell has been going through Ruth's things, he orders her to take everything off and put it back in its rightful place. Eddie leaves to continue his work, giving Nell the opportunity to invite Jed to visit her in person. Before he arrives, Nell sits down at the dressing table to apply some of Ruth's lipstick. A closeup of her wrists show scars from an obvious suicide attempt.

With whiskey bottle in hand, Jed arrives at suite 809. Nell lies to Jed about her reasons for being in the hotel. When Jed mentions his occupation, she reveals (more to the audience than to Jed) in her delusional ramblings that her fiancé Phillip was also a pilot, but he died while piloting a plane over the Pacific. Thinking he was only missing and that he's now returned to her, Nell kisses Jed. He doesn't object.

Bunny wakes up and wanders out of her bedroom, interrupting their moment of passion. It's an interruption that infuriates Nell, and when she shakes the little girl and orders her back to bed, Bunny says something that makes it apparent to Jed that Nell is a babysitter. Nell confesses that Bunny was telling the truth.

Jed consoles Bunny by offering her some kindly words and a drink of water. When the little girl complains that she's feeling hot, Nell offers to open the window to let in some air. As Bunny looks out the window, Nell's mood shifts and her hand rises toward the little girl's back. She thinks about pushing her to her death. Jed hears a bloodcurdling scream and he rushes across the room to pull Bunny back from the window in time. The scream came from busybody hotel guest Emma Ballew (Verna Felton). She witnessed the window incident from across the way and she tries to convince her husband (Don Beddoe) that it must be reported to the hotel detective. In the meantime, Nell has taken Bunny back to bed and accuses the terrified child of spying on her. She tells her to go back to sleep and not to make another sound.

Waiting in the other room for Nell to return, Jed realizes that he's in a situation that he wants out of; he decides to make up with Lyn and leave the room. Nell begs him to stay and when she tries to kiss him, Jed pulls her hands away. He sees the scars on her wrists and Nell admits that she cut herself with a razor when her boyfriend died.

When Eddie comes back to check on Nell, Jed hides to avoid a scene. When Nell opens the door and Eddie sees her dressed in the same clothes he told her to get out of, he rubs off her lipstick and berates her. Nell loses control and hits him over the head with a heavy ashtray stand. He falls into the bathroom, where Jed is hiding. Spying through the keyhole of her door, Bunny sees everything and starts sobbing uncontrollably just as her mother calls to inquire about her welfare. Nell tells her that Bunny is asleep and hangs up. Ruth returns to the banquet, but she feels something isn't right. As Jed tends to Eddie's bleeding head, Nell wanders off toward Bunny's room. At this stage, Bunny is still crying. When Nell returns to the bathroom to see Jed and Eddie, the little girl's room is quiet.

By now, the Ballews are knocking on the door. Fearing he'll lose his job, a nervous Eddie hides, as does Jed. Nell opens the door and speaks with the elderly couple. While Nell is preoccupied, Jed sneaks into Bunny's room so that he can exit from the other door, without Nell noticing. He calls to Bunny and asks if she's asleep. No answer. In the darkened room, he fails to notice that the little girl is now bound and gagged on the bed. Thinking she's sound asleep, he exits into the hotel corridor, but the Ballews see him and assume, by Nell's odd behavior, that he's been keeping her captive. The Ballews contact the hotel detective.

Realizing Jed has gone, Nell locks Eddie in the closet. The Ballews are still preoccupied and talking on the phone, totally unaware of Nell's trance-like state. She mutters that Bunny is to blame for Jed's departure and she goes toward the girl's room to get her final revenge.

Back in the hotel bar, Jed tells Lynn what went on in the room and she is impressed by how emotionally affected he is. As he's telling the story to Lyn, Jed realizes that Bunny was on the wrong bed when he left her room. Feeling something is terribly wrong, he races back upstairs to check on her.

Ruth leaves the banquet to return to her suite to check on her daughter. Though she's bound and gagged, Bunny has managed to wriggle to a sitting position on the floor beside her bed. Nell finds her and lectures her about ruining her chances with Jed. The implication is that Nell is about to kill Bunny. Ruth enters her room just in time.

Nell attacks Ruth, but Jed saves her. He throws Nell to the floor and helps Ruth untie Bunny. Jed then rescues Eddie from the locked closet. Eddie tells Jed that Nell just finished a three-year stint in a mental hospital. During all the commotion, Nell slips out of the suite unnoticed.

Jed frantically searches the hotel for Nell. Finding her in the hotel lobby with a razor, she threatens to harm herself. She still believes that Jed is her deceased boyfriend Phillip and so he talks her into giving him the razor. Eventually Nell realizes that Phillip is dead and that Jed isn't him. Lyn witnesses the gentle, emotional exchange between Jed and Nell and she sees him in a whole new light. Nell is taken away to the hospital for treatment and Lyn and Jed rekindle their relationship.

Don't Bother to Knock marked Anne Bancroft's film debut. Later in her career, she remembered the emotional final scene between Widmark and Monroe: "There was just this one scene of one woman seeing another woman who was helpless and in pain. It was so real… [Monroe] moved me so that tears came into my eyes (Buskin, *The Films of Marilyn Monroe*).

There's an interesting May 5, 1950, memo in the Twentieth Century–Fox files on *Don't Bother to Knock*:

> Please remember that at no time should Nell be identified as or called a *Baby Sitter*. Everybody has unions these days and possibly Baby Sitters are organized, too, and it would be awful if our nice picture were to be picked by the Baby Sitters of America.

Zanuck had issues with Nell's violence, particularly towards the end of the story. While all of the characters feel sorry for Nell, he, as a reader of the script, didn't have the same feelings of empathy, especially during the finale where she apparently attempted to kill the child and engaged in the fight with the mother:

> It must be perfectly clear before she goes into the child's room the last time that there is no premeditation, no will to damage anyone, no less kill anyone. Nell must be very child-like, really very frightened. She is all alone in a pretty scary world.

More emphasis on "the great sense of loss in this girl" needed to be worked into the script, wrote Zanuck; otherwise, "we are in trouble with this character." He concluded with:

> While in rational moments the audience might know that such people have to be helped, in an emotional moment during the picture they would probably say, "The world is better off without her. Why make an effort to save her?" If this feeling ever leaks into it, we are in trouble.

Richard Widmark said:

> I liked Marilyn Monroe... Murder to work with, because she was scared to death of acting—even when she had become big... [But] something happened between the lens and the film. Nobody knew what it was. On the set you'd think: "Oh, this is impossible; you can't print this." You'd see it and she's got everyone backed off the screen [Haspiel, p. 32].

Philip K. Scheuer of the *Los Angeles Times* reviewed *Don't Bother to Knock* on July 31, 1952, and ripped the storyline and Monroe's performance apart:

> [Monroe] is supposed to be a "sick girl" and she plays the part like a sick girl. This may have the sound of praise; but when you see her you will be uneasily aware that her portrayal is reinforced by virtually no acting resources whatsoever. The paradox is that here is a woman of sensuous physical beauty who, although she arrays herself briefly in finery, conveys the over-all impression of being lackluster and drab. Her voice seems as dead as her spirit...

Edwin Martin of the *San Diego Union* (August 18, 1952) felt differently about her performance:

> Miss Monroe shows signs of having considerable dramatic power. She plays her role quite effectively, with sympathy and understanding, scoring nicely in a part that not only marks a change of pace for her in her buildup as a glamour girl, but that demands certain dramatic knowledge.

O. Henry's Full House
(1952)

Marilyn Monroe appeared as a Street Walker in "The Cop and the Anthem," one of five vignettes in an all-star anthology based on the stories of O. Henry (aka William Sidney Porter). Twentieth Century–Fox. 117 minutes. Working *Title: Baghdad on the Subway*. UK *title: Full House*. Director of the episode "The Cop and the Anthem": Henry Koster. *Producer:* Andre Hakim. *Screenplay:* Lamar Trotti. Story: O. Henry *Original Music:* Alfred Newman. *Cinematography:* Lloyd Ahern, Lucien Ballard, Milton R. Krasner and Joseph MacDonald. *Costume Design:* Edward Stevenson, Sam Benson and Charles LeMaire. *Production dates for "The Cop and the Anthem":* January 2 to mid–January 1952. *Release Date:* August 7, 1952. *Genre:* Drama. Black and White. Other Cast for "The Cop and the Anthem": Charles Laughton (Soapy), David Wayne (Horace), James Flavin (Cop), Robert Foulk (Cop), Tom Greenway (Cop), Marjorie Holliday (Cashier), Richard Karlan (Headwaiter), Jack Mather (Cop), William Vedder (Judge), John Steinbeck (Narrator). *Taglines:* A dozen top stars—five famed directors bring you the best stories of O. Henry!

Charles Laughton plays Soapy, a kindly tramp with his sights set on committing a petty crime that will land him in a warm jail cell for the duration of a harsh New York winter. A day of unsuccessful attempts at getting arrested follows, including a 90-second scene with Marilyn Monroe playing a lady window-shopper that Soapy sees as an easy target. Unaware that Monroe is a prostitute, he saunters by her side and starts a conversation. He hopes she will alert a nearby policeman to his unwanted advances, but she is quite willing to accept his attention. Yet another failed attempt at arrest.

O. Henry's Full House (1952) 75

Monroe plays a streetwalker in "The Cop and the Anthem," one of five stories told in the anthology film *O. Henry's Full House* **(1952).**

Night falls and Soapy is exhausted and frustrated at his inability to catch a policeman's eye. After hearing organ music coming from a nearby church, Soapy and his friend and fellow tramp Horace (David Wayne) enter the place of worship to reflect on life and its hardships. Once inside, Soapy has an emotional breakdown. Fed up with his useless existence, he decides to turn over a new leaf. He'll get a job and become a respectable citizen. After leaving the church, Soapy recalls a kindly man who was willing to give him an honest job years before. As he tells Horace of his plans to seek his potential employer out the following day, the sound of a policeman's footsteps is reason enough for Horace to run off. Muttering to himself about his future plans, Soapy is unaware of his friend's departure or the impending arrival of the policeman. A tap on the shoulder follows:

> "Okay, come along," says the policeman.
> "Huh? Officer, what have I done?" Soapy asks.
> "Never mind. Come along. Don't give me any of your lip or I'll bash you in that skull of yours," says the policeman.

The following day, despite his pleas of innocence, Soapy stands before an unsympathetic judge and is sentenced to three months in jail for loitering and vagrancy, with no visible means of support.

"The Cop and the Anthem" followed O. Henry's usual formula of good-natured wit, common folk and an ironic twist ending. As with many of his stories, New York City at the turn of the 20th century was the backdrop. The story was originally published in the *New York World* on December 4, 1904, and in 1906 it was reprinted in a book of O. Henry's collected works, *The Four Million*. The book title came from the population of New York City during the time O. Henry penned most of the stories. He started the book with the following explanation of the *title:*

> Not very long ago someone invented the assertion that there were only "Four Hundred" people in New York City who were really worth noticing. But a wiser man has arisen—the census taker—and his larger estimate of human interest has been preferred in marking out the field of these little stories of the "Four Million."

The 1952 film is a faithful retelling of the original tale. The other four episodes making up the film were "The Clarion Call," starring Richard Widmark and Dale Robertson and directed by Henry Hathaway; "The Last Leaf," starring Anne Baxter, Jean Peters and Gregory Ratoff and directed by Jean Negulesco; "The Ransom of Red Chief," starring Fred Allen, Oscar Levant and Lee Aaker and directed by Howard Hawks; and "The Gift of the Magi," starring Jeanne Crain and Farley Granger and directed by Henry King.

Now in the public domain, O. Henry's original prostitute scene from "The Cop and the Anthem" reads as follows:

> A young woman of a modest and pleasing guise was standing before a show window gazing with sprightly interest at its display of shaving mugs and inkstands, and two yards from the window a large policeman of severe demeanour leaned against a water plug. It was Soapy's design to assume the role of the despicable and execrated "masher." The refined and elegant appearance of his victim and the contiguity of the conscientious cop encouraged him to believe that he would soon feel the pleasant official clutch upon his arm that would insure his winter quarters on the right little, tight little isle. Soapy straightened the lady missionary's readymade tie, dragged his shrinking cuffs into the open, set his hat at a killing cant and sidled toward the young woman. He made eyes at her, was taken with sudden coughs and "hems," smiled, smirked and went brazenly through the impudent and contemptible litany of the "masher."
> With half an eye Soapy saw that the policeman was watching him fixedly. The young woman moved away a few steps, and again bestowed her absorbed attention upon the shaving mugs. Soapy followed, boldly stepping to her side, raised his hat and said:
> "Ah there, Bedelia! Don't you want to come and play in my yard?"
> The policeman was still looking. The persecuted young woman had but to beckon a finger

and Soapy would be practically en route for his insular haven. Already he imagined he could feel the cozy warmth of the station-house. The young woman faced him and, stretching out a hand, caught Soapy's coat sleeve.

"Sure, Mike," she said joyfully, "if you'll blow me to a pail of suds. I'd have spoke to you sooner, but the cop was watching."

With the young woman playing the clinging ivy to his oak, Soapy walked past the policeman overcome with gloom. He seemed doomed to liberty. At the next corner he shook off his companion and ran.

"The Cop and the Anthem" was also made as a silent film, released in June 1917 and directed by and starring Thomas R. Mills. Additionally, Red Skelton's Freddie the Freeloader took center stage in a version of "The Cop and the Anthem" presented on the 1954 Christmas episode of *The Red Skelton Show*.

O. Henry frequently wrote his stories with a bottle of Scotch beside him. His heavy drinking eventually affected his work and health and he died on June 5, 1910, at age 47. O. Henry's reputation as one of America's greatest storytellers stands to this day. Since 1919, the O. Henry Award is an annual prize given to the best short stories of the year.

Monroe does her best with a minuscule part in "The Cop and the Anthem," perhaps shining more than she otherwise would because her window-shopping prostitute (dressed from head to toe in a costume faithful to the era, not necessarily befitting her character's profession) is the only female speaking part in the episode.

Monkey Business (1952)

Marilyn Monroe appeared as Miss Lois Laurel. Twentieth Century–Fox. 97 minutes. *Alternate Titles: Be Your Age*; *Darling I Am Growing Younger*; and *Howard Hawks' Monkey Business*. *Director:* Howard Hawks. *Producer:* Sol C. Siegel. *Screenplay:* Howard Hawks, Ben Hecht, Charles Lederer, I.A.L. Diamond. Story: Harry Segall. *Original Music:* Leigh Harline. *Cinematography:* Milton Krasner. *Costume Design:* Travilla. *Production Dates:* March 5 to April 30, 1952. *Production Cost:* $1,615,000. *Domestic Box Office Receipts:* $2 million. *Release Date:* September 2, 1952. *Genre:* Comedy. Black and White. *Other Cast:* Cary Grant (Dr. Barnaby Fulton), Ginger Rogers (Mrs. Edwina Fulton), Charles Coburn (Mr. Oliver Oxly), Hugh Marlowe (Hank Entwhistle), Henri Letondal (Dr. Jerome Lenton), Robert Cornthwaite (Dr. Zoldeck), Larry Keating (G.J. Culverly), Douglas Spencer (Dr. Brunner), Esther Dale (Mrs. Rhinelander), George Winslow (Little Indian), Esther, the chimp (Peggy, the chimp), Rudolph, the chimp (Bingo, the chimp). *Awards:* 1953 Golden Globe (USA): Best Motion Picture Actress, Musical/Comedy—Ginger Rogers (nominated). *Taglines:* CARY Grant gets younger for the sake of science! GINGER Rogers goes along for the sake of Cary! MARILYN Monroe stays just as she is for the sake of everybody!; When a scientist like Cary starts doing Research on Marilyn ... and a Gal like Ginger finds Lipstick on Hubby...That's Really *Monkey Business*!; *Monkey Business*—The Funniest Picture of The Year!

Dr. Barnaby Fulton (Cary Grant), an eccentric, often-forgetful scientific chemist, is developing an anti-aging formula. He is summoned to the office of his boss, Oliver Oxly (Charles Coburn), of the Oxly Chemical Factory. Oxly's secretary, Miss Laurel (Marilyn Monroe), hikes up her skirt and gives Barnaby a thigh-high view of her leg, but it's all in the name of work. She tells him that she's wearing one of the first pair of no-run pantyhose designed by Barnaby. Needless to say, Barnaby is very appreciative of the exclusive view.

Oxly calls Barnaby into his office and excitedly shows him the new ad campaign for the formula that's yet to be perfected, B-4—The Revival Vitamin, Barnaby feels pressured that an ad has already been developed to promote a product that is yet to be proven.

As he urges his boss to be patient, Oxly gets a phone call to say that Rudolph, an elderly lab monkey (Bingo, the chimp), has broken loose and is acting strangely. At first, everyone thinks the formula has at last taken effect, but it's only a case of mistaken identity. The energetic primate is the six-month-old Esther (Peggy, the chimp), and she's wearing Rudolph's uniform. Barnaby puts Esther back in her cage and he returns to work. When he momentarily leaves the lab, Esther escapes from her cage, mixes her own batch of the youth formula and pours it into the water cooler.

Against the advice of his worried assistant Jerome Lenton (Henri Letondal), Barnaby takes a dose of his own concoction. Washing it down with water from the cooler, he begins to feel immediate side effects, followed by a feeling of youthful exuberance. He no longer feels the pains of a middle-aged man and his eyesight improves to the point that he no longer needs his thick glasses. Before returning home to his wife, Edwina (Ginger Rogers), he gets a crewcut, buys a loud plaid jacket and a convertible.

When Lenton tells Oxly that Barnaby took his own formula and bounced around like a man decades younger than his actual age, Oxly sends Miss Laurel out to find him. Barnaby takes Miss Laurel out for an afternoon of fun. Speeding around town in his new car, he crashes into the side of a truck. While they're waiting for it to be repaired, they go roller skating and swimming. Miss Laurel gets the wrong idea and kisses Barnaby, who then confesses that he's a married man. The formula wears off and Barnaby loses his 20/20 vision while driving back to the chemical plant with Miss Laurel. Once again he crashes, this time into a wire fence.

After the effects of the formula have completely worn off, Barnaby remembers everything he did while under its influence. He recounts what happened to Edwina, including an explanation for Miss Laurel's lipstick mark on his cheek, and he then tells her that he wants to take more of the formula, this time a much stronger dose.

Barnaby makes a new batch and then goes into the other room to get his jacket. While he's gone, Edwina takes the formula—followed by a sip of water from the cooler. She soon begins to act mischievous, and for the next few hours Barnaby sees the side effects of his anti-aging experiment. When Edwina insists that she and Barnaby spend the night at the hotel they honeymooned in, he plays along. While at the hotel, Edwina's energy doesn't wane and an exhausted Barnaby can't keep up with her.

As they get ready for bed, Edwina starts to cry for her mother and an argument begins. When Barnaby drops his glasses on the floor and pushes her away to save them from being trodden on, she tosses him out of their room and proceeds to call her ex-flame Hank (Hugh Marlowe) to inform him that she's filing for divorce. Hank is unaware that Edwina has taken the formula, and his hopes are raised at the thought of Edwina becoming a single woman again.

After being evicted from his room without his glasses, Barnaby falls down a chute and spends a rough night in the laundry room. Edwina awakens the next morning no longer under the influence of the youth formula, and wondering where her husband has gone.

After experiencing the effects of his experiment for himself and then witnessing the effects of it on his wife, Barnaby believes his concoction causes nothing but trouble. He returns to the lab and considers destroying it. As he and Edwina discuss the consequences of destroying years of work, Edwina uses the water from the cooler to brew a pot of coffee. After several cups, she and Barnaby start acting like children.

Oxly and members of his board of directors ask Barnaby for the formula recipe but the spiked coffee causes both he and Edwina to run rampant. All sorts of mayhem ensues at the meeting and eventually Barnaby asks his boss for a zillion dollars for the formula.

As Barnaby and Edwina walk home, they antagonize each other along the way and get into a paint fight. Once home, Edwina calls Hank and tells him that she's covered in paint, and it's Barnaby's fault. Barnaby overhears the phone call and he joins a group of neighborhood kids who are playing a game of Cowboys and Indians. As Edwina falls asleep on the bed, Barnaby hatches a plan with the kids to capture and scalp his love rival, Hank.

Edwina wakes up with the effects of the formula worn off and wonders where Barnaby is. While she's been sleeping, the neighbor's baby has climbed up onto the bed next to her. She instantly thinks that Barnaby has regressed back to infancy and she hurries to the lab with him in a cab.

When a concerned Hank arrives at the house to see Edwina, he's greeted by the Cowboy and Indian kids who trick him into playing a game with them. After they tie him to a pole, Barnaby emerges from the bushes and he and the kids do a war dance before giving Hank a Mohawk haircut.

A tearful Edwina arrives at the lab and tells Oxly that the baby she's holding is her husband. Edwina then realizes that she always returns to normal after going to sleep, so she puts the baby down on the lab couch in the hope that he'll fall asleep and reawaken as his adult self.

As Barnaby's colleagues gather around and wait for Barnaby to return to normal, they all take water from the cooler that has been spiked with Esther's version of the youth formula. When Oxly tastes the water, he complains that it tastes bitter and he orders the rest of it to be poured out.

Following Hank's "scalping," Barnaby leaves his Indian tribe and climbs through the window of his lab. He takes a nap next to the baby and is discovered by his relieved wife. By this time, the cooler water has taken effect on Oxly and his board members and they all begin to run around the lab like children. When Miss Laurel appears in the doorway, she's confused by their rowdy behavior. Oxly invites her in and then he proceeds to chase her with squirts of water from a Seltzer bottle. Barnaby realizes that the *real* youth formula was concocted by Esther. With the remaining solution poured down the sink, the magic monkey recipe for eternal youth will remain a mystery. The moral of the story: Being young once is quite enough!

The original name for Barnaby's formula was Cupidone but because this gave the implication that it was some sort of aphrodisiac love potion, for censorships reasons the name was changed to indicate it was more of a vitamin tonic. The Production Code Administration also insisted that Oxly's lecherous behavior towards Miss Laurel be toned down.

In the opening credits, Cary Grant opens the front door of his house. As he is about to walk out, a voice says, "Not yet, Cary." Grant then shuts the door. This occurs a couple of times, before and after the main cast credits appear. The voice directing Cary Grant is the director of the film, Howard Hawks.

During filming, Marilyn Monroe was hospitalized for "nerves." The production company released a statement saying she had a sudden attack of appendicitis. While she *did* come down with appendicitis during production, her nervous state was eliminated from media reports. Hawks wanted to fire her over the production delays her illness had caused, but according to Grant biographer Marc Eliot, it was Grant who persuaded Hawks to keep her on. In *Cary Grant: A Biography* (2004), Eliot writes:

> Monroe's future in Hollywood owed a debt to the compassion of Cary Grant, at a time when she was considered to be just one more dumb blonde in an industry that purchased them twelve at a time for ten cents a pack. Had she been fired at this early juncture, she would most likely not have been given another chance in Hollywood.

With the pressure of imminent Hollywood success upon her, Monroe was in a fragile state. Grant said:

> I had no idea she would become a big star. If she had something different from any other actress, it wasn't apparent at the time. She seemed very shy and quiet. There was something sad about her. She came to the set early, went into her room, and read. She would stay there until we called her. When the studio workers whistled at her and made remarks that I certainly did not want to hear, it would embarrass her a lot... She was a victim of the Hollywood system [Nelson, p. 175].

Monkey Business began filming during the early days of Monroe's relationship with Joe DiMaggio. When she invited him to the set to watch her work, studio photographer Roy Craft seized the opportunity to capture the moment. Cary Grant was pictured with Monroe and DiMaggio, but the next day, when the photo appeared in newspapers across the country, Grant had been artfully cropped out, supposedly at DiMaggio's insistence.

Monroe appeared on her first *Life* magazine cover in April 1952, and on April 28, she was admitted to Cedars of Lebanon Hospital in Los Angeles for the removal of her appendix. It was an operation that should have been done weeks before, but Monroe was adamant about finishing *Monkey Business* before undergoing surgery so as not to hold up the production. Prior to the operation, she stuck a handwritten note to her tummy, pleading with the doctor not to leave a major scar.

Journalist Erskine Johnson tracked down Monroe's mother Gladys, who had been institutionalized for much of her daughter's life, and broke the story to the world. What made the situation worse was that Monroe had just given an exclusive interview to journalist Jim Henaghan of *Redbook* magazine, where she spoke at length about her heartbreaking childhood, and about being raised as an orphan after both her parents *died*. Henaghan, furious, phoned the Fox publicity department, called Monroe a liar and demanded an explanation. Monroe smoothed the waters, writing a letter to *Redbook* that said, in part:

> I frankly did not feel wrong in withholding from you the fact that my mother is still alive ... since we have never known each other intimately and have never enjoyed the normal relationship of mother and daughter [Taraborrelli, p. 191].

From her hospital bed, Monroe called Erskine Johnson to say that she was shuttled from one foster home to the next, had an appointed guardian and had spent time in the Los Angeles Orphans' Home. She also said that becoming Marilyn Monroe was her choice; being hounded by the media was not something Gladys could cope with. So Monroe's "lie" didn't come from shame, it was a story to protect her mother. She told Johnson that she maintained contact with her mother (however sporadic it was, mostly due to Gladys' hostility) and helped her financially. Monroe's business manager Inez Melson was appointed conservator of Gladys, and she kept Monroe up-to-date on her condition.

On February 9, 1953, Monroe moved her mother to Rockhaven Sanitarium, a private facility that would give her additional protection from the outside world. The media circus surrounding her existence and the inevitable press inquiries about her movie star daughter made it impossible for her to stay in a public facility. At the time, Monroe was still only earning $750 a week, and with her own expenses mounting, there was little money left over. But she continued to pay for her mother's care until her death, after which a bequeath in Monroe's will continued to support her care.

Hot on the heels of the nude calendar scandal, this new revelation about her mother's existence threatened to ruin her credibility with the public, and possibly even threaten her upcoming starring role as the evil seductress Rose Loomis in *Niagara* (1953). It did neither. Monroe had such a unique way of talking herself out of a sticky situation, she usually managed to gain public sympathy in the process. Remembering scripted lines for her films was always a problem, but when it came time to answer questions from reporters, she was a glib professional.

Despite widespread critical praise, *Monkey Business* failed to resonate with audiences. Director Hawks felt the premise was too unbelievable. He was right. The absurdity killed the humor. Certainly, the story was as goofy as anything that Hawks had done in the past, but *Monkey Business* didn't have the same magic that the earlier Grant-Hawks collaboration *Bringing Up Baby* (1938) had.

Kaspar Monahan of *The Pittsburgh Press* (September 25, 1952) praised Monroe's performance: "[T]he best laughs are provided by Marilyn Monroe as a dumb babe serving as [Charles] Coburn's secretary who can't type. 'After all,' says Coburn, 'anybody can type.'"

Despite a ho-hum response to the film, it grabbed the tenth spot on the list of top-grossing films of 1952. *The Greatest Show on Earth* was in the number one spot. *We're Not Married!* was in fifteenth position, followed by *Don't Bother to Knock* in twentieth place.

Niagara
(1953)

Marilyn Monroe appeared as Rose Loomis. Twentieth Century–Fox. 92 minutes. *Director:* Henry Hathaway. *Producer:* Charles Brackett. *Writers:* Charles Brackett, Walter Reisch and Richard L. Breen. *Original Music:* Sol Kaplan. *Cinematography:* Joe MacDonald. *Costume Design:* Dorothy Jeakins. *Production Dates:* Early June to mid–July 1952. *Release Date:* January 21, 1953. *Production Cost:* $1.67 million. *Domestic Box Office Receipts:* $2.35 million, $6 million (worldwide). *Genre:* Drama-Thriller. Technicolor. *Other Cast:* Joseph Cotten (George Loomis), Jean Peters (Polly Cutler), Max Showalter aka Casey Adams (Ray Cutler), Denis O'Dea (Inspector Starkey), Richard Allan (Patrick), Don Wilson (Mr. J.C. Kettering), Lurene Tuttle (Mrs. Kettering), Russell Collins (Mr. Qua), Will Wright (Boatman). *Soundtrack:* "Kiss": Music by Lionel Newman. Lyrics by Haven Gillespie. *Tagline:* Marilyn Monroe and *Niagara*—a raging torrent of emotion that even nature can't control!

In a September 19, 1951, pre-production report relating to the September 14, 1951, conference about the treatment for *Niagara*, Darryl Zanuck suggests a list of suitable actors alongside the character names to help aid the writers in telling the story. Zanuck writes, "[P]lease keep these [actors names] *CONFIDENTIAL* for the time being."

One-sheet poster for *Niagara* (1953).

None of the suggested actors ended up being cast in the film. For the role of "George," Zanuck had only one suggestion, Louis Jourdan. Joseph Cotten got the part. For the role of Rose, three actors were suggested: Anne Baxter, Maureen Stapleton and Constance Smith. Marilyn Monroe got the part. For the role of Ray, two actors were suggested, Scott Brady and Jeffrey Hunter. Max Showalter got the part.

For the role of Polly (the character's name was initially Louise), two actresses were suggested, Anne Francis and Jeanne Crain. Anne Baxter was the original Polly, but she left soon after filming took place when her role was severely reduced. Jean Peters took over. For the role of Inspector Starkey, two actors were suggested, Millard Mitchell and Michael Rennie. Denis O'Dea got the part.

The story involves two married couples, Polly Cutler (Jean Peters) and her husband Ray (Max Showalter) and Rose Loomis (Marilyn) and her husband George (Joseph Cotten). The happily married Cutlers are visiting Niagara Falls on their delayed honeymoon and upon their arrival they encounter the unhappily married Loomises who are still occupying the cabin the Cutlers have booked. The Cutlers agree to a different cabin after Rose apologizes for not moving out sooner, telling them her husband's been unwell. The Cutlers see how unwell he is after he storms out of his cabin one evening and breaks the record that Rose had requested be played. George is a Korean War veteran with battle fatigue. Rose is a calculating sex bomb who plays on her husband's neuroses and is in the midst of an affair with Ted Patrick (Richard Allan).

When George disappears right around the time that Rose and Ted have planned to kill him, the plot takes an unexpected Hitchcock-esque turn. As Rose skillfully plays the role of the mournful widow for the sake of the police, she does her wifely duty and identifies the body at the morgue—only it *isn't* her husband. Rose faints at the sight of the body—her lover's body! She's sedated and hospitalized, after which we discover that George killed his wife's lover in self-defense. Realizing it was a murder plot hatched between his wife and her lover to get rid of him, he's out for revenge. When Rose regains consciousness, she leaves the hospital. George tracks her down and chases her up the many steps to the top of a bell tower. Rose pleads for her life to no avail. George strangles her, and the carillon bells, which are a pivotal plot point when they're chiming, are silent as Rose's lifeless body lies beneath them.

When Polly is awakened in her room by George, until that moment she, like everyone else, assumed he was dead. She screams and he runs away. With Rose now dead, Polly is the only person who knows that George is alive. She alerts the police and with the law on his tail, George takes a motorboat with the idea of crossing the Canadian–US border to escape. Polly is also on the boat. A struggle ensues; Polly falls and hits her head and a panicked George takes off with her still on-board. As Polly regains consciousness, the boat runs out of fuel and the pair coast in the rapids and into the main current of the treacherous falls. Before reaching his inevitable fate, George does what's right and puts Polly onto a nearby rock to safety. As she desperately clings to the slippery rock, she watches as George and the boat plummet over the falls. A Coast Guard helicopter rescues Polly and she's reunited with her husband.

Monroe's sensually cool portrayal of the manipulative femme fatale, the wondrous backdrop of Niagara Falls, a fine supporting cast, skillful direction by Henry Hathaway, a suspenseful storyline, Technicolor—it's a collective combination of elements that mesh perfectly, making *Niagara* a first-rate film noir thriller.

Hathaway was one of Hollywood's most temperamental directors. He was so methodical about the length of time a scene should take, he timed them down to the second. Monroe was her usual late self coming to the set. Her tardiness did nothing to endear her to a director who was meticulous about making every second count, both on-screen and off.

Niagara has a couple of moments that are often referred to as "highlights" and both involve Monroe. As the record of the song "Kiss" is played, Monroe, dressed in a daring figure-hugging dress that her on-screen husband aptly describes as "cut down so low in front you could see her kneecaps," croons along to the tune. In the film, "Kiss" is partially sung by Marilyn Monroe when the record is played on the phonograph. As Cotten suggested, Monroe's dress left little to the imagination. But in reality, there was no imagination needed. She showed it all! Monroe was notorious for going without underwear, especially during the summer heat, and she was so immersed in the "Kiss" take that her skin-tight skirt had crept up to her waist. After several more takes, the crew placed a blanket over her legs to protect her modesty while the closeups were shot.

In a group setting, Monroe had trouble making conversation. She was often physically sick when she was required to be in that type of social situation. The cluster of people required to make a film set was a living nightmare for her. One-on-one she was a natural talker and at ease with herself and her surroundings. It was yet another conflict of personalities for her to be so casual about showing her body while immersed in a situation that truly terrified her.

There were plans for "Kiss" to be released as a single, with Monroe singing a solo version. Composer Lionel Newman suggested a promotional campaign that was sure to make the record a number one hit, and said that an impression of Monroe's lip prints be stamped directly onto the vinyl. While she was enthusiastic about the proposal, the studio had weathered enough controversy over the film's provocative tone and they nixed the idea.

Monroe has several walking sequences in the film and they caused quite a sensation. So much so, women's groups across the United States were outraged, saying Monroe's "frank characterization" was indecent (*Variety*, February 1953). A reviewer for the *Monthly Film Bulletin* (undated, 1953) wrote that Monroe's character was "vulgar and faintly repulsive." The Niagara Falls representative to the Ontario legislature was equally outraged by the plot and characterizations in the film, saying it "did the honeymoon capital nothing but harm" (*Los Angeles Herald-Examiner,* April 1953).

While it may seem strange that a simple "walking sequence" could cause such a stir, this isn't just any walk; it's Marilyn Monroe's walk. She had the ability to make a jaw-dropping impression upon entering the frame, and an equally jaw-dropping impression upon exiting the frame. The most talked-about Hollywood walk is the 116 feet of film it took to film Monroe sashaying away from the camera, dressed in a tight black pencil skirt, white blouse and red cropped jacket, her signature wiggle on full display. The scene is often referred to as "the longest walk in cinema history."

The *New York Times* (January 22, 1953) wrote:

> Perhaps Miss Monroe is not the perfect actress at this point. But neither the director nor the gentlemen who handled the cameras appeared to be concerned with this. They have caught every possible curve both in the intimacy of the boudoir and in equally revealing tight dresses. And they have illustrated pretty concretely that she can be seductive—even when she walks.

On the set of *Niagara*. Monroe was asked by reporter Sidney Skolsky what she wore to bed. Her unexpected answer was, "Why, Chanel No. 5, of course." At the time, Monroe seemed to be carrying on her own personal shock-and-awe campaign. Her flagrant nudity set tongues wagging, at least at first. After a few weeks, it was commonplace. She wore no underwear under her outfits and showed little concern about who saw what; she insisted on being naked under the sheets in the bedroom scenes and during the shower scene. Director Hathaway kept yelling at her to step back from the shower curtain and away from the light. While her silhouette was a feature of the scene, Monroe's insistence on also pressing her naked form against the wet shower curtain was, at the time, equivalent to soft porn. In order to pass the censors, the raunchy scene was darkened by the special effects department in post-production.

While this type of exhibitionism seemed deliberate, there were other times when it seemed entirely innocent. Darryl Zanuck had given Max Showalter the extracurricular job of looking out for Monroe during the course of production. He made sure they had adjoining rooms at the General Brock Hotel and Monroe asked Showalter to leave the adjoining door to their rooms unlocked at all times. Prior to shooting her first scene in the early hours of the morning, a stark-naked Monroe entered Showalter's room, jumped on his bed and said, "Please don't do anything to me but just hold me....just help me with my lines. Help me" (Buskin, *Blonde Heat: The Sizzling Screen Career of Marilyn Monroe*, p. 126). Despite the

George Loomis (Joseph Cotten) has just strangled his flirtatious, philandering wife Rose (Marilyn Monroe) in the carillon bell tower in a shocking scene from the Technicolor film noir, *Niagara* (1953). This was the only time a Monroe character died on screen.

obvious distraction, Showalter helped her with her lines. He said there was a certain quality about her that made you want to help her.

Another time, she was standing naked in front of her hotel room window in clear view of the street below. She called Showalter into the room to ask why all the men were looking up at her. When Showalter pointed out the obvious, she seemed genuinely surprised—so much so that he felt it was an entirely innocent reaction. It was this provocative versus pure conflict that pulled people in. At times she was so overtly sexual, she knew what she was doing and she knew the reactions that came from it. Then there were times like the window incident, where she reacted to the moment like the naïveté of a child who didn't know better. Was she really that clueless? Or was she just *that* good an actress?

In Joseph Cotten's 1987 autobiography, *Vanity Will Get You Somewhere,* he wrote that he found her to be "charming" and "defensively shy." He also wrote of her self-deprecating sense of humor and quick wit. In describing her overall demeanor, Cotten moved to a darker place and was far more analytical in tone, writing:

> At times she glowed with the joy of discovery and then, suddenly, her focus would move into outer space, thrusting her into a cloud of blankness. This dilution of thought, this quick snapping of concentration sometimes happened to her in the middle of acting a scene, and recovery was not always easy for her. At the time, it seemed to me that she was cursed with less than her share of confidence and more than her share of insecurity, both dark synonyms for fear... I enjoyed her company. I enjoyed working with her.

As on most of her films, Monroe was anti-social. She didn't mix with the cast and crew after hours. Cotten's room was the go-to place for a drink and to wind down after a day of shooting in the stifling summer heat. Monroe never showed up.

Niagara was the first of three monumental Marilyn Monroe films released in 1953; *Gentlemen Prefer Blondes* and *How to Marry a Millionaire* followed, making the year the most successful of her career. The three films grossed in excess of $25 million at the box office worldwide.

Gentlemen Prefer Blondes (1953)

Marilyn Monroe appeared as Lorelei Lee. Twentieth Century–Fox. 91 minutes. *Director:* Howard Hawks. *Producer:* Sol C. Siegel. *Writers:* Charles Lederer (screenplay). Based on the musical comedy by Joseph Fields and Anita Loos. *Original Music:* Jule Styne and Leo Robin. *Cinematography:* Harry J. Wild. *Costume Design:* Travilla. *Production Dates:* November 17, 1952 to January 22, 1953 (additional scenes shot in February 1953). *Release Date:* July 1, 1953. *Production Cost:* $2.26 million. *Domestic Box Office Receipts:* $5.1 million. *Genre:* Comedy-Drama-Musical-Romance. Technicolor. *Other Cast:* Jane Russell (Dorothy Shaw), Charles Coburn (Sir Francis "Piggy" Beekman), Elliott Reid (Ernie Malone), Tommy Noonan (Gus Esmond Jr.), George Winslow (Henry Spofford III), Marcel Dalio (Magistrate), Taylor Holmes (Mr. Gus Esmond, Sr.), Norma Varden (Lady Beekman), Howard Wendell (Watson), Steven Geray (Hotel Manager). *Soundtrack:* "When Love Goes Wrong": Music by Hoagy Carmichael. Lyrics by Harold Adamson. Performed by Marilyn Monroe and Jane Russell. "Anyone Here for Love?": Music by Hoagy Carmichael. Lyrics by Harold Adamson. Performed by Jane Russell. "A Little Girl from Little Rock": Music by Jule Styne. Lyrics by Leo Robin. Sung by Marilyn Monroe and Jane Russell. "Diamonds Are a Girl's Best Friend": Music by Jule Styne. Lyrics by Leo Robin. Performed by Marilyn Monroe (with high notes dubbed by Marni

Nixon). "Bye Bye Baby": Music by Jule Styne. Lyrics by Leo Robin. Performed by Jane Russell and Marilyn Monroe. *Awards:* 1954—Writers Guild of America, WGA Award: Best Written American Musical—Charles Lederer (nominated). *Tagline:* The Two M-M-Marvels of Our Age in the Wonder Musical of the World!

On her 26th birthday, June 1, 1952, Marilyn Monroe received a present of grand proportions: She was cast as Lorelei Lee in Fox's *Gentlemen Prefer Blondes*. It was big news and it was a huge break for Monroe. The film was originally slated for Betty Grable and Ginger Rogers. (With Judy Holliday in mind for the role of Lorelei Lee, Columbia had negotiated for the film rights, but Fox won out.)

At the time, Grable was commanding a whopping $150,000 per picture, so Fox went with the cheaper option, Monroe. While her co-star Jane Russell pulled in $100,000 as a freelance player, Monroe was under contract at $1,500 per week. In total, she received $18,000 for her iconic role of Lorelei Lee (Summers, p. 119–20).

The stage play of the same name opened at Broadway's Ziegfeld Theatre on December 8, 1949. Carol Channing played Lorelei Lee and Yvonne Adair played Dorothy Shaw. The play lasted for 740 performances, closing on September 15, 1951. A London production opened on August 20, 1962. It ran for 223 performances. Dora Bryan played Lorelei Lee and Anne Hart played Dorothy Shaw.

An adaptation entitled *Lorelei* opened at Broadway's Palace Theatre on January 27, 1974. It ran for 320 performances and closed on November 3, 1974. Carol Channing reprised her role as Lorelei Lee and Tamara Long played Dorothy Shaw. A Broadway revival of the original play opened at the Lyceum Theatre on April 10, 1995, and closed on April 30, 1995. KT Sullivan played Lorelei Lee and Karen Prunzik played Dorothy Shaw.

In her 2002 memoir, *Just Lucky I Guess: A Memoir of Sorts*, Channing wrote that Twentieth Century–Fox purchased tickets for Marilyn Monroe to study the play. She sat third-row center for exactly one month. Channing wrote, "Our orchestra never ever saw anyone that beautiful before." Despite Monroe's viewings of the show, Channing said in an e-mail to the author that she never met Monroe. "Marilyn always left immediately following the curtain call and never came backstage to meet."

While Channing admitted that *Gentlemen Prefer Blondes* was one of Monroe's finest films, she didn't think it was funny. The studio strayed from the dialogue of Anita Loos' original book, which Channing said was "hilarious and which was what constantly kept the stage musical on a higher level."

The film begins with Lorelei Lee (Marilyn Monroe) and Dorothy Shaw (Jane Russell) dressed in matching floor-length, figure-hugging red sequined dresses with a thigh-high split on the left leg. As they sing and dance their way through "A Little Girl from Little Rock," in the audience is Gus Esmond, Jr. (Tommy Noonan), the smitten, very rich, nerdy fiancé of Lorelei. When Lorelei and Dorothy travel by ship to France, without Gus, they're tailed by Ernie Malone (Elliott Reid), a private detective hired by Lorelei's distrustful future father-in-law (Taylor Holmes) to keep tabs on her.

For Lorelei, the main aim of the trip is to snare herself a millionaire, or billionaire— any man richer than the one she's already got. Dorothy goes along as her chaperone, but she's far more interested in looks over loot. Lorelei only has the voyage to France to find a replacement for Gus, because when she gets there, she's agreed to marry him. The diamond-obsessed Lorelei plays the dumb blonde role to perfection, but she's smarter than she appears

We get only a glimpse of this gold-pleated Travilla dress in *Gentlemen Prefer Blondes* (1953) as Monroe dances seductively and sings "Down Boy" to a smitten Charles Coburn. While much of the movie's dialogue borders on the provocative, this scene crossed the line and the censors put their foot down. As a result, the gold dress is only seen briefly; through a window aboard the ship, we see Monroe from behind, dancing with Coburn and swaying her famous derriere.

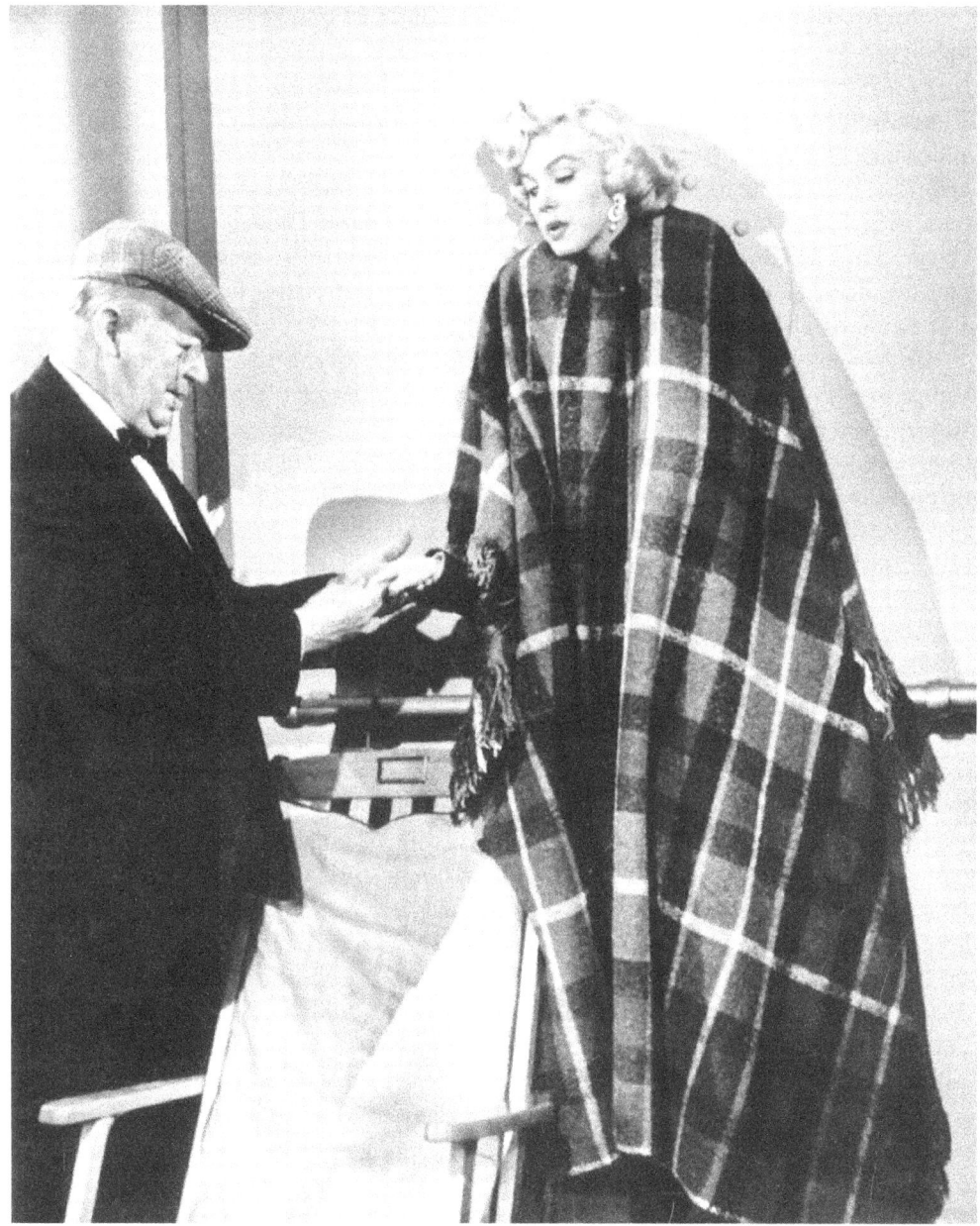

Stuck in the porthole window, Marilyn Monroe attempts to disguise her predicament from Charles Coburn with a well-placed blanket in one of the many comedic scenes from *Gentlemen Prefer Blondes* (1953).

to be, and surprisingly likable. The woman is a self-confessed gold digger, but Monroe's usual blend of seduction with a child-like innocence makes her impossible to dislike.

Aboard the ship, Lorelei runs into the much-older Sir Francis "Piggy" Beekman (Charles Coburn), the owner of a South African diamond mine. She sets her sights on him, despite the fact that he's married and traveling with his stuffy wife.

Ernie takes a genuine liking to Dorothy but continues to try to catch Lorelei in an act of betrayal. When he snaps a photo of Lorelei and "Piggy" in an embrace (which in actuality is an innocent demonstration by "Piggy" of how a python chokes a goat), the girls set out to get a-hold of the incriminating photo. After drugging Ernie, Lorelei finds the roll of film and immediately gets it developed. "Piggy" is thankful that Lorelei has intercepted the photo before his wife saw it in the papers and insists on giving her something as a thank you. Lorelei tells "Piggy" that she only wants one thing—his wife's tiara! Though he's hesitant at first, "Piggy" gives her the tiara. Upon her arrival in Paris, Lorelei is accused by "Piggy's" wife (and her insurance agent) of stealing it. "Piggy" disappears to Africa, but not before denying ever giving Lorelei the tiara in the first place.

To protect her friend from the law, Dorothy, impersonates Lorelei, (complete with a blonde wig), in a comedic courtroom scene that puts an end to the "tiara fiasco." "Ain't There Anyone Here for Love" is a musical number featuring Dorothy with a group of scantily-clad men, introduced as Olympic Athletes, who cavort shirtless around her, their only attire being flesh-colored swim trunks. It's so homoerotic, it's surprising it got past the censors. In fact, the entire film cleverly dances around the strict censorship codes of the time. Its sexual innuendos, both verbal and visual, make it even more enjoyable to watch.

While the Olympic athletes do their exercise routine to Dorothy's song, the finale sees Dorothy bend down in front of the pool; the athletes dive into the pool one by one, the last one clipping her enough for her to lose her balance and fall in. To Russell's credit, she pops up out of the water and finishes the song with a smile. Russell going into the pool was not scripted, but director Howard Hawks felt that it was the best take of the athletes diving into the pool and in the end it served to give the performance a comedic finale that fit the overall tone of the film.

Monroe has a chance to show off her physical comedy skills in a scene with Henry Spofford III, played by child actor George Winslow. On board the ship, Lorelei tries to escape Eddie's room (after unsuccessfully looking for the incriminating roll of film) by measuring her hips with her hands and then comparing the width with the porthole window. Convinced she'll fit, she proceeds to climb through to the deck—and she gets stuck. Her escape attempt is interrupted by a curious Henry, a boy with a deep voice who is convinced that he caught Lorelei in the act of a burglary. When "Piggy" approaches, Henry gives Lorelei a blanket to pull up high around her neck and the boy hides underneath it. "Piggy" is unaware that Lorelei is stuck in the window and that Henry is hiding beneath the blanket; as a result, the conversation that follows, with husky-voiced Henry joining in (though he's never seen), is a comedy highlight. Lorelei says she is catching a cold, which explains her deep voice.

Gentlemen Prefer Blondes is the "buddy story" of two very different women, with two very different personalities, the blonde Monroe and the brunette Russell. Both actresses have their solo time to shine throughout, and when they come together, there's no grandstanding from either one. Their collaborative scenes are warm, funny, and delightful to watch. *Gentlemen Prefer Blondes* is a battle-of-the-sexes musical comedy that's everything a 1950s musical should be: brilliant song and dance numbers, a charming, feel-good story, perfect chemistry between Monroe and Russell, stunning costumes by Travilla, and all presented in vivid Technicolor. It is the epitome of the genre.

Monroe's iconic "Diamonds Are a Girl's Best Friend" number is the solo musical highlight, and once again we see Lorelei's conservative fiancé Gus in the audience. The end scene is a double wedding with Lorelei and Dorothy dressed as identical brides, walking down the aisle to their husbands-to-be, the loyal Gus and Ernie the private detective.

There are several publicity shots showing Monroe and Russell dressed in black-sequined corseted leotards with a contrasting ruffled floral bodice, a strategically placed yet sexually suggestive gathering of draping long cords at the crotch and Napoleonic hats. The costumes were donned for a routine that was performed with an Eiffel Tower backdrop and a similarly dressed group of female dancers bearing swords. It wasn't used in the film, but a snippet survives in the trailer.

Monroe's infamous gold lamé halter dress with sunburst-pleats was worn in a deleted scene with Charles Coburn as "Piggy." Through a window on the ship's deck, Dorothy sees Lorelei dancing with "Piggy." The song, "Down Boy," was sung by Lorelei to "Piggy" while they were dancing. While the number originally made the cut, it was considered inappropriate and too sexually suggestive and the dress didn't help matters. Its plunging neckline (open to Monroe's waist) was too raunchy for the censors. The full scene was cut following the first preview, but there is one snippet in the film that shows Monroe cha-cha-ing from behind. A third song, "When the Wild Women Go Swimmin' Down in the Bimini Bay," was also cut.

The Hays Code constantly warned Twentieth Century–Fox about the skimpiness of Monroe's *Gentlemen Prefer Blondes* costumes, saying, "The business of the girls' dressing should be kept within careful limits of good taste…" Complying with the prudish censorship regulations was a thorn in the side of every Hollywood designer, but most laughed off the stifling rigidity of the censors and worked their magic to get the fashion police pioneers to approve their designs—eventually. With any signs of cleavage being taboo, Edith Head once called the Hays Office employees "The Bust Inspectors." Fellow designer Irene Sharaff got around the censorship rules on a technicality, saying, "So long as there was a covering, however thin, the studio could claim that the actress was fully clothed" (Nadoolman, *Dressed: A Century of Hollywood Costume Design*, p. 182).

Edwin Schallert of the *Los Angeles Times* (August 1, 1953) wrote:

> Miss Monroe sparkles much of the time just as the diamonds do. Her work is insidiously intriguing in this picture, and at the same time almost childlike in its utter lack of guile. Her portrayal demonstrates that much may be maneuvered in her instance in the future to humorous advantage. She discloses a surprising light comedy touch.

Bosley Crowther of the *New York Times* (July 16, 1953) wrote:

> There is not much class in this picture. The humor is mainly in such things as Miss Monroe's finding it difficult, for anatomical reasons, to squeeze her way through a porthole, or she and Miss Russell's conspiring to pull the pants off a gentlemen friend … and yet, there is that about Miss Russell and also about Miss Monroe that keeps you looking at them even when they have little or nothing to do.

Academy Award–winning actor-dancer-singer George Chakiris shared his memories of working as a chorus dancer on *Gentlemen Prefer Blondes* with the author:

> I know it's been said many times, but I'd love to reiterate how exquisitely beautiful Marilyn Monroe was. Even in rehearsal with no makeup, there was something about her personal quality, who she was as a person, that was beautiful as well. A sweetness, a kindness, in her case the camera definitely did not lie. I remember the different times I was around her, that she was quiet. She came into the room or soundstage or set quietly. One of the things I remember during the filming of the "Diamonds Are a Girl's Best Friend" number was that whenever [choreographer]

Jack Cole or the camera operator called "cut" for any reason and we had to start over, she never looked in the mirror to check her makeup, she never went to her dressing room, she went right back to her starting position and waited to begin again. She was incredibly disciplined and concentrated. Thinking back, I feel she cared very deeply about her work. I know everybody cares [about their work], but I always felt it was much more for her. I remember thinking that the two people I was lucky enough to be around and who seemed to have this deeper caring, were Marilyn Monroe and Jerome Robbins, and I hope that's saying something. They were both incredible, and that deeper caring is something that sets them apart from the rest. Jerry was such a perfectionist, and I suppose she was too, but her desire to do right by everyone bred inner anxieties, which in turn made her appear unprofessional to some.

Another time during a break in shooting, I was near enough to see Marilyn listening to Jack Cole and her acting coach Natasha Lytess at the same time. Jack was saying something to her about the number and behind him stood Natasha. Jack wasn't aware that Natasha was behind him. She quietly and very slightly, but also very seriously, shook her head "no" to whatever he was saying to Marilyn, in a sort of, "I'll talk to you about that later" manner, and Marilyn was having to pay attention to both of them. She showed diplomacy and courtesy in a very difficult situation.

My favorite credit is saying that I was "one of the guys behind Marilyn Monroe in the "Diamonds Are a Girl's Best Friend" number. It's such a great number and people always love to hear her name. It's an impressive credit, really. It took three days to shoot that number. We went until

Marilyn Monroe is coached by her drama teacher, Natasha Lytess, on the set of *Gentlemen Prefer Blondes* (1953).

9 p.m. on the third day. In those days everyone had to wait until they were told the film was okay, or something like that. So everyone was standing around and waiting. They finally gave us the okay sign and everyone slowly started to leave. When Marilyn discovered that Jack [Cole] had already gone (he was catching the red eye to New York), she ran out of the sound stage in her beautiful pink gown. I always assumed she wanted to try and catch up with him to say thank you.

On June 26, 1953, shortly before the film was released, Marilyn Monroe and Jane Russell put their hand and footprints into the wet cement outside Grauman's Chinese Theatre. Monroe suggested that her behind and Jane Russell's breasts be imprinted as well, but the request was denied. Additionally, Monroe wanted to dot the "i" in Marilyn with a diamond, but a rhinestone was used instead. The cheaper option didn't prevent a tourist from chiseling it out and taking it home as a souvenir.

Russell helped Monroe's insecurities, and in turn, helped director Howard Hawks get the best possible performance out of her. Hawks said, "It wasn't easy, that film, but it wasn't difficult either because I had Jane there... I'd hear them talking, Marilyn would whisper, 'What did he tell me?' Jane wouldn't say, 'He's told you six times already,' she'd just tell her again" (McCarthy, p. 506).

Greg Schreiner is a world-renowned Marilyn Monroe collector and president of Marilyn Remembered, a fan club in existence since 1982. Over the years he developed close friendships with many of Monroe's friends and peers, including Jane Russell. He recalls a conversation with her about Monroe's work ethic on the set of *Gentlemen Prefer Blondes*:

> Jane and Marilyn became good friends... She always called Marilyn "Blondel." Marilyn would have difficulty coming to the set. She had many insecurities about her looks and acting ability [so] Jane would swing by her dressing room each day and say, "Come on, Blondel, let's go to the set!" and Marilyn would then garner up her courage and join Jane. Neither was a great dancer, but through the help of choreographer Jack Cole, they were able to look proficient on the screen. Jane said that when she become exhausted rehearsing, Marilyn would still stay late in the night with Jack to really perfect her movement.

Once again, Monroe's drama coach Natasha Lytess made her presence felt on set. Hawks kept his temper in check and indulged Monroe most of the time. In one scene, Monroe nailed her first take. Hawks was happy with her performance and he was ready to move on, but just off to the side, Lytess gave Monroe the silent nod in the negative. To keep the peace, Hawks agreed to redo the scene, but the do-over went on for at least ten more takes, and none of them came near the first one.

Hawks eventually wielded his authority and banished Lytess to Monroe's dressing room. But when it was time to shoot her scenes, Monroe stayed in her dressing room with her. In order to keep the production moving, Hawks allowed her back on set, but she was ordered to sit much further away to prevent any further distractions. Hawks dealt with the Monroe-Lytess combination better than most directors, but when Darryl Zanuck asked Hawks how filming could be sped up, he responded with, "[I have] three wonderful ideas: replace Marilyn, rewrite the script to make it shorter, and get a new director" (McCarthy, p. 506). And whenever Monroe would politely ask if she could try the scene "just one more time," Hawks would agree, then turn around and mouth, "There's no film in the camera, is there?" before nodding for her to continue (McCarthy, p. 506).

Gentlemen Prefer Blondes ended up being the second most successful film of Hawks'

Marilyn Monroe (left) and Jane Russell in a promotional still for *Gentlemen Prefer Blondes* **(1953).**

career, playing second fiddle only to *Sergeant York* (which grossed $6 million). Opening at the Roxy Theater in New York City on July 15, 1953, the film grossed $128,500 in its first week and a total of $625,000 in its exclusive six-week run, making it America's number one film for the first week of August.

Nine years after the film was made, and a few weeks before her untimely death, Monroe spoke with associate editor Richard Meryman of *Life* magazine. The interview was aptly titled "A Last Long Talk With a Lonely Girl" and published twelve days after her death. Monroe said, "I remember when I got the part in *Gentlemen Prefer Blondes*, Jane Russell ... got $200,000 for it and I got $500 a week [it was $1,250 a week], but that to me was, you know, considerable. She, by the way, was quite wonderful to me." After being constantly told that she was not the star of the film, or a star *period*, Monroe said, "Look, after all, I am the blonde and it is *Gentlemen Prefer Blondes*...whatever I am, I *am* the blonde."

Marni Nixon, renowned singing voice for many of Hollywood's classic stars, dubbed the high notes for Monroe on the song "Diamonds Are a Girl's Best Friend." Twentieth Century–Fox initially wanted Nixon to dub Monroe on the entire song. In her 2007 memoir *I Could Have Sung All Night*, Nixon wrote, "Thank goodness they let her sing her own way. That breathy, sexy sound suited her screen persona perfectly, even if she did need a little help on the high notes."

"As Lorelei Lee, who believes that diamonds are a girl's best friend, Marilyn Monroe does the best job of her short career to date," *Time* magazine's critic wrote on July 27, 1953. "[She] sings remarkably well, dances, or rather undulates all over, flutters the heaviest eyelids in show business, and breathlessly delivers such lines of dialogue as 'Coupons—that's almost like money,' as if she were in the throes of a grand passion."

How to Marry a Millionaire (1953)

Marilyn Monroe appeared as Pola Debevoise. Twentieth Century–Fox. 95 minutes. Alternate *Title: The Greeks Had a Word for It*. *Director:* Jean Negulesco. *Writer-Producer:* Nunnally Johnson. *Original Music:* Cyril Mockridge. *Musical Director:* Alfred Newman. *Cinematography:* Joe MacDonald. *Costume Design:* Travilla. *Production Dates:* March 9 to mid–April 1953. *Release Date:* November 4, 1953. *Production Cost:* $1.87 million. *Domestic Box Office Receipts:* $7.3 million. *Filming Locations:* Twentieth Century–Fox Studios (Stage 14), Sun Valley, Idaho, Hudson River, NY, George Washington Bridge, Manhattan, 36 Sutton Place South, Sutton Place, Manhattan. *Genre:* Comedy-Drama-Romance. Technicolor and CinemaScope. *Other Cast:* Betty Grable (Loco Dempsey), Lauren Bacall (Schatze Page), David Wayne (Freddie Denmark), Rory Calhoun (Eben), Cameron Mitchell (Tom Brookman), Alex D'Arcy (J. Stewart Merrill), Fred Clark (Waldo Brewster), William Powell (J. D. Hanley). *Awards:* 1954 Academy Awards (USA): Best Costume Design—Charles Le Maire, Travilla (nominated). 1954—Writer's Guild of America (USA): Best Written American Comedy (WGA Award, screen)—Nunnally Johnson (nominated). 1955—BAFTA Film Awards: Best Film from any Source (USA—nominated). How to Marry a Millionaire: The Most Glamorous Entertainment of Your Lifetime in CinemaScope. You See It Without Glasses!

When Professor Henri Chretien developed the anamorphic lens for use in tank periscopes during World War I, little did he realize the impact he would have on the evolution of motion pictures. After some further development to suit Hollywood's needs, CinemaScope was first introduced to audiences in 1953.

How to Marry a Millionaire, the smash-hit comedy of 1953 about three gold-digging women looking for money over love, starred (l to r) Betty Grable, Lauren Bacall and Marilyn Monroe. Writer Nunnally Johnson, showcased Monroe's comedic timing to perfection with his cleverly crafted script. *How to Marry a Millionaire* was the first film shot in CinemaScope, though it was released *after* the 'Scope religious epic *The Robe.*

With promotional taglines such as "The First Picture on the New Miracle Curved Screen" and "No Glasses Needed" (a reference to 3D), the Henry Koster–directed religious epic *The Robe* made a healthy box office profit and won several industry awards. Despite *How to Marry a Millionaire* being the very first film to ever be shot in the widescreen format, Fox decided to release *The Robe* first, making *How to Marry a Millionaire* the second CinemaScope release. Fox very smartly copyrighted the invention and then proceeded to sell their exclusive license to other companies clamoring to use the specially designed anamorphic lens.

The conventional screen aspect ratio was 1.33:1; CinemaScope produced a much larger ratio of 2.35:1, meaning theaters needed a screen that was two and a half times the standard size to show the picture. While Hollywood's newest invention was exciting, it was not without its faults. The magnification of CinemaScope was on such a grand scale that even the slenderest Hollywood actress was considerably widened in the process. Closeups were distorted and the voluminous fifties skirts that Lauren Bacall, Betty Grable and Marilyn Monroe were slated to wear in *How to Marry a Millionaire* looked enormous. Monroe went on a strict diet before production began and she also insisted on wearing tight skirts to combat the problem.

Aside from its aforementioned faults, CinemaScope also limited costumers in the patterns and textures used in their designs. Horizontal stripes, large florals and strong textures were forbidden because of CinemaScope's distortion. Despite its shortcomings, CinemaScope (now called Panavision) was a groundbreaking invention. So long as the rules were followed (few, if any closeups, the right costumes, etc.), the final result of a film shot with an anamorphic lens is unmatched in its beauty, vibrancy, and impact on audiences (Landis, p. 178).

In her 2005 memoir *By Myself and Then Some*, Bacall wrote that, in Cinemascope, the actors were required to be constantly moving, but not too close together because of the restrictions of the long and narrow screen. Longer scenes were also shot, up to six script pages at a time. It was a method that Bacall felt comfortable with, likening the technique to working on the stage.

According to Bacall, "Marilyn was frightened, insecure—trusted only her coach and was always late." That said, Bacall wrote that Monroe was impossible *not* to like, saying, "[S]he had no meanness in her—no bitchery." Understandably, Monroe's insistence on printing only *her* best take irked even her most good-natured co-stars. Yet, even when she got everything right, she still wasn't able to determine which take was her best, at least not without a nod of approval from Natasha Lytess first.

The simplest of tasks and the actions required of her would terrify her into making mistakes that would cause lengthy delays, and this was in addition to her problems with her lines. In one *Millionaire* scene, her character, Pola, is awaiting a telephone call, and Monroe's nervousness caused her to constantly pick up the phone before it rang. Likewise, when she was called upon to pour some coffee and take a sip, she'd take a drink from an empty cup, forgetting to first pour the coffee. Bacall said that it wasn't unusual for a scene to go for fifteen takes, sometimes more, which meant that both she and Betty Grable had to be at their best in all of them. It wasn't possible.

Somehow, through all the repetition, Monroe would work herself up to her best take. Most actors lose their spark and natural momentum with repeated takes, but Monroe only gained more confidence. And so the rule was set in stone: So long as Monroe's co-stars got their lines right, if it was Monroe's best take, then *that* was the one that was used. Nothing else mattered.

It wasn't an easy way to work, and reason enough to despise Monroe for wielding that type of control over the production, yet Bacall and Grable (both veterans of the industry at that point) still went out of their way to make her feel secure and liked, giving her the genuine feeling that she could rely upon them, not just as co-stars, but as friends too.

But even with people who expressed kindness toward her, Monroe had major trust issues. If she didn't get too close she wouldn't get hurt; at least that was her thought process. On the other hand, with many of the relationships that came and went throughout her life, both friendships and romances, she'd become so immersed in the life of the other person she'd lose herself in the process.

Monroe either snubbed people or smothered them. There was rarely a middle ground. She was both needy and cold. Bacall wrote, "There was something sad about her—wanting to reach out—afraid to trust—uncomfortable...[Monroe] made no effort for others and yet she was nice."

The press (and the studio) invented a feud between Monroe and Grable, the two sexy platinum blondes of the Fox lot. By the time *How to Marry a Millionaire* was produced, Grable was the "old hand" and Monroe was "the rising star." The eager press were chomping at the bit for some juicy news about on-set catfights, but they didn't happen. With Hollywood's "out with the old and in with the new" attitude, of course, there *had* to be tension, or so they hoped. In reality, it was the quite the opposite. Grable did everything in her power to befriend Monroe. Though Monroe was hesitant to trust her, Grable's warmth chipped away at Monroe's protective wall and they became quite close throughout the production.

By 1953, Grable was in her late thirties, married to bandleader Harry James (her second husband after a short-lived marriage to child star Jackie Coogan) and had two young daughters. She had given her best acting years to Fox. She was a top box office star and now she was being pushed out. While she *did* feel disposable and slighted, none of her resentment was directed toward Monroe. Instead, she went straight to the root of the problem: Darryl Zanuck.

After filming for *How to Marry a Millionaire* was complete, Grable stormed into Zanuck's office and tore up her Fox contract in front of him. She had five years left on it, but she didn't care. She was done. After Grable's departure, the studio's final attempt at proving there really was bad blood between the two stars was to order photographers to get a shot of Monroe posing in front of her new dressing room door. It was hot on the heels of Grable's dramatic exit but it was no accident that her name was *still* on the door. The manipulation was obvious. The photo would imply that Monroe had pushed her out and succeeded her. Monroe's loyalty was steadfast: She refused to pose for the photo.

Grable's last two feature films, both released in 1955, were *Three for the Show* and *How to Be Very, Very Popular*. The latter *almost* re-teamed her with Marilyn Monroe but the script wasn't to her liking and Sheree North took over Monroe's would-have-been role. Grable passed away from lung cancer on July 2, 1973. She was fifty-six years old.

Preceding the opening credits, *How to Marry a Millionaire* begins with a must-watch rendition of Alfred Newman's "Street Scene" overture, with Newman conducting the orchestral presentation himself. In a story of money versus love, three models, Schatze (Lauren Bacall), Loco (Betty Grable) and Pola (Marilyn Monroe) set themselves up in a lavish New York penthouse that is owned by Freddie Denmark (David Wayne), a tax evader who is avoiding the wrath of the IRS by living overseas. Thinking they'd have a better chance of attracting a millionaire husband if they seemed to have their own wealth, the crafty gals gets off to a rough start when their lack of affluent suitors forces them into selling off the fugitive's lavish penthouse furniture in order to buy themselves some extra time.

Schatze, the ringleader of the gold-digging trio, insists that finding a husband is a task that should be ruled by the head, not the heart. She's adamant that her "next husband" won't be the usual "gas pump–jockey" type that she typically falls for. She then instructs Loco and Pola on the fine art of marrying for money.

After Loco scams the likable Tom Brookman (Cameron Mitchell) into buying her groceries, she brings him home to meet the other ladies. He takes an instant liking to Schatze, and she finds him attractive, but Schatze is convinced that he's just another good-looking, blue-collar loser. Although she initially rebuffs his repeated attempts to woo her, she eventually agrees to date him. Though Schatze enjoys spending time with him, strictly on the basis of his "assumed" lack of finances, she informs him that she "never wants to see him again" after each and every date. Setting her sights on the exceedingly wealthy, much older widower J.D. Hanley (William Powell), Schatze follows her own theory of "money over love" and accepts his marriage proposal.

In the meantime, Loco agrees to go to Maine with a married businessman, but only because she assumes there'd be a chance of meeting a rich available man during her stay. Nothing could be further from the truth, and when she gets the measles, she's forced to hibernate in an isoated cabin until she's well. Her recovery is helped along by the handsome Eben (Rory Calhoun), a local forest ranger whom she mistakes for a landowner after he takes her out to look at "his land." By the time she realizes that he's only the caretaker and fire-spotter, it's too late: She's fallen in love with him. Love wins over money and they marry.

Pola is as blind as a bat, so many of Monroe's scenes have "visual" gags incorporated in order to play up her near-sightedness. Though she has glasses, she refuses to put them on whenever a man is within spitting distance. Pola thinks she's snared herself an Arab oil tycoon, but he's really a hustler. Unaware of his scam, she plans on taking a plane to meet him, but once again her eyes fail her and she ends up on the wrong flight. Coincidentally, she's seated next to the bespectacled owner of her apartment, the tax evader Freddie Denmark. When Freddie sees Pola reading her book upside down, he prompts her to put on her glasses and embrace the look. Freddie, we find out, isn't a crook after all. He's going to Kansas to clear his name and track down the dishonest accountant who absconded with his IRS payment. When Freddie finds him, he gets a beating for his trouble; however, he gains a wife. He and Pola get married and she wears her glasses for the remainder of the film.

Newlyweds Loco and Pola show up with their husbands in time to witness Schatze marry her millionaire. Loco and Pola failed in their quest for a wealthy man but they're happily in love. Before long, Schatze realizes that a marriage should be based on love, not the size of a man's bank account, and she backs out of her marriage to J.D. She confesses to the very gracious J.D. that she's in love with Tom Brookman, the usual "gas pump jockey" type that she's always attracted to. When Tom shows up to Schatze's nuptials unannounced, J.D. knows exactly who he is and exactly how much he's worth. When J.D. tells Tom that Schatze didn't go through with the marriage because she's in love with him, he agrees to keep his wealth a secret until after they're wed. Against her better judgment, and still thinking her husband is a working class bum, Schatze marries him—for love.

In the last scene, the three women and their new husbands celebrate their nuptials over cheeseburgers and beer at a modest diner, or a "greasy spoon" as Schatze refers to the place. Tom says he estimates his wealth at two hundred million. As he casually begins to reel off his long list of impressive assets, the others laugh and mock him. It's not until he pulls out a wad of $1,000 bills to pay for the modest post-ceremony meal that they realize he's serious. The realization that he's a multi-millionaire, together with the sight of so much cash, causes all three women to faint, falling off their stools to the floor. To end the film, Tom, Eben and Freddie make a toast to their wives.

Monroe's character being self-conscious about wearing glasses was an art-imitating-life situation. Monroe initially wanted to play Grable's role, but only because her character Loco wasn't scripted to wear glasses. In the end, *because* she was near-sighted and *because* of the way Monroe played up the handicap, it was Pola who got all the laughs.

Several exceptionally witty in-jokes were incorporated into the script. Loco makes a reference to Grable's real-life husband, bandleader Harry James. "Good ol' Harry James," she says, as his music plays on the radio in the cabin in Maine. Likewise, in a conversation with the much older, J.D., Bacall's character Schatze mentions her real-life husband Humphrey Bogart, "I've always liked older men," she says, "Look at that old fellow, what's-his-name in [*The*] *African Queen*. Absolutely crazy about him..."

When Monroe's character Pola models a red swimsuit, she's introduced with the line, "You know, of course, that diamonds are a girl's best friend..."—a nod to Monroe's show-stopping number in the smash-hit released in the same year, *Gentlemen Prefer Blondes*. Lastly, when Monroe's character pulls out something to read on the plane, the title of her book is *Murder by Strangulation*, the fate of her character in the 1953 film noir *Niagara*.

Bosley Crowther of the *New York Times* (November 15, 1953) called *How to Marry a Millionaire* "an average wisecracking comedy, stretched out like a rubber band." Audiences disagreed because *Millionaire* was the fifth highest grossing film for the year. *Gentlemen Prefer Blondes* came in sixth, with *Niagara* grabbing eleventh spot. As with the previous year, the top twenty most popular/top grossing films for 1953 included *three* Marilyn Monroe films.

River of No Return (1954)

Marilyn Monroe appeared as Kay Weston. Twentieth Century–Fox. 91 minutes. *Directors:* Otto Preminger (and Jean Negulesco [post-production retakes]). *Producer:* Stanley Rubin. *Screenplay:* Frank Fenton. Story: Louis Lantz. *Original Music:* Cyril Mockridge. *Cinematography:* Joseph LaShelle. *Costume Design:* Travilla. *Production Dates:* July 29 to September 29, 1953; retakes in mid–November and mid–December 1953. *Release Date:* April 30, 1954. *Filming Locations:* Banff National Park, Alberta, Canada. Jasper National Park, Alberta, Canada. Lake Louise, Alberta, Canada. Twentieth Century–Fox Studios (Stage 9). *Genre:* Action-Adventure-Western. Technicolor and CinemaScope. *Other Cast:* Robert Mitchum (Matt Calder), Rory Calhoun (Harry Weston), Tommy Rettig (Mark Calder), Murvyn Vye (Dave Colby), Douglas Spencer (Sam Benson). *Soundtrack:* "River of No Return": Lyrics by Ken Darby. Music by Lionel Newman. Performed by Marilyn Monroe, Robert Mitchum and Tennessee Ernie Ford. "One Silver Dollar": Lyrics by Ken Darby. Music by Lionel Newman. Performed by Marilyn Monroe. "I'm Gonna File My Claim": Lyrics by Ken Darby. Music by Lionel Newman. Performed by Marilyn Monroe. "Down in the Meadow" (and reprise): Lyrics by Ken Darby. Music by Lionel Newman. Performed by Marilyn Monroe. *Taglines:* Reckless, Roaring, Adventure of the Great Northwest Gold Rush Days!; MARILYN MONROE...Sultry, flaming, exciting as never before—on a desperate river journey ... experiencing the violence and madness of desperate men!

Like *Niagara*, *River of No Return* is as much about the scenery as it is about Marilyn Monroe. It's set in the Canadian Rockies and filmed in color with multi-track stereophonic sound and the awesome spectacle of CinemaScope. What started out to be a rather small B-western (originally to be filmed in Idaho) grew bigger due to Darryl Zanuck's enthusiasm. It also became more expensive and more complicated as time rolled along. The revised script and the decision to film it in CinemaScope more than doubled the original studio estimates of a cost of under a million dollars. Coming in at a cost of $2.195 million, *River of No Return* made $3.8 million in ticket sales during its first release.

A clash of personalities (Monroe, Lytess and director Otto Preminger), together with the location shooting which often called for Monroe to be soaked to the skin, made for one of the most stressful and physically grueling shoots of Monroe's career. Preminger was a dictator: brash, loud, opinionated and unsympathetic to Monroe's insecurities, including her security blanket Natasha Lytess.

Monroe plays Kay, a late 1800s dance hall songstress who looks out for Mark (Tommy Rettig), the ten-year-old son of widower Matt Calder (Robert Mitchum). Calder is released from jail after serving a sentence for murder and returns to claim

Robert Mitchum pins Marilyn Monroe to the ground in this attempted rape scene from *River of No Return* (1954).

his son, but the boy has no memory of him. With promises of father-son hunting and fishing adventures and a life on the farm, Matt promises his son that he'll more than make up for lost time and the love-starved little boy embraces the return of his dad.

Kay's fiancé Harry (Rory Calhoun) has won a gold mine in a poker game. He tells Kay that they have to travel to Council City to file the deed, so they set out down the river on a very dodgy-looking log raft. When they get into trouble amidst the rapids, they just happen to be near Matt and Mark's farm, and father and son pull them to safety. When Matt refuses Harry's offer to buy his rifle and horse in order to reach Council City by land, Harry gets violent, hitting Mark with the rifle and stealing the weapon and the horse. With Matt, Mark and Kay now stranded, the threat of Indians loom and the three must escape downstream on Harry's raft.

The rest of the film examines the complexities of the developing relationship between Matt and Kay, the shock revelation that the father Mark worships is a murderer, a mountain lion attack and the arrival of prospectors who are out to get Harry for stealing their claim. The treacherous ride through the rapids almost gets them killed, but they eventually arrive in Council City in time to confront Harry.

The climax of the film allows Mark to understand that his father is not the cold-blooded murderer he thought he was, and that sometimes killing one man is what has to be done to save another. While Kay takes up singing at the local saloon, Matt physically claims her and puts her in his wagon for the ride home with him and Mark.

Preminger was on salary with Fox and earning a regular weekly paycheck of $2,500, whether he was working or not. The studio assigned him *River of No Return*, but he was less than enthusiastic about the script or about Marilyn Monroe as his signed and sealed female lead. Producer Stanley Rubin said Preminger was so unhappy with Monroe being cast that "it was very possible that if we hadn't cast Monroe before we hired Preminger, he would have fought against Monroe. Her style of acting, which was rather self-conscious, probably annoyed him ... then with the addition of Natasha Lytess, and the imbroglio that happened because of it, they were on the wrong foot from the word go" (Fujiwara, p. 154). Prior to production, Rubin let it slip that Preminger was down the list for choices as director and William Wellman, Raoul Walsh and Henry King were all considered earlier.

Preminger was assigned *River of No Return*, his first film in CinemaScope, but on many levels and for various reasons he was a reluctant participant. His hostility towards the studio overflowed to the set. His no-nonsense attitude was on full display and he was quick to brand Lytess a phony. Her usual interference caused disharmony between the cast and crew and her constant reminders for Monroe to use her stilted diction and over-enunciate each word drove Mitchum to distraction. Whenever she overdid it, Mitchum would slap her ass and remind her to act like a human. While his jolt of reality did the trick on more than one occasion, Monroe's devotion to her teacher was clear. As usual, Lytess would override the vision of Preminger. His opinion meant little to nothing, which further cemented his thoughts that the film was not for him. Preminger found himself on location, often in weather that was less than ideal, with an actress who couldn't function without her drama teacher and a leading man who drank too much. Though filming had barely begun, communication between Monroe and Preminger had broken down completely and Mitchum played the go-between as best he could. When Lytess wasn't interfering with Monroe, she would offer her unwanted advice to the rest of the cast, including child actor Tommy Rettig. The little boy was playing Mitchum's son in the film, and doing a damn good job at that. He was often line perfect and could teach many of the adult actors a thing or two about professionalism. Lee Server, author of *Robert Mitchum: Baby I Don't Care*, recalled the day that Lytess rattled the little boy's confidence to such an extent that Preminger banned her from the set:

> Natasha would wander among the rest of the cast offering unsolicited advice in gloomy Garbo-like tones, as when she told the boy playing Mitchum's son, Tommy Rettig, that child actors lost their talent at just about his age. Rettig immediately began having trouble with his lines and sobbing before a take. Preminger had Lytess barred from the set. Then Monroe refused to come out of her dressing room [Server, p. 249].

Monroe kept her usual distance from the other adults on set, preferring to spend her free time with Rettig. It wasn't unusual for her to gravitate toward child actors in a film or play games with the children of co-stars when the cameras weren't rolling (probably because there were never any expectations from children about the way she should act or look). She could leave the sex symbol persona behind and just be herself. Rettig was old enough to clearly remember his time on the film, and even as an adult, his opinion of Monroe never wavered. He said she was attentive, friendly and fun to be around.

In Darryl Zanuck's notes (December 2, 1953), he states that a great improvement was made with the recent cuts made to the film. He was also pleased with some scenes that were added, with the exception of "the attempted rape of Marilyn by Mitchum." Zanuck wanted to "retake" that sequence, "picking it up when he first tries to kiss her." Zanuck emphasized the need for this to be a violent, aggressive scene, further explaining that it's the very reason why Mitchum's character later refers to himself as "an animal."

Zanuck breaks the scene down in great detail:

> We must remember that Marilyn has practically offered herself to him. He is convinced that she loves Harry (Rory Calhoun) so much that she will sleep with anyone to save Rory. This annoys the hell out of Mitchum. After all, he has lived a long time alone in the woods and she is not hard to take. What really infuriated him is the fact that this little "tramp" resists and repulses him. He is so sure of her invitation that he is now sore because he has made a damned fool of himself—so he decides to take it.

When Mitchum grabs Monroe to kiss her, she pushes him away and socks him one. As Zanuck states, "[I]t should be a real sock." As she turns to run, he grabs her and pulls her back to him, kissing her again. She beats him with her hands and furiously kicks at him. Zanuck suggests that she should kick him hard enough in the shins that it breaks Mitchum's hold on her and gives her the chance to escape his clutches. Zanuck then goes one step further, suggesting they might want to imply "a knee in the crotch—if it is done below camera level."

The controversial scene's climax sees Mitchum make a flying leap to grab Monroe's leg as she runs from him. Zanuck explains that his lunge and grab will, "in a natural way, get them both down on the ground." Now on the ground, Mitchum pins a defeated Monroe and kisses her again. Then they hear the cry of the boy. Zanuck says that the audience should feel at this point that Monroe is "utterly exhausted and that [Mitchum] would have raped her if the boy had not cried out."

Zanuck goes on to discuss a new sequence in the cave, scheduled to be included after Monroe faints on the raft. The inclusion, he says, will serve to give the film "an amazing change of pace." Saying this particular scene can be "loaded with sex and showmanship," Zanuck states that audiences expect both these elements in a film starring Monroe and Mitchum and if they don't get it, "they will feel that we are cheating them."

A perilous situation on the river involving Monroe, Mitchum and Rettig almost got all three of them drowned. Their raft was was anchored to a rock, but it came loose and off they went downstream with five sets of falls between them and Calgary. Tommy Rettig was physically tied down and Mitchum said, "I told Marilyn to lie down because the sweep was going back and forth and I couldn't control it. I knew I could make it to shore, but on the other side of the river. The rescue boat finally came out…[then] I realized what the problem was with the rescue boat. Coming out they had hit a rock and there was a hole in the side of the skiff. I just plugged that up with my elbow. And we finally made it back to shore" (Mitchum, Champlin and Roberts, p. 125, p. 126).

Despite the obvious dangers, Preminger was hellbent on featuring the stars of his film battling the rapids, and Zanuck was all for it. In an April 22 studio memo, Zanuck said, "These episodes of the raft going down the river have got to stand an audience on its ear. It has got to be the Cinerama [*sic*] equivalent of the roller coaster."

But the scenes were risky, and Monroe had more than one close call. The *Los Angeles Times* (August 14, 1953) ran the headline, "Marilyn Monroe Nearly Drowned" on a small article that described her as stumbling in swift waters while rehearsing a scene. After she slipped on a rock, her high wading boots filled with water and dragged her under. Mitchum, along with a dozen crew men, leaped into the water to pull her ashore. A seriously sprained ankle kept her from filming for several days. Production stopped until Monroe had sufficiently recovered, but many believed that Monroe's injury was far less serious than she was making out. She was fitted with a walking cast and was photographed with crutches. Though he suspected Monroe's injury was played up for sympathy, Preminger subsequently changed his attitude toward her.

As usual, Monroe had trouble with lengthy dialogue sequences. Preminger did what he could to ease the burden, filming scenes in short takes to accommodate her. When asked why he decided to help Monroe by shortening the takes, he said, "[Because] I didn't want to spend my entire life in Canada" (Fujiwara, p. 155).

In early September, additional river scenes with closeups of Monroe, Mitchum and Rettig were filmed in a tank in Los Angeles. Preminger finished the film on time (September 29) and on budget, but he despised the experience so much, he paid $150,000 to get out of his Fox contract (Hirsch, p. 207). Shortly after filming was completed, he departed for a much-needed European break, leaving producer Rubin and editor Louis R. Loeffler to contend with a post-production mess. Several retakes were needed for continuity purposes so director Jean Negulesco took over, doing what he could to fill in Preminger's gaps and complete the film. For years, Preminger was bitter about the film and harsh about Monroe's performance, both on and off the set. However, by January of 1980, he had a change of heart. In an interview with the *New York Daily News*, he gave Monroe the closest thing to a compliment that she would ever get from him: "She tried very hard, and when people try hard, you can't be mad at them."

Critical reviews were mixed. Many reviewers noted that the magnificent scenery had taken over the film and instead of the location adding to the spectacle of it, the breathtaking landscape was a distraction, only serving to make the story and actors minor elements in a very expensive travelogue that promoted the beauty of Canada. Bosley Crowther of the *New York Times* (May 1, 1954) wrote:

> Certainly, Scriptwriter Frank Fenton has done the best he could to arrange for a fairly equal balance of nature and Miss Monroe. He has bluntly confronted Robert Mitchum, as a hardy fellow of the Northwest frontier, with a menacing situation compounded of generous portions of the two. Not only does Mr. Mitchum have to spend several days guiding a flimsy log raft down a raging mountain stream, relentlessly stalked by Indians who make it perilous for him to come ashore, but he also has to ward off temptation in the shape—and we mean shape!—of Miss Monroe.

Edith Lindeman of the *Richmond Times Dispatch* (May 15, 1954) wrote,

> Histrionically, the picture makes few demands on the players. Mitchum is adequate as the outdoor man. Miss Monroe would have been more credible as a saloon singer if she had dropped her perfect diction as easily as she lowers her shoulder straps. She sings four numbers rather nicely, including the title song.

The *Springfield Union* reviewed the film on May 14, 1954:

> Marilyn Monroe is strong on form but weak in the talent necessary for dramatic characterization. She has certain undeniable charms which are more suited to musical comedy. In *River of No Return* she shows her ability to put over a good tune, especially the haunting title song, but in dramatic scenes she substitutes a monotonous and over-precise enunciation of her lines for sincere feeling. Robert Mitchum and Tommy Rettig are admirably suited as father and son.

Following the release of the film, Monroe's sexually suggestive rendition of "I'm Gonna File My Claim" was released as a single and sold 75,000 copies in the first three weeks of issue. *River of No Return* was the 12th highest grossing film for the year.

There's No Business Like Show Business (1954)

Marilyn Monroe appeared as Vicky Hoffman/Vicky Parker. Twentieth Century–Fox. 117 minutes. *Director:* Walter Lang. *Producer:* Sol C. Siegel. *Screenplay:* Phoebe and Henry Ephron. *Story:* Lamar Trotti. *Original Music:* Earle Hagen, Bernard Mayers, Alfred Newman, Lionel Newman, Hal Schaefer and Herbert W. Spencer. *Cinematography:* Leon Shamroy. *Costume Design:* Travilla and Miles White. *Production Dates:* May 29 to July 8, 1954. *Production Cost:* $4.34 million. *Domestic Box Office Receipts:* $4.5 million. *Release Date:* December 16, 1954. *Genre:* Comedy-Drama-Musical-Romance. Color and CinemaScope. *Other Cast:* Ethel Merman (Molly Donahue), Donald O'Connor (Tim Donahue), Dan Dailey (Terence Donahue), Johnnie Ray (Steve Donahue), Mitzi Gaynor (Katy Donahue), Richard Eastham (Lew Harris), Hugh O'Brian (Charles Biggs), Frank McHugh (Eddie Dugan, Vicky's Agent), Rhys Williams (Father Dineen), Lee Patrick (Marge), Eve Miller (Hatcheck Girl), Robin Raymond (Lillian Sawyer). *Soundtrack:* "After You Get What You Want You Don't Want It": Written by Irving Berlin. Performed by Marilyn Monroe. "Heat Wave": Written by Irving Berlin. Performed by Marilyn Monroe. "Lazy": Written by Irving Berlin. Performed by Marilyn Monroe, Mitzi Gaynor and Donald O'Connor. "There's No Business Like Show Business": Written by Irving Berlin. Performed by ensemble cast (also sung solo by Ethel Merman). "You'd Be Surprised": Written by Irving Berlin. Performed by Marilyn Monroe. "Alexander's Ragtime Band": Written by Irving Berlin. Performed by ensemble cast. "A Sailor's Not a Sailor ('Til a Sailor's Been Tattooed)": Written by Irving Berlin. Sung by Ethel Merman and Mitzi Gaynor. "A Man Chases a Girl (Until She Catches Him)": Written by Irving Berlin. Sung by Donald O'Connor and Marilyn Monroe. "A Pretty Girl Is Like a Melody": Written by Irving Berlin. Sung by Ethel Merman. "Simple Melody": Written by Irving Berlin. Sung by Ethel Merman. "When the Midnight Choo-Choo Leaves for Alabam": Written by Irving Berlin. Sung by Ethel Merman and Dan Dailey (also performed by Mitzi Gaynor and Donald O'Connor). "If You Believe": Written by Irving Berlin. Sung by Johnnie Ray. "Let's Have Another Cup o' Coffee": Written by Irving Berlin. Sung by Ethel Merman. "Remember": Written by Irving Berlin. Sung by Ethel Merman and Dan Dailey. "Marie": Written by Irving Berlin. Performed in nightclub by uncredited male trio. "I've Got My Love to Keep Me Warm": Written by Irving Berlin (instrumental played in nightclub). *Awards:* 1955 Academy Awards: Best Costume Design—Charles Le Maire, Travilla, Miles White (nominated). Best Music: Scoring of a Musical Picture—Alfred Newman and Lionel Newman (nominated). Best Writing: Motion Picture Story—Lamar Trotti (nominated). 1955 Writers Guild of America (WGA Award, Screen): Best Written American Musical—Phoebe Ephron and Henry Ephron (nominated).

Pre-production on *There's No Business Like Show Business* had begun as early as December 1951 (filming began on May 29, 1954). Prolific Hollywood producer and screenwriter Lamar Trotti was on board to write the story but his unexpected death at age fifty-one on August 28, 1952, meant the film was not off to a good start. With his treatment almost complete, the rest of the characterizations were built around the solid foundation that he had created. Zanuck initially hired writer I.A.L. Diamond to fill in the gaps, but Zanuck lost faith in his abilities to further develop the complex characters and relationships. Diamond was soon replaced with Henry and Phoebe Ephron. Phoebe was less than enthused with the job, saying, "I won't go to see it, why should I write it?" (Bergreen, p. 518). Despite her lack of enthusiasm, the Ephrons were nominated for a Writers Guild of America Award for their work. Lamar Trotti received a posthumous Academy Award nomination for his story.

In Twentieth Century–Fox conference notes (dated January 26, 1953) from Darryl Zanuck to producer Sol Siegel, Zanuck states that it is "a very great story in its present shape" and that the current rewrite is an "enormous improvement over the original." His personal opinion was that some clever scene-writing could make it "probably one of the best musicals ever made." Originally, the Donahue family were called the Monahan family up to and including the third re-write. In closing, Zanuck summed up the core story in his conference notes to Siegel:

> I show two young people start together as a vaudeville team. I show them raise a family until they become the Five Monahans. Then I show the "pleasant and human" disintegration of the family as the children go their various ways until a tragedy brings them together again. This is a pretty good story to tell—especially when loaded with entertainers who have real talent and music that has importance.

During production, Mitzi Gaynor sprained her ankle and was unable to dance for several days, and Ethel Merman was briefly hospitalized to "stave off an appendectomy" (Flinn, p. 263). The usual delays by Monroe were again a factor during filming, but all in all, filming was relatively trouble-free.

In two memos (December 13 and 17, 1952) to composer, Irving Berlin, Zanuck wrote:

> Almost every great musical has contained an emotional last act. The really great musicals make you cry: *Show Boat, Alexander's Ragtime Band*, etc. I believe our new last act can top them all and that we can emerge with a four star picture as well as a "four handkerchief" picture

Donald O'Connor and Marilyn Monroe in a scene from *There's No Business Like Show Business* (1954).

"There's No Business Like Show Business" is a loving tribute to the glitz and glamour of life in the entertainment industry. The song was originally written by Berlin for the Broadway musical *Annie Get Your Gun* (1946), starring Ethel Merman; it's safe to say that by the time she sang it in the 1954 film, Merman knew it back to front. After all, she played the legendary American sharpshooter Annie Oakley and sang the song for three years, in over one thousand Broadway performances. It is perhaps fitting that the emotional last act of the film gives Merman her chance to belt out the song, *her* song (before the ensemble cast steps in), and it be recorded for all time. The original song slated for the finale was "God Bless America," and while it's a patriotically stirring anthem in its own right, "There's No Business Like Show Business" perfectly enforces the film's title and all that the Donahue family stood for and endured throughout the story (Flinn, p. 257).

Promising her the lead role of "The Girl" in *The Seven Year Itch* (1955), Fox struck a deal with Monroe. In order to boost its box office potential, she eventually agreed to appear in the musical. Though she was less than enthusiastic with the role of "Vicky" she desperately wanted the part in *The Seven Year Itch*. After signing, several of the film's song and dance numbers were added or switched to accommodate her late inclusion.

Monroe's controversial "Heat Wave" routine was originally slated for Ethel Merman's character, the Donahue family matriarch Molly. When Donald O'Connor's character, Tim, tells his family that Vicky will be doing the "Heat Wave" number instead of them, the film mirrors what actually happened behind the scenes. The switch did nothing to endear Merman to Monroe, and on-screen, ironically, the switch did nothing to endear Merman's character, Molly, to Monroe's Vicky. In the film, Tim is smitten with Vicky and it's a relationship that Molly strongly opposes. Stealing her son is bad enough, but when she steals *her* song ... it's war!

The day the "Heat Wave" number was filmed, Joe DiMaggio stood to the side and watched his wife perform the most sensual song and dance number of the film. Of all the days to show up to set, this was the worst of them. He was eerily silent in his rage. DiMaggio made it no secret that he despised Hollywood and show biz "types," but it was a world he was forced into because of his association with Marilyn. Many of those "types" got to see how much he despised them, and the feelings were returned, with few having anything good to say about him.

Monroe had worked hard on the routine and she was more than ready to film it, until she saw her seething husband in the wings, disgusted and furious at his wife's exhibitionism. As soon as her eyes shifted to him, she faltered. She forgot the lyrics and fell down during the dance routine. While crew members from all departments fawned over her, DiMaggio stood stone-faced. He didn't move. Thinking the support of her husband would help her confidence, a publicity man led her over to DiMaggio and suggested they be photographed together. He refused on the grounds that she looked indecent.

The die was cast. Marilyn Monroe was also one of those "types" that he despised, only she just happened to be his wife (but not for long). Monroe regrouped and got through the next take without a hitch. Her ability to do so under the stress and heartache that Monroe was subjected to right before nailing the number that did make the film proves how gutsy she really was, not only as a performer but also as a woman.

Monroe would often show up to set with bruises that had to be covered with makeup. No one asked how she got them; no one needed to ask. They all knew. But it was anyone's guess as to how long she'd put up with DiMaggio's violent, controlling ways.

DiMaggio married Marilyn Monroe—movie star. But from the day they were married, he was hellbent on making her into a dutiful 1950s housewife. He despised Hollywood, he despised his wife's career and he was constantly at her to give it up. Of course, it was a ludicrous notion. Despite his anger issues, and despite the fact that she was often on the receiving end of his physically violent, jealous rages, Monroe truly loved her husband, but she had worked too hard and been through too much to turn her back on her career, even for him (Taraborrelli, p. 242).

In her "Hollywood" column (June 15, 1954), Hedda Hopper wrote:

> You haven't heard "Heat Wave" until you watch Marilyn sing it... I counted 52 people on the set of *There's No Business Like Show Business* watching her rehearse her "Heat Wave" number. Some were on business, but most of the visitors came to ogle Marilyn.

Dressed in a sultry flamenco-style costume and surrounded by a mob of fawning male dancers, Monroe's jazz-inspired performance of "Heat Wave" was seductive, sexy and boldly suggestive. Censorship regulations required designer William Travilla to ensure that his tropical-inspired costume completely covered Monroe's navel, and it did. But between her gyrating hips and her suggestive vocal inflections with the song's lyrics, you have to wonder how the performance passed the censors without a word of warning to tone things down a notch.

Marilyn in the controversial "Heat Wave" number from *There's No Business Like Show Business* (1954).

Academy Award–winning actor-dancer-singer George Chakiris shared his memories of working as a chorus dancer on the film:

> The choreographer was Robert Alton. Everyone loved working for him. He knew everybody's name and you never felt like a chorus dancer. He also had a wonderful sense of humor. I think he was the only choreographer that got single frame credit. He also did Broadway shows and some of the great MGM musicals, like *Easter Parade* [1948] and *The Barkleys of Broadway* [1949]. He was contracted to do all the musical numbers for *There's No Business Like Show Business* but Marilyn wanted Jack Cole to do [her] "Heat Wave" number. When Mr. Alton choreographed his "Heat Wave" number for her, he started by screening the "I'm Gonna File My Claim" number from *River of No Return* [1954], which Jack Cole had staged for Marilyn. He let a couple of us [me and Pepe De Chazza] sit down in front in the screening room. Jack Cole was known for having humor in his work, "double entendres." Pepe and I really loved the number and we "got" the humor. Mr. Alton thought it was vulgar. That's not a putdown of Mr. Alton, it's just that his taste was different. He liked double entendres as much as the next person, but in his own way. In his version, Mr. Alton used his female dance assistant, Joan Weamer [who was great], to dance in for Marilyn. Johnny Brascia partnered her [he had partnered Vera Ellen in *White Christmas*] and four guys to dance behind them. I was one of those four guys. We rehearsed for four weeks on his "Heat Wave" number for Marilyn. When it was finally ready, she came in one afternoon to see the number. She came alone. She was quiet, sweet and very courteous. I remember she was wearing a very simple, soft, orange-colored knit dress. We did the number for her and when we finished, she thanked Mr. Alton and Joan and left as quietly as when she came in. Jack Cole did the number that we see in the film. She loved Jack's work, and with all due respect to Mr. Alton, who was wonderful, his and Jack Cole's choreographic styles were really very different. Marilyn was right to want Jack to do the number. Her instincts were kind of perfect.
>
> Another time, at the end of a rehearsal, a sort of cocktail party was held on the sound stage for a number of people, and the dancers were also included, which was very nice. So there were men in suits, Mitzi [Gaynor], Ethel [Merman] and others, but then Marilyn arrived with a couple of people. She wore black pedal pushers and simple heels. I don't remember what blouse or top she wore but I do remember the pedal pushers. She looked great. Beautiful. Again, she arrived quietly.
>
> My dance partner was a girl named Drusilla Davis. We were standing not too far from Marilyn, and Drusilla said, "Why don't I ask her to give you a kiss on the cheek?" I said, "Noooo!" but she did it anyway. She went over to Marilyn and asked if she would give "that boy a kiss on the cheek." Marilyn looked in my direction. She then very sweetly and honestly said, "But I don't know him." Well, to me, that spoke volumes. I loved her integrity of not going over to just anyone and giving him a kiss on the cheek. I thought that was terrific.
>
> For the grand finale, everybody was arriving on the set in the morning to shoot it, which included all the stars of course. Ethel Merman looked great in her white gown and Mitzi, with her gorgeous figure, looked sensational in her red gown. But when Marilyn arrived—quietly—in her soft blue gown, everybody else disappeared—just disappeared. Maybe it was just me, but I don't think so. She was truly breathtaking, but it was always much more than just the way she looked. It was *her*. She had an extraordinary personal quality.
>
> I was in Japan in August of 1962 [the year he won his Best Supporting Actor Oscar for *West Side Story*]. That's where I heard about Marilyn's death. I was really so saddened by the news. I was really so sorry, like everyone else. I cried for her. Marilyn Monroe—dead! So unbelievable, so unbelievably sad. After that terrible day, I was back in Los Angeles and I overheard the owner of Schwab's Drugstore saying the Seconals that she presumably ingested came from his drugstore. It was horrible! Name-dropping is one thing, but pill-dropping takes the cake! And being proud of it! I guess some people, in their own way, wanted to be part of something. I don't know.

Bosley Crowther of the *New York Times* (December 17, 1954) praised the film, calling it "a huge, sprawling, sentimental show. Lots of laughing and crying. Lots of singing." But when it comes to Monroe's song and dance numbers, he wrote that her "wriggling and squirming to 'Heat Wave' and 'Lazy' are embarrassing to behold."

It's been over five decades since *There's No Business Like Show Business* was released, yet Monroe's performance of "Heat Wave" is still a sit-up-and-take-notice scene. Though controversial in its day, it's now a highlight of the film. That said, the number is almost an entity unto itself, not really fitting into the look and feel of the rest of the production; it's as if Monroe's character, Vicky, is almost forgotten for a moment. Suddenly, it's not Marilyn Monroe playing Vicky, it's Marilyn Monroe playing Marilyn Monroe. And the explanation is obvious.

Legendary jazz pianist and composer Hal Schaefer was brought in by Fox to specially arrange a few of Monroe's numbers. The tempo of "Heat Wave" was purposefully slowed down to suit Monroe's temptress style, thus giving it that unique sexed-up jazz feel. Additionally, Monroe insisted that choreographer Jack Cole be brought in to choreograph her routines. The reason why Monroe's performances (especially "Heat Wave") look, sound and feel different in comparison to the rest of the cast's musical numbers, is because Travilla, Schaefer and Cole were all working exclusively for her. (Miles White designed the other costumes, while Robert Alton choreographed the other production numbers.)

During "Heat Wave," watch for the moment where Monroe clings to a tree for some more hip-swinging, pelvic thrusts to the sounds of the bongo drums. As she grips the flame-red tree branch, her left hand comes around and pokes one of the male dancers in the eye. He flinches but continues with his part. Though Monroe stayed focused on her performance, she was obviously aware of the mistake. To acknowledge the mishap, before turning back around to face the camera to finish the song, she gives the dancer a quick, unscripted kiss (obvious, though her back is to the camera).

In a contrived attempt to attract a younger audience, singing sensation Johnnie Ray was cast as one of the three Donahue children. Two of his biggest hits, "Cry" and "The Little White Cloud That Cried," had taken him to the top of the music charts in 1951 and Fox banked on his legion of fans to support him at the box office too.

Ray's character, Steve, does a lot of soul-searching throughout the first half of the film, not appearing to fit in or feel the same desire to carry on the Donahue name in the entertainment industry for another generation. He finally confesses to his parents that he has decided to dedicate his life to the Church and become a priest. Initially, his show-biz family is devastated by his confession and their strong, emotional reactions to his career choice gives the audience the very clear impression that the decision to join the priesthood really means that their son has just come out of the closet as a gay man. Being a priest would give him a level of social respectability and serve as a guise for his homosexuality, a taboo topic in the mid-fifties.

While the ever-loyal Donahues throw an intimate party for their son to celebrate his impending placement as a priest, Ray stands up and leads his guests in a rousing, emotionally charged rendition of Irving Berlin's "If You Believe." His gospel-inspired performance showcases Ray in his usual delivery. The rest of the partygoers clap their hands and enthusiastically sing along, suddenly transforming them from family and friends into his first church congregation.

According to a 2007 Ethel Merman biography, Fox and the Breen Office exchanged a barrage of letters over the scene. The studio even brought in a "Catholic authority" to supervise the song and the way it was handled, ensuring "accurate and respectful treatment" (Flinn, p. 265).

Critical reaction to *There's No Business Like Show Business* was mixed. C. A. LeJeune of the *London Sunday Observer* (February 6, 1955) wrote one of the film's most scathing reviews:

> It is always horrible to see or hear a human being make a public exhibition of his weaknesses, and the agonies of Mr. Ray and Miss Monroe apply themselves to song were to me almost unendurable. Both seemed to be in agony; he, approaching God with a desperate piston-action of the jaws; she, in urgent need, perhaps, of a nice, quiet "lay-down"... [A]t the risk of seeming prim, I would call [this] a vulgar picture; suggesting to me at least an insult to intelligence, religion, music, Ethel Merman, good taste and the human soul.

While Monroe's singing and acting was as good as any of her co-stars, critics were determined to note their repulsion at her sexually inappropriate choreography. Their disdain for the latter unfairly overshadowed anything else she did in the film.

Then and now, Ray's weak, nasally performance is cringe-worthy to watch. He certainly stands out, but that's only because he's so bad. It's no surprise that his acting career began and ended with this film. Asked why he never made other films, he said, "[T]he answer is I was never asked" (www.imdb.com).

Though Ray had a brief marriage to Marilyn Morrison (daughter of Mocambo nightclub owner Charlie Morrison), he was a closeted homosexual. The marriage was doomed from the very beginning. Morrison was certainly not blind to her husband's sexual preferences but she naively thought she could change him, telling a friend that she would "straighten it out" (www.glbtq.com). Ray was arrested a couple of times (1951 and 1959) for soliciting men for sex and his career (at least in the United States) started a steady decline. His years of alcohol and tranquilizer abuse took their toll. Following decades of frail health, on February 24, 1990, he died of liver failure at age sixty-three.

Not surprisingly, Monroe's self-imposed segregation caused friction with her fellow cast members. Merman's biographer wrote, "Monroe's moods swerved from one extreme to the other. Some days she was garrulous and charming, but most of the time she kept to herself. Merman and Gaynor gave up asking her to lunch" (Flinn, p. 264).

Monroe continually complained about Donald O'Connor's youthful appearance and small frame. Though O'Connor was a year older than her, she was concerned that they were horribly miscast as lovers. She said that people would look at them together and think of her as his mother! In the "Lazy" number with O'Connor and Gaynor, Monroe refused to consider doing the routine barefoot. Even though she was inches above O'Connor with shoes, she insisted on keeping them on.

The passage of time often creates new memories, or clouds the reality of what actually happened, and it appear that O'Connor suffered from this malady during his 2001 on-air interview with Larry King. Talking about the making of *There's No Business Like Show Business,* he mentioned that director Walter Lang thought that his and Monroe's scenes would play out better if Monroe went barefoot, bringing her down to O'Connor's height. Monroe was usually wearing heels, and her hairstyle gave her some extra height too. O'Connor didn't mention the aforementioned "Lazy" number; instead he cited Monroe's rehearsal of the

"Heat Wave" number in front of the bandstand. According to O'Connor, instead of asking Monroe to ditch her shoes, Lang asked O'Connor to stand on an apple box to give him the extra height needed. Refusing to be emasculated in this way, O'Connor went to Monroe and explained the height dilemma to her, and he said she immediately kicked off her shoes without a fuss. He then quoted her as saying the director was "an idiot" for not asking her himself.

Though Monroe's feet aren't seen in the "Heat Wave" rehearsal scene, she's still clearly a few inches taller than O'Connor. And, throughout the rest of the film, she's visibly wearing shoes.

The Seven Year Itch (1955)

Marilyn Monroe appeared as The Girl. Twentieth Century–Fox. 105 minutes. *Director:* Billy Wilder. Producers: Charles K. Feldman and Billy Wilder. *Screenplay:* Billy Wilder and George Axelrod. Based on the play by George Axelrod. *Original Music:* Alfred Newman. Cinematographer: Milton Krasner. *Costume Design:* Travilla. *Production Dates:* September 1 to November 5, 1954; additional sequences filmed on January 10, 1955. *Filming Locations:* Twentieth Century–Fox Studios (Stage 10); Trans-Lux Theater, 52nd and Lexington, Manhattan; (original, yet unusable, subway scene, shot on September 15, 1954, at 1 a.m.), 164 East 61st Street, Manhattan (exterior shots of Richard's apartment). *Release Date:* June 1, 1955 (star-studded world premiere at Loew's State Theatre in Times Square, New York). *Genre:* Comedy-Romance. Color and CinemaScope. *Production Cost:* $3.2 million. *Domestic Box Office Receipts:* $6 million. *Other Cast:* Tommy Ewell (Richard Sherman), Evelyn Keyes (Helen Sherman), Sonny Tufts (Tom MacKenzie), Robert Strauss (Mr. Kruhulik), Oscar Homolka (Dr. Brubaker), Marguerite Chapman (Miss Morris), Victor Moore (Plumber), Donald MacBride (Mr. Brady), Carolyn Jones (Miss Finch), Doro Merande (Waitress). *Awards:* 1956 BAFTA Film Award: Best Foreign Actress: Marilyn Monroe (nominated). 1956 Director's Guild of America (DGA Award): Outstanding Directorial Achievement in Motion Pictures: Billy Wilder (nominated). 1956 Golden Globes (USA): Best Motion Picture Actor in a Musical/Comedy: Tom Ewell (won). 1956 Writers Guild of America (WGA Award): Best Written American Comedy: Billy Wilder and George Axelrod (nominated). The Seven Year Itch *taglines:* It TICKLES and TANTALIZES!—The funniest comedy since laughter began!; [T]he 3 year Broadway COMEDY sensation is now on the screen!

For a number of reasons, *The Seven Year Itch* was a monumental event in Marilyn Monroe's life and career. At her own initiative, it would be her last film under her restrictive and low-paying Fox contract. She would be suspended from the studio for refusing to see out their arrangement, but after retreating to New York for almost a year, she would return to Los Angeles triumphant. Monroe signed a lucrative new contract with the studio at a higher salary and with creative control. She also started Marilyn Monroe Productions, her own production company (with photographer, Milton Greene), whereby the studio would allow her to pursue her own film projects, independent of Fox. Considering the harsh confines of her previous Fox contract, it was as though she had been set free. Following the formation of her company, she talked about her dissatisfaction with her contractual studio work, saying, "I now want to do movies which won't make me feel, after I drive away from the preview, that I ought to drive off a cliff" (Lyons, *Advocate*, July 5, 1956).

Monroe's nine-month marriage to Joe DiMaggio ended before filming did, and her relationship with her long-time drama teacher Natasha Lytess was about to come to a screeching halt too. In fact, the film's title could also refer to the end of their seven-year collaboration. *The Seven Year Itch* was their last film as teacher and student. Though Lytess was disliked by almost everyone that Monroe associated with, their relationship, though professional, was also a personal one. They were friends. As difficult as Lytess was, Monroe remained with her and relied on her for as long as she did for a reason. As hard and tough as Lytess appeared to be on the outside, she had grown somewhat dependent on her student too. Lytess left her position at Columbia Studios to exclusively coach Monroe. She put all of her eggs in one basket, as the saying goes, and while her run was a good one, by the end of filming on *The Seven Year Itch*, without a word to Lytess, Monroe went on strike and left for New York. Lytess remained in Los Angeles on the Fox payroll as the drama coach of a star who was not only no longer working, she was no longer in the same state! Not surprisingly, she was soon let go. Monroe had left her high and dry.

In New York, Monroe began work at the Actors Studio, under the direction of Lee Strasberg and his wife, Paula. With no explanation, Monroe refused phone contact from Lytess. When she returned to Los Angeles, she avoided personal contact with her. In order to support herself and her child, Barbara Lytess scrambled to get private students and survive on the payments from those sessions, but her salary was nowhere near the amounts earned as a private teacher to Monroe and an employee at Columbia and Fox Studios. When Lytess played the sympathy card and revealed that she was dying of cancer, Monroe sent Lytess a check for $1,000. Since it was the first and only form of contact that Lytess had received from Monroe in so long, she felt there was hope for reconciliation. She was wrong.

Lytess showed up to speak with Monroe in person, but she was turned away at the door by MCA agency president Lew Wasserman. "You don't understand, Marilyn needs me," Natasha told him. "Marilyn needs no one," Wasserman snapped, slamming the door in her face (Taraborrelli, p. 280).

As Lytess turned to leave, looking back, she saw Monroe staring down at her from an upstairs window. No expression, no smile, no wave, no acknowledgment—nothing. The two women locked eyes for a brief moment, then Monroe closed the drapes. That was the last time they saw each other. Natasha Lytess died of cancer in 1964, two years after Monroe. She was fifty years old. Shortly before her death, she said:

> I wish I had one-tenth of Marilyn's cleverness. The truth is, my life and my feelings were very much in her hands. I was the older one, the teacher, but she knew the depth of my attachment to her, and she exploited those feelings as only a beautiful younger person can. She said she was the needy one. Alas, it was the reverse. My life with her was a constant denial of myself [Victor, p. 176].

The Seven Year Itch was the beginning of a four-film streak that could arguably be described as the greatest run of her career. As an actress, she was at her peak. As a person, she was crumbling from the inside out. To her testament, all four films (*The Seven Year Itch, Bus Stop, The Prince and the Showgirl* and *Some Like It Hot*) captured her beauty and perfectly showcased her abilities, not only as an actress but as a comedienne. She had proven herself to be more than a "one-hit wonder," and even her harshest critics were forced to admit it.

The Seven Year Itch tells the story of a neurotic fortyish man, his wife ... and a girl. Not just any girl, "The Girl," played by Monroe. When Richard Sherman's wife Helen (Evelyn Keyes) and his young son Ricky (Butch Bernard) leave the stifling New York summer heat for a stint in Maine, Richard stays behind to work. While he initially relishes the peace and tranquility of his temporary bachelorhood (no noisy kids' television programs, no nagging wife), Richard's world is turned upside down when, on his first night alone, The Girl locks herself out of the upstairs apartment that she's renting for the summer. She rings Richard's bell for help. The Girl *is* Marilyn Monroe and Marilyn Monroe *is* The Girl. No need for a character name.

Many of Richard's scenes are solo; he talks a lot and has a number of daydream sequences, most of which involve him being desired by the women he's been in everyday contact with.

Though his wedding ring never leaves his finger, when The Girl asks Richard if he lives alone, he initially says, "Yes." Later, The Girl sees the ring and realizes he's married. The Girl now admits to feeling safer and more comfortable with their developing relationship because he's married. Richard assures her that he's not only married, he's *very* married, and that he has no intentions of asking her to marry him (though it doesn't stop his fantasies). They laugh, sip champagne, eat potato chips, listen to Rachmaninoff and play "Chopsticks" on the piano. While Richard thoroughly enjoys his "date" with The Girl, suddenly his conscience kicks in and he sends her home.

Richard's paranoia increases. The following morning he goes to his boss, Mr. Brady (Donald MacBride), and asks for two weeks' leave so he can join his wife and son in Maine, thus escaping the temptations of The Girl upstairs. Mr. Brady refuses his request because it's the busiest time of year in the publishing industry, and so Richard is forced to stick around. He frantically retreats to his office and looks up the theories surrounding the plight of husbands who have been married for seven years, an ailment that he learns is known as the Seven Year Itch. He now seeks the advice of psychiatrist Dr. Brubaker (Oscar Homolka). His paranoia deepens further when he imagines The Girl using her regular television spot for Dazzle Dent toothpaste to tell the entire country about their rendezvous.

Richard calls Maine to speak to Helen and when he's told that she's out taking a hay ride, he imagines it to be a hay ride for two, Helen and family friend Tom Mackenzie (Sonny Tufts), in a rollicking moment of unbridled passion. Infuriated by their imagined betrayal, Richard goes home to his apartment and The Girl. With guilt-free contentment, their blossoming relationship continues.

Richard and The Girl retreat to an air-conditioned movie theater to see *Creature from the Black Lagoon* (1954). As they leave the theater, the infamous subway scene occurs. Upon returning home, Richard invites The Girl into his air-conditioned apartment and she accepts the invitation. Not wanting to return to the stifling heat of her place upstairs, she asks if she can stay at Richard's for the night (in the chair, of course). While he initially agrees to let her stay, this arrangement is rudely interrupted by the nosy janitor, Mr. Kruhulik (Robert Strauss). Though Richard tries to block his view from the door, he sees The Girl's leg hanging over the arm of the chair and assumes Richard is having an affair. Richard talks his way out of it, and to avoid further rumors, he apologetically sends The Girl back upstairs while Mr. Kruhulik is watching.

Later, The Girl does some crafty renovations, removing the boards that block the original access of the duplex apartments and she gains instant access from her floor down to Richard's apartment via the internal stairs that joined the two places. She ends up spending the night in Richard's bed, but not with him. He takes the couch.

In the morning, Richard's imagination gets the better of him again. As he makes a coffee and cinnamon toast breakfast for two, The Girl is in the shower and Richard talks himself into a state of panic. In his imaginings, Helen shoots her way through the apartment door and holds a gun on her "philandering" husband. As he pleads for his life, she shoots him multiple times. He falls dead at the bottom of the stairs. Richard's wild imagination has now reached fever pitch.

In the end, Richard realizes his wife loves him for his odd yet gentle ways and he loves her too. Leaving The Girl in his apartment and giving her full use of it while he's gone, despite his boss' objections, he decides to join his wife and son in Maine for a couple of weeks. The Girl gives Richard a lingering kiss goodbye and he giddily runs out of the apartment without his shoes. She runs to the window and tosses them down to him. Leaving the innocent summer fling that didn't quite happen in his apartment until he returns, a content Richard races eagerly to the train station to be with his family.

The Seven Year Itch has many glorious moments, witty lines, hilarious dream sequences and great chemistry between Monroe and Ewell. But the conversation that tops everything else is toward the end of the film, between Richard and family friend, Tom MacKenzie. As Tom bursts into the apartment, oblivious to The Girl finishing breakfast in the kitchen, Richard goes off the deep end (in part because he's convinced himself that Tom had a roll in the hay with Helen). Of course, Tom is entirely innocent and he accuses Richard of being drunk. During his verbal rampage, the conversation continues with:

> RICHARD SHERMAN: I can explain everything. The stairs, the cinnamon toast, the blonde in the kitchen!
> TOM MACKENZIE: Now wait a minute, Dickie Boy, let's just take it easy. What blonde in the kitchen?
> RICHARD SHERMAN: Ohhhhh, wouldn't you like to know?! Maybe it's Marilyn Monroe!

While the script was written and rewritten to placate the censors, a couple of scenes were cut in post-production for being too raunchy, namely, part of the iconic subway sequence and a bathtub scene. When Monroe gets her toe stuck in the faucet of the bath, the plumber (Victor Moore) beckoned to rescue her drops his wrench into the tub and reaches down into the bubbles to fetch it. While part of this scene exists in the film, the wrench-grabbing part was deleted. And when Monroe stands over the subway grate as one of the trains go by and the wind lifts up her skirt, she coos, "Oooh, here comes another one. This one's even cooler. Must be an express. Don't you wish you had a skirt? I feel so sorry for you in those hot pants."

Both of these seemingly innocent portions were deleted from the final film. Luckily, they weren't destroyed, remaining in the Fox vaults for decades. Nowadays, many of the restored DVD versions of *The Seven Year Itch* include these deleted scenes within the special features. Tame by today's standards, the scenes are an example of what was considered offensive filmmaking in the mid–1950s. But, was it all really offensive to the public, or was it an assumption by the Breen Office that it would be invariably received that way? Four years later, Billy Wilder would prove a point and get his revenge for the stifling restrictions placed upon him on *The Seven Year Itch. Some Like It Hot* (1959) was not only one of the most popular films of the year, it was also the highest grossing comedy in film history to date.

Gary Cooper and William Holden were originally considered for the male lead in *The Seven Year Itch,* but they were both deemed too handsome, with neither one fitting the part of a believable "everyday man." Jimmy Stewart fit the description, and he was interested, but other work commitments prevented him from taking the part. Walter Matthau shot a screen test and while director Billy Wilder was pleased with his performance, the studio didn't want to take a gamble on a newcomer. Finally Tom Ewell was screen tested and got the part, reprising his Tony Award–winning Broadway role as the scrawny worry-wart.

Darryl Zanuck stated in a September 20, 1954, studio memo: "If I had read the script at the time we were casting the picture, I would never have recommended William Holden or anybody else except Tommy Ewell. No one I can think of can play this particular script. I didn't quite understand it at the time, but in re-reading it again I now believe that Holden would have been as big an error as Gary Cooper...In spite of the enormous success of this play on the stage it would not be, in my opinion, 50 percent of the picture it will be with Marilyn Monroe. She is an absolute must for this story" (www.tcm.com).

American theater was far less restrictive in what was deemed acceptable to show. Hollywood, however, was at the mercy of the Breen Office, and the rules were clear. Adultery must never be the focus of comedy and *The Seven Year Itch* was based on just that. It was Wilder and Axelrod's job to eliminate all traces of blatant adultery from the script. Given the story was based on a man's affair with the woman upstairs when his wife goes away for the summer and his subsequent guilt being the comic relief, it was a difficult, almost impossible task. Several kissing scenes (both fantasy and reality) were as far as the "adultery" went. The majority of the romance is played out as a fantasy, all of it going on in the irrational head of Richard.

In the play, Richard and The Girl have sex. There's no mistaking the status of their relationship. It's adulterous. The husband cheats on his wife, which propels the guilt and paranoia to a whole different level.

Despite Axelrod and Wilder's obvious frustrations in adapting the play to suit the Hollywood censors, they were masters at the double entendre. Most of their skillfully crafted rewrites got past the Breen Office guidelines. Though toned down, the sexual implications were still there, and they still had Marilyn Monroe as The Girl. By 1968, the censorship code was revised and the ratings system was introduced, thus allowing filmmakers the artistic freedom to include sex, violence and coarse language so long as it was appropriately rated to reflect the film's content, warning audiences what to expect.

The Hollywood Reporter (May 4, 1955) wrote that Fox paid Axelrod and the play's producers an additional $175,000 for the right to release the film six months earlier (while the Broadway play was still running) than contractual agreements initially stated. Publicity for the film was on such a grand scale, a four-story cutout of Marilyn Monroe posing with her skirt blowing up over her knees was hung over the Loew's State Theatre marquee in New York City. However, the Catholic Legion of Decency objected to the image and it was soon replaced with a more conservative version of the same iconic pose (*Hollywood Reporter*, May 24, 1955). In the interim, Loew's enjoyed the additional publicity and the film gained extra attention that did nothing to hurt its box office return. *The Seven Year Itch* was the top-grossing film of the summer. Additionally, Monroe sent the media and public into a frenzy when she unexpectedly showed up to the New York premiere of the film with ex-husband Joe DiMaggio as her date. It was also her 29th birthday. DiMaggio may not have been husband material, but he was a consistent source of comfort and support for Monroe for the rest of her life.

Playing at the Fulton Theatre, *The Seven Year Itch* was a Broadway hit for close to three years (November 20, 1952–August 13, 1955), with Ewell playing the husband with the wandering eye for 1141 performances. The Girl was played by Austrian-born actress Vanessa Brown on the stage. Ewell won a Tony Award for the play and then a 1956 Golden Globe Award for Best Actor in a Comedy/Musical for his character reprisal in the film.

Harold V. Cohen of the *Pittsburgh Post-Gazette* (June 23, 1955) compared the film to the play and in doing so he was disappointed.

> Not all the laughs but a lot of them have been drained out of *The Seven Year Itch*. The play was a barrel of fun. The picture is considerably less so. It does have Miss Marilyn Monroe, however… [P]eople who didn't see the play may possibly find the movie version entirely satisfactory, but they'll never know the fun they missed. Miss Monroe is some compensation but not that much.

Bosley Crowther of the *New York Times* (June 12, 1955) wrote:

> Miss Monroe is becoming a singular symbol on the order of our old friend, Mae West. She doesn't have to act in a picture, she just has to wiggle, bat her eyes, twist her mouth in those oval contortions and speak vapidly in that toothpaste voice. This may be very stimulating to a certain clientele, but it can also become monotonous.

In a 1987 television interview, Tom Ewell discussed the infamous subway scene and described the atmosphere of the balmy night and the altercation that Monroe had with then-husband DiMaggio as a result of that very scene. With bleachers set up across the street from where the scene would be shot (the Trans-Lux Theater, 52nd and Lexington, Manhattan), thousands of curious spectators crammed themselves into the designated area to witness the filming.

Gina Lollobrigida visited the set to meet Monroe; also present was Monroe's stand-in Gloria Mosolino. Thirty extras from the Screen Actors Guild participated in the scene as fellow moviegoers coming out of the Trans-Lux. Theater manager Wally Beach protested *Creature from the Black Lagoon* replacing the real film showing at the movie house (*Lili*, which was in its 80th week at the theater), that is, until director Wilder explained that the title chosen for the in-film marquee had a specific meaning within the script (*Springfield Union*, September 20, 1954).

Ewell explained that Monroe was averse to wearing underwear during the summer months (even in the film, The Girl confesses to keeping her underwear in the freezer to keep it cool), and the temperature that night almost insured that she would be naked underneath that infamous ivory halter dress (designed by William Travilla). The pleated skirt, a Travilla trademark, was hand-folded and sewn into place, the hem was rolled and the halter neck was boned in metal to ensure proper cleavage coverage.

Monroe's dress was designed to be sexy, while also pleasing the censors. Axelrod and Wilder had tweaked the script to suit the censors and now it was Travilla's turn to tweak the wardrobe. There was an art to designing a dress that had a "wow" impact and still stayed within the boundaries of what was morally acceptable. Monroe's halter-neck "subway dress," as it's most often referred, discreetly covers her curves. The low-cut bodice, though open to the waist, is quite full, the tucks and pleats are in all the right places, but not a hint of cleavage is seen. Implying more than it shows, the dress is a masterful design that gives the illusion of showing way too much, without showing too much at all. While Travilla's job was done, no one predicted what would happen next. Unbeknownst to Monroe and Ewell, Wilder had placed a powerful fan underneath the subway grate to give the pleated skirt some extra lift when the train passes. Under ordinary circumstances, a subway train passing would give a quick burst of cool air to the person standing over the grate on the sidewalk above. As Ewell and Monroe started their scene, the fans were turned on and a sudden blast of powerful air shot up through the grate. Monroe's dress blew all the way up over her head.

DiMaggio's intimidating visit to the *There's No Business Like Show Business* set and his negative reaction to his wife's raunchy "Heat Wave" routine was no secret to those in the know, and it was at columnist Walter Winchell's insistence that Joe accompany him to the Trans-Lux Theater on Lexington Avenue for filming of the now famous "subway scene." Winchell knew what the scene entailed and DiMaggio knew too. DiMaggio felt that his presence wouldn't be a good idea, not good for himself or his wife. He didn't want to go but Winchell insisted. Against his better judgment, DiMaggio accompanied Winchell to the shoot. The fan frenzy, along with several photographers lying on the pavement and shooting their flashbulbs up his wife's billowing skirt, sent DiMaggio into yet another rage. Winchell's premeditated plan to lure DiMaggio into a situation that would essentially get him a story worked. He got his story all right.

DiMaggio and Winchell sat amongst thousands of screaming, whistling fans. Having just witnessed his wife's immodest display and the uproarious reaction that followed, he was furious. As Ewell and Monroe went to regroup, DiMaggio followed. Director Billy Wilder described the look on DiMaggio's face as "the look of death." Wilder's recollections differed from Ewell's version of events: He said Monroe was not only wearing panties to protect her modesty, she wore *two* pairs to ensure the bright klieg-lights wouldn't illuminate through just one pair. However, under the powerful lights, the material was still see through (Taraborrelli, "Joe DiMaggio Wanted Marilyn Monroe to Be His Demure Housewife So When She Posed for This Picture He Beat Her Up").

DiMaggio stormed into the theater lobby to confront his wife. Ewell remembered DiMaggio's stern warning to Monroe: "If you go back out there—we're through!"

Monroe looked at him and responded with, "I'm going."

Ewell said they were the last words she said to him before putting on the necessary undergarments to protect her modesty on the next take. They went out and reshot the scene again and again, until they got it right.

According to the aforementioned Taraborrelli article (September 1, 2009), DiMaggio seethed as he waited in their hotel room for his wife to return. When she did, he beat her up. There was so much noise coming from their room, other guests reported the room number to hotel management. The following day, Gladys Witten, a studio hairdresser, noticed bruising across Monroe's shoulders and covered them with makeup. Sportswriter Stacy Edwards said that Monroe's decision to leave DiMaggio was because of his physical and mental abuse in their hotel room on the night after shooting the skirt-blowing scene. No doubt it wasn't the first time that Monroe was on the receiving end of her husband's volatile temper.

A few weeks later, Edwards confronted DiMaggio about the incident. Admitting that "things got out of hand," he went on to say, "[S]he pissed me off so much. She didn't care what I thought about anything, she just wanted to do what she wanted to do." Edwards admitted that she lost a lot of respect for DiMaggio after his confession, saying that she immediately thought, "How could any man hit such a beautiful creature?"

Ironically, the scenes shot on that tumultuous night were unusable due to the crowd noise. Wilder later re-created the street scene at the studio. Even so, that was the night that ended their marriage. Monroe filed for divorce citing "mental cruelty" as the reason. They officially divorced in November of 1954.

One of the most iconic Hollywood images of all time: Marilyn Monroe does little to protect her modesty in the subway grate scene from *The Seven Year Itch* (1955). This ivory halter-neck Travilla-designed dress was later owned by actress Debbie Reynolds for decades. It was auctioned in 2011 and almost tripled its pre-sale estimate, selling for $4.6 million, with an additional $1 million in fees.

Monroe received $1,500 per week for her work in *The Seven Year Itch*. Despite there being four years left on her Fox contract, on January 7, 1955, Monroe held a press conference (with celebrity photographer Milton H. Greene) announcing the development of her own production company, Marilyn Monroe Productions, Inc. With 101 shares of stock making up the company, Monroe held 51 as president and Greene held 50 as vice-president.

The Seven Year Itch was the year's fifth highest grossing film. Following its success, Fox buckled and renegotiated Monroe's contract on *her* terms. Toward the end of 1955, the new contract saw Monroe's salary rise to $100,000 per film (including $500 per week in expenses) and she was only obligated to do four films within the contractual seven years. As well as story, director and cinematography approval for each film she made at Fox, she could also make another film with a rival studio. She was free to record songs, appear on radio and make up to six TV appearances annually. Additionally, she received a compensation payment of $142,500 as well as $200,000 for the rights to a screenplay (based on the novel *Horns for the Devil*) owned by Marilyn Monroe Productions, Inc. (Buskin, *Blonde Heat: The Sizzling Screen Career of Marilyn Monroe*, p. 189).

Monroe's holdout, while initially thought to have been a career killer, was an unheard-of victory for a lone actress against a major studio. While most studio contracts during that time (and in the past) gave little consideration to the wants and needs of the actor, whether she knew it at the time or not, Monroe not only stood up for herself, she paved the way for actors to negotiate their contracts on *their* terms and not be told which films to star in and how many.

The Seven Year Itch made a good showing at the box office but Billy Wilder was adamant: "I'll never work with Monroe again" (Curtis and Vieira, *Some Like It Hot, Me, Marilyn and the Movie*, p. 27). Famous last words.

In the early–1980s, almost two decades to the day since Monroe's death, Tom Ewell embarked on a tour of the U.S. giving readings of American humor. There wasn't a performance that went by without questions from the audience about Monroe. When asked for his opinion as to why she continues to capture the interest of the public, he said, "I think it's because she had everything in the world that the average woman wants—fame, sex, glory—yet she still was unhappy. People realize that what appeared to be the American dream turned out to be empty." Ewell would tell audiences about he and Monroe eating lunch together every day during the filming of *The Seven Year Itch*. He said she would read the Bible in-between takes, but she'd make sure she placed it inside a *Life* magazine so no one would know. She explained why to Ewell: "Every time I turn around, people think I'm doing some publicity stunt. I don't want them to think that about reading the Bible" (*Springfield Sunday Republican*, August 1, 1982).

Ironically, the real Marilyn Monroe existed behind a fake facade, just like her Bible.

Bus Stop
(1956)

Marilyn Monroe appeared as Cherie. Twentieth Century–Fox. 96 minutes. *Alternate Title: The Wrong Kind of Girl*. *Director:* Joshua Logan. *Producer:* Buddy Adler. *Screenplay:* George Axelrod. Based on the plays *Bus Stop* and *People in the Wind* by William Inge. *Original Music:* Cyril Mockridge and Alfred Newman. *Cinematography:* Milton Krasner. *Costume Design:* Travilla. *Production Dates:* March 15 to May 29, 1956. *Production Cost:* $2.2 million. *Domestic Box Office Receipts:* $4.5 million. *Filming Locations:* Twentieth Century–Fox Studios (Stage 8 and Stage 14), Sun Valley, Idaho, Phoenix, Arizona (exterior shots), North Fork Store, National Forest, Idaho, Ketchum, Idaho. *Release Date:* August 31, 1956. *Genre:* Comedy-Drama-Romance. Color and CinemaScope. *Other Cast:* Don Murray (Beauregard "Bo" Decker), Arthur O'Connell (Virgil Blessing), Betty Field (Grace), Eileen Heckart (Vera), Robert Bray (Carl), Hope Lange (Elma Duckworth), Hans Conried (*Life* Magazine Photographer), Casey Adams (*Life* Magazine Reporter). *Soundtrack:* "That Old Black Magic": Harold Arlen and Johnny Mercer. Sung by Marilyn Monroe. "The Bus Stop Song": Ken Darby. Sung by The Four Lads (and passengers on the bus). *Awards:* 1957 Academy Awards: Best Actor in a Supporting Role: Don Murray (nominated). 1957 BAFTA Awards: Most Promising Newcomer to Film: Don Murray (nominated). 1957 Directors Guild of America (DGA Award): Outstanding Directorial Achievement in Motion Pictures: Joshua Logan (nominated). 1957 Golden Globes (USA): Best Motion Picture (Musical/Comedy, nominated) and Best Motion Picture Actress: Marilyn Monroe (Musical/Comedy, nominated). 1957 Writers Guild of America (WGA Award, screen): Best Written American Comedy: George Axelrod (nominated). *Taglines:* The coming of age of Bo Decker ... and the girl who made him a man!; Give this boy enough rope and he'll land Marilyn Monroe!

Based on William Inge's Broadway play, *Bus Stop* was the first film following Monroe's lengthy absence from Hollywood and the first film since signing her groundbreaking new contract with Fox (December 31, 1955).

Since observing and studying at the Actors Studio in New York, Monroe had adopted the Method technique. She had transformed her style in a genuine attempt to be taken seriously as a "real actress." Monroe was fed up with fluff roles, and determined to gain control over her own career. That new mindset began with controlling herself. At the Actors Studio, she was taking dramatic lessons and, in her own words, "learning to be an actress." Many speculated as to why a woman with a perfectly viable Hollywood career would walk away from a studio contract and travel to the East Coast to become an acting student, but when Monroe was interviewed by Joe Hyams for the *Youngstown Vindicator* (November 28, 1955), she explained why:

> I don't think I'll ever be through studying, so I want to live in New York, where I'll be going to [acting] school. Fox can do anything they like with me as long as I get parts and good directors... I don't want to be the highest paid star in Hollywood. When I'm old and in a rocking chair, I'll need a roof over my head, but I want to have memories of having been a real actress.

Monroe's holdout with Fox paid off. She stood her ground and utilized her spare time by perfecting her craft. It seemed the only people who took her seriously at the time were her acting coaches Lee and Paula Strasberg and her fellow Actors Studio students. Monroe was terrified of performing live, but a scene with Maureen Stapleton from *Anna Christie* in front of her class brought a standing ovation with thunderous applause. That reaction may not seem abnormal for a worthy performance, but at the Actors Studio, no one applauded *anything*. It was just the way it was; everything was about observation.

Following her scene in *Anna Christie*, the rules were broken, not because she was Marilyn Monroe, but because she was *that good*. But even then, Monroe couldn't quite believe she was worthy of such adulation. Though she had often forgotten her lines in rehearsals, when it came time to perform the scene in front of her class, she was faultless. But *she* felt her performance was horrible and she began to sob uncontrollably. The applause from her audience, the praise from the Strasbergs, none of it mattered. Despite the arduous studying and the

In *Bus Stop* (1956), Don Murray is a lovestruck cowboy who tries to convince a doubtful Marilyn Monroe (as Cherie) that he's a good catch. After a year of studying with acting coach Lee Strasberg at the Actors Studio in New York City, Monroe received some of the best reviews of her career for this film.

A UK poster for *Bus Stop* (1956).

desire to be the best she could possibly be, even when she was at her best, she didn't know it. She didn't feel it. She wouldn't allow herself the moment.

Despite her continued lack of self-worth, whether she knew it or not, Monroe was becoming the "real actress" that she wanted to be. But many in Hollywood believed she had been gone too long, burned too many bridges. However, when the new contract was signed, the snickering stopped. The *Los Angeles Mirror News* (January 5, 1956) ran the headline, "Actress Wins All Demands from Studio." The article stated: "Marilyn Monroe, victorious in her year-long sit down strike against 20th Century–Fox, will return to the studio next month with a reported $8,000,000 deal. Veterans of the movie scene said it was one of the greatest single triumphs ever won by an actress."

Monroe's first choice for director on *Bus Stop* was John Huston, but his unavailability meant that Joshua Logan, a friend of Strasberg, stepped in. Strasberg assured Logan that Monroe could do the job, but he would have to coddle the performance out of her. Not one to step away from a challenge, he agreed to the task. Likewise, from Monroe's viewpoint, any directorial recommendation that came from Strasberg gave her the security that she desperately needed.

Of all the directors Monroe worked with, Joshua Logan understood her best. By the time *Bus Stop* was filmed, Logan had already had two nervous breakdowns and was hospitalized as a result; he was eventually diagnosed as manic depressive. Despite the issues that arose during production, Logan considered Marilyn Monroe to be the "most brilliant" actress that he ever directed (Rosenfeld, Megan. "Joshua Logan Steps Into Another Role—As Teacher").

During pre-production, costume ideas were presented to Monroe for her role as Cherie, the hillbilly lounge singer. While they were beautifully constructed, they were far too "Hollywood" and she instantly knew they were all wrong for her character. Logan knew it too, but he withheld his opinion until Monroe saw the costumes for herself. When she told him she hated them, Logan was thrilled because at that moment he knew that Monroe "got" her character.

Cherie was a poor girl from the wrong side of the tracks, with dreams of making it big. She was a bad singer in a two-bit saloon. Expensive-looking costumes compromised everything the character portrayed. So she and Logan decided to shop for Cherie's costumes themselves. Within the cluttered racks of the studio wardrobe department, they found exactly what they were looking for. Everything Monroe wore in the film was recycled and only slightly modified; nothing was made exclusively for her and she wanted it that way. The sequined leotard costume that Cherie wears in the saloon, as well as the raggedy pea-soup–colored coat that she wears throughout the second part of the film were both found on one of those racks. It was Monroe who suggested some rabbit fur be added to the coat as a touch that Cherie, in her lowly way, would consider classy. Logan was amazed. This woman, a Hollywood star, who he expected to be difficult and unprepared, was so in tune with her character that she put her own glamor aside so that she could portray Cherie authentically, just like a "real actress." But just as fast as his hopes were raised, they would soon be dashed.

Broadway actor Don Murray in his debut film role beat out thirty other hopefuls for the role of the lovestruck, dim-witted cowboy "Bo" from Montana's Susie-Q ranch who falls for Cherie, the sexy, talentless chanteuse of the Blue Dragon Cafe in Phoenix, Arizona. For greater authenticity, Logan took the cast and crew first to Phoenix, where the annual rodeo was in progress, then on to Sun Valley, Idaho, for scenic shots. Ten thousand spectators became "extras" in the rodeo scenes.

While Murray fell for Monroe in the film, in real life, he fell for his co-star Hope Lange (she, like Murray, was appearing in her debut film role). Murray and Lange were married on April 14, 1956, and two children followed: a son, Christopher, and a daughter, Patricia. They divorced on July 7, 1961.

At the time of filming, Monroe was in a serious relationship with Arthur Miller, but that didn't matter. She fully expected Murray to be smitten with her. From the very beginning, Murray's affections were with Lange and it was a scenario that Monroe wasn't used to experiencing with her leading man, or any man. She was *always* the center of attention. He was supposed to fall in love with *her*, not her co-star. Instantly, Monroe saw Lange as a rival instead of a co-star and she insisted that Lange's hair be dyed a deeper shade so that she was the only blonde in the film. As requested, Lange's hair was darkened.

It wasn't long before Monroe starting showing up late, sometimes hours past her call time. While everyone else waited, she'd be preparing for her scene with Paula Strasberg. These preparations often meant staring into her mirror, retouching her makeup, deep breathing, shaking her hands to loosen herself up, searching deep within herself for a moment from her past that she could draw upon to evoke Cherie from within her. This was Marilyn Monroe taking everything she learned from Lee Strasberg's method acting technique to the max, and putting it into practice for the first time. As Monroe psyched herself up, Paula sat patiently and fanned herself in silence. Every now and then Strasberg would pipe up in a monotone voice, boosting Monroe's confidence by telling her how brilliant she was. Logan would be so infuriated at waiting for Monroe to arrive, on more than one occasion he physically went to get her to bring her to work. The rose-colored glasses were not only gone, they were crushed! *This* was the Marilyn Monroe that he was warned about, and she was living up to her reputation.

On May 21, while filming a studio scene in the Blue Dragon Café, Murray was supposed to grab at the sequined tail of Monroe's costume as she flees his unwanted advances. As cameras rolled, Murray's tug was too meek for Monroe to react accordingly and enable her own rage to come through in the scene. Feeling the moment had been ruined, Monroe grabbed at the sequined tail and whipped Murray across the face with it. The sequins slashed him near his eye and Murray left the set. He later demanded an apology and told Logan that he wouldn't return to set until he got one. While Monroe initially agreed to apologize, she never did. Tempers cooled and filming continued, but between this incident and Monroe's tardiness and inability to remember her lines, to say there was tension on set was an understatement of grand proportions.

Monroe earned a $100,000 fee, plus an additional $500 per week for expenses. Her coach Paula Strasberg received $1,500 per week to be on set and calm Monroe's nerves. *Bus Stop* was the first film that Fox made with Marilyn Monroe Productions, Inc., and it was the film that made critics sit up and take notice. Some went as far as to eat their words, admitting that Monroe's *Bus Stop* performance proved she could act and that it was one of the best films to come out of Hollywood that year. Richard Griffith of the *Los Angeles Times* (September 18, 1956) wrote:

> Joshua Logan has got her to do a great deal more than wiggle and pout and pop her big eyes and play the synthetic vamp in this film. He has got her to be the beat-up B-girl of William Inge's

play, even down to the Ozark accent and the look of pellagra about her skin. He has got her to be the tinseled floozie, the semimoronic doll, and what's most important, he has got her to light the small flame of dignity that sputters pathetically in this chippie and to make a rather moving sort of her.

Monroe held a very powerful position on the film. She was no longer just the star. This was her film, made for her production company. But her insecurities were still there. She gained little confidence from her landmark contract agreement with Fox. The pressure to produce a smash hit as the star of the film was always with her, only this time it was her production company on the line too. Logan knew Monroe's nerves prevented her from remembering her lines. He also knew that as long as he didn't yell "Cut," even if she muffed her scene, she'd start over and stay in character. As soon as Monroe heard "Cut," she deflated like a balloon and it was anyone's guess how long it would take for her to work herself up to a performance. As cameras rolled, Logan allowed her to keep going. He knew he'd have to piece the scene together in the editing room, and he did. When it came time for Monroe to recite a lengthy stretch of dialogue on the bus to Lange's character, Elma, Logan knew it'd be an impossible task for Monroe to remember the dialogue in full, so he didn't ask her to. The scene was constructed from the fragments he got from her, and again, her perform-

Eileen Heckart and Monroe in a scene from *Bus Stop* (1956).

ance was pieced together in the editing room. When Monroe saw the rushes of her lengthy speech, she was thrilled. However, time constraints meant the film had to be cut down, so the greater part of Monroe's speech was cut for length, which in her opinion eliminated her chances of receiving an Oscar nomination. That said, Logan's perseverance and technique had enabled Monroe to pull off one of the greatest performances of her career.

Academy Award–winning actress Eileen Heckart (1919–2001) plays Vera in the film. On-screen and off, she was a mother figure of sorts, not only for Monroe's character, Cherie, but also for Monroe herself.

In *Just Outside the Spotlight: Growing Up with Eileen Heckart* (2006), written by Heckart's son Luke Yankee, he discusses the relationship that developed between his mother and Monroe while they were shooting *Bus Stop*. Heckart's two older sons, Mark and Phillip, were four and two at the time, but they both spent time on the set with their mother, and in doing so, they found a new friend in Monroe. Monroe was desperate for her own children, and the children who came and went throughout her life, be it her stepchildren or the children of her peers and friends, were all doted upon. At the end of a long shooting day, Heckart's young sons would wait for her to appear on the balcony above them. "Wanna play a little catch?" she'd shout down to them. The answer was always, "Okay!" And so began the nightly ritual of grapefruits and oranges (taken from the various gift baskets that were constantly sent to her) being thrown down from Monroe's balcony, to the balcony below, and the little Heckart boys laughing and scrambling to catch the citrus bombs before they exploded everywhere. Two-year-old Philip didn't catch many, so when his near-misses rolled off the balcony and down another five flights to the pool deck below, the clean-up would inevitably be their mother's job. Heckart would describe the nightly game to her husband during their telephone calls, saying:

> Oh sure, Marilyn's playing catch with the boys on the terrace again. They're having the time of their lives. And guess who's gonna have her raggedy ass down at the pool at two in the morning picking up all those goddam grapefruits and oranges? It ain't Miss Monroe, that's for sure! [Yankee, p. 85].

During the early months of 2012, Luke Yankee shared his mother's memories of the production and Marilyn Monroe for this book. He said:

> *Bus Stop* was shot on location in Phoenix. There were many crowd scenes, especially at the rodeo where Vera and Cherie were in the stands together watching "Bo" compete. The extras were ecstatic to be sharing the same air with the sexiest, most glamorous movie star in the world. At the end of a long day of crowd shooting, everyone was tired and restless. Sweaty and exhausted, Mama and Marilyn started to head back to their trailers. As they walked, extras and locals who had been sitting in the rodeo stands all day started asking Marilyn for autographs and to pose for pictures. "Hey Marilyn!" one of them shouted, "Look over here!" Marilyn paused momentarily to indulge them and kept walking. And then a few more. And more still. With each request, those in the ever-growing crowd who felt they weren't getting their fair share started to get hostile.
>
> "Hey, wait a minute!" a young woman shouted. "I didn't get a picture!"
>
> Then a large man protested, "How come you signed *his* book and not *mine*?!" Mama had never witnessed an angry mob before and it scared her.
>
> Marilyn gave the appearance of total calm and never stopped walking. Finally, in an edgy whisper, she said to Mama, "Whatever happens, just stay beside me." She picked up her pace, scribbling autographs to as many of the outstretched arms as she could reach while she kept

moving. Walking and signing, signing and walking, with ever-increasing velocity. Through her panic, Mama thought, "How can Marilyn move that fast in four inch heels?" She also wondered why there didn't seem to be a cop or a security guard in sight. By this point, the malevolent crowd was screaming, shoving and closing in on them. Marilyn grabbed Mama's arm and dragged her the last twenty feet to the trailer. Once they escaped inside, Marilyn locked the door and threw her body against it as the belligerent hordes pounded on the walls, practically overturning the Winnebago. Mama looked at Marilyn with panic. It was one of the most terrifying moments of my mother's life.

One day, there were lots of entertainment reporters and gossip columnists on the set. As a result, Marilyn hadn't even looked at her dialogue for that morning's scene. Director Joshua Logan was shooting a scene with Mama, Arthur O'Connell as Virgil, the fatherly, older rancher, and Marilyn. Arthur had six lines in the scene, Mama had four lines and Marilyn had only two. They wound up having to shoot the scene thirty-seven times because Marilyn didn't know her two lines.

For the first three or four takes, Marilyn was apologetic and made a joke of it. She'd shrug her shoulders, titter and say, "I'm such a silly ole ninny!" Since time and money are precious commodities on a film set, after a few more takes, the tension began to increase. Eventually, Marilyn needed a scapegoat. First she'd start on the makeup man. "Mah nose is shiny!" A willing participant rushed in and powdered Miss Monroe. Three or four takes later, it would be, "Mah curls are gone! How can I act when mah hair has fallen?" The on-set hairdresser rushed in with bobby pins and styling gel for Miss Monroe. A few takes later, it would be the continuity supervisor, the prop man and on down the production chain—anything other than shouldering the responsibility herself.

While my mother had the outward appearance of success as a character actress (certainly not the super stardom that Marilyn had—nor did she want that), I am not sure that she ever conquered many of her particular demons (after all, do any of us *fully* conquer them?). Her mother was an alcoholic who had five husbands in an era when this behavior was truly scandalous. Some of these husbands just didn't want a kid around, so my mother was often shipped off to her grandmother for weeks or even months at a time. I wonder if this sense of abandonment was one of the things that she related to in Marilyn. As I said in my book, whenever my mother spoke of her, she either spoke of the spoiled starlet with a sense of entitlement, or she literally burst into tears as she remembered this sad, vulnerable lady so desperate to have a child, to be loved, to fit in. I never saw her behave that way over anyone else. She really didn't like to talk about her, probably because it took her to a very dark, emotional place within herself.

I recently heard Shirley MacLaine talking about her dear friend, Elizabeth Taylor, and the fact that she had a Cerces complex—she had to believe that every man in the room (if not every person) was in love with her. I'd never heard of this, but it certainly seems to apply to Marilyn as well.

One of the reasons I was so impressed with the film *My Week with Marilyn* [2011] was that it seemed to embody exactly the characteristics my mother spoke of with Marilyn. You wanted to kill her and take care of her all at the same time.

My mother was very upset about Marilyn's death. There was a piece (I believe in *The New York Times*) at the time of her death that said (I am paraphrasing), "Her co-star in *Bus Stop*, Eileen Heckart, said Miss Monroe was difficult to work with and unprofessional." My mother was absolutely livid and made them print a retraction. It was the only time in her fifty-year career she made any journalist do that. She never talked much about Marilyn's death, but I think that she believed she was murdered (as do I).

Monroe's pasty-white appearance in *Bus Stop* was a deliberate look to fit her character Cherie, the second-rate saloon chanteuse. Since she slept all day and performed most nights, she saw little sunshine and was devoid of color. While the chalky, talcum-powdered appearance was an attempt to further accentuate the physical sacrifices that Cherie made for her work, in some scenes Monroe's face is so blotched with powder, it detracts from the scene.

Allan "Whitey" Snyder was her makeup artist on the film, but when her business partner, Milton Greene, suggested they use clown white on her face, Monroe agreed. It was two against one. Despite Snyder being the makeup artist, he had a fight on his hands. Insisting it would be too white if used on its own, he dulled it down with some other colors. "I think it was still too white," he said. "But [Monroe] wanted it that way. I tried it a shade or two darker and it made her look so much prettier—her teeth stood out better—but I was overruled and so I thought, 'What the hell, I don't care'" (Buskin, *Blonde Heat: The Sizzling Screen Career of Marilyn Monroe*, p. 202).

Critics raved about Monroe's performance in *Bus Stop*, noting that it was, quite possibly, the best of her career. The praise was well deserved. She's charming, funny, sympathetic and, best of all, she sings "That Old Black Magic" with a hillbilly accent and stilted poses that perfectly fit her character's abilities as a mediocre performer. Five years after Monroe's death, Joshua Logan reflected on that very scene:

> [*Bus Stop*] was Marilyn's greatest role, a total characterization. But even more memorable was her remarkable one-take for ["That Old Black Magic"]. She sang it straight through, with all the comedic touches to put it across. That was a live vocal, not a prerecorded job of mouthing the song to a playback soundtrack. I didn't want the velvet perfect sound of prerecording for that scene… (Lesner, "Joshua Logan Feels *Camelot* His Finest").

Bosley Crowther of the *New York Times* (September 1, 1956) gave Monroe a glowing review: "Hold onto your chairs, everybody, and get set for a rattling surprise. Marilyn Monroe has finally proved herself an actress in *Bus Stop*. She and the picture are swell!" On September 9, Crowther wrote another lengthy *Times* review, praising the overall film and adding that the movie "marks her as a genuine acting star, not just a plushy personality and a sex symbol, as she has previously been." *Bus Stop* was the sixth highest grossing film of the year.

In 1956, papers were filed to legally change her name to Marilyn Monroe. On March 12, she attended a hearing where she stated, "I have been using the name I wish to assume, Marilyn Monroe, for many years and I am now professionally known by that name" (Taraborrelli, p. 274).

In a series of e-mails to the author, actor Christopher Riordan revealed memories that were long buried and very difficult to revisit, starting with his "accidental" introduction to Monroe following the filming of *Bus Stop*, right through to how he heard about her death. To this day, Riordan still wears the 18k gold link bracelet that Monroe gave him, and despite the numerous compliments he gets on it, he freely admits that he rarely reveals how he came to own it because it leads into a conversation that is far too painful. He said:

> My actual introduction to Marilyn occurred sometime in late '56, or early '57. She had just finished work on *Bus Stop*, and was closing the house on Beverly Glen, as she was heading to New York to meet with Arthur Miller.
> I had been asked to join a friend of mine who was going to a pool party. At first, I didn't think I wanted to go; but he had just bought a new Karmann Ghia, and enticed me with the promise that we would drive to the party in this new car. Nothing was said about whose house we were going to, or who was giving the party. We arrived and were escorted to the backyard where everyone was sitting by the pool, drinking, smoking and enjoying the sunshine. At some point, I asked where the rest room was. I was directed, but found them occupied. Therefore, I ventured back inside the house, and started my search there. I couldn't find anything that wasn't busy. So, I figured, "Well, I'm only going to the loo, so I'll go upstairs."

When I hit the landing, I heard someone almost whisper, "Hi." And there was this sweet-looking girl, sitting at her mirror and combing her hair. For a good long time, I didn't even realize who I was talking to. We began chatting, and I suddenly found we had a great feeling of already knowing each other. While talking, I took note of the many boxes that were packed and waiting to be taken away. The whole scene seemed terribly surreal to me. Marilyn never did introduce herself. It seemed a given that I knew who she was. And, as I said, our conversation was conducted as though we had been friends for years. We both, I think, seemed to sense that we had much in common.

At some point, I heard my friend call my name; so I excused myself and ran downstairs. I never did go to the bathroom. I received a little scolding for going into the house, but when I assured my friend that everything was all right, it was forgotten. Most of us stayed until around four o'clock, I'd say. And Marilyn never did come downstairs, or anywhere near the pool. Of course, on the way home, I asked, "Why didn't you tell me where we were going?" The answer was, "Because she almost never comes out. She's never 'ready enough.' And I didn't want you to be disappointed."

Years later, I became a neighbor of Inez Melson, Marilyn's business manager. I told her the story, and she laughed. "That's Marilyn," she said. And some time after that, I met Rupert Allan, who was Marilyn's publicity agent. Rupert was, in fact, a very dear friend of my adoptive "dad," Lewis Milestone, and his wife Kendall. Suddenly, I was emerged in all of this social circle.

Oddly enough, I noticed: If Marilyn wasn't in attendance at a gathering, she was the topic of conversation. After she died, Rupert and I spoke quite frequently of Marilyn. However, he never speculated about her death to me. Still, he knew how I felt. And he knew I had other connections. I will say, he never argued with me. By saying, "other connections," I mean...I knew many people who knew her, some people who worked for the Kennedys when they were in town. I knew Peter Lawford too. Personally, I felt then, and I feel now...Marilyn was murdered. Rupert was called to Marilyn's side *very* often. I don't think there was anything, job or otherwise, that Rupert didn't run to her.

From what I understood, the relationship with Miller started falling apart quite a bit before *The Misfits*. Which, from what I was told, was *why* he started writing the story. I know that Marilyn was devastated that she had had miscarriages. She really wanted to have a baby. She wanted to give a child everything she never got. I understood that perfectly. Fortunately, I got to fulfill my wish.

As you must understand by now ... it's hard to just write a couple of things about this woman. There are *so* many layers. I've known a lot of movie stars in my day, but I never knew anyone like her. No one was so fragile, so vulnerable. And yet, at times she could put her foot down, and there was *no* changing her mind.

By the time Marilyn was "killed," I had worked with Sinatra, Dean Martin, etc., several times. My "dad" had directed the entire Rat Pack in the original *Ocean's Eleven* [1960] so comments were made, rumors had started, and so on. Plus, a very close friend of mine had been working for Tony Curtis at that time.

Oddly enough, when Marilyn died ... everyone seemed to *shut up*. Dean and Frank became *very* quiet. And DiMaggio sensed their pulling back, and banned them all from the funeral. For Peter [Lawford], it destroyed him. He immediately began to drink more, and abuse himself to such a point that he was often incoherent.

There is much I'd like to say about the "killing" (I guess I'm safe in saying that). But I too, will not be going into great detail. It's just too dangerous. I will say that at the end, Marilyn was in a pretty good place, despite the fact that Fox had fired her. Many are, or were, sure that she would be put back on the picture. However, she had many irons in the fire, and she was *thrilled* at finally having her own home.

In my book, I write about coming home from a cast party and thinking, "I should call Marilyn and let her know that she has supporters." That party was held on the evening of her death. The next morning, I was awakened by a phone call from a friend. He said, "Sit down, I have some bad news." And that's how I learned Marilyn was no longer with us. It didn't take long for people to start speculating, putting two and two together. There seem to be [two] "camps," those who wish to think she "finally" took too many pills and those who feel that someone very powerful saw to it that she was silenced.

The Prince and the Showgirl (1957)

Marilyn Monroe appeared as Elsie Marina ("The Showgirl"). Warner Bros. Pictures and Marilyn Monroe Productions. 117 minutes. *Working Title: The Sleeping Prince. Director:* Laurence Olivier. *Producers:* Milton H. Greene, Laurence Olivier and Marilyn Monroe (uncredited). *Writer:* Terence Rattigan (screenplay and play *The Sleeping Prince*). *Original Music:* Richard Addinsell. *Cinematography:* Jack Cardiff. *Production Designer:* Roger Furse. *Costume Designer:* Beatrice Dawson. *Production Dates:* August 7 to November 16, 1956. *Domestic Box Office Receipts:* $1.6 million. *Release Date:* June 13, 1957. *Filming Locations:* London, England, and Pinewood Studios, Iver Heath, Buckinghamshire, England. *Genre:* Comedy-Romance. Technicolor. *Other Cast:* Laurence Olivier (The Regent), Richard Wattis (Northbrook), David Thorne (The Foreign Office), Jeremy Spenser (King Nicolas), Sybil Thorndike (The Queen Dowager), Harold Goodwin (Call Boy), Gladys Henson (Dresser), Jean Kent (Maisie Springfield), Charles Victor (Theatre Manager), Daphne Anderson (Fanny), Vera Day (Betty), Gillian Owen (Maggie), Esmond Knight (Hoffman), Paul Hardwick (Major Domo). *Awards:* 1957 National Board of Review (USA): Best Supporting Actress: Sybil Thorndike (won). 1958 BAFTA Awards: Best British Actor: Laurence Olivier (nominated); Best British Film, Best British Screenplay: Terence Rattigan (nominated); Best film from any Source, Best Foreign Actress: Marilyn Monroe (nominated). 1959 David di Donatello Awards (Golden Plate): Best Foreign Actress of 1958: Marilyn Monroe (won). 1958 Laurel Awards (Golden Laurel): Top Female Comedy Performance: Marilyn Monroe (nominated, fourth place). March 1959, Crystal Star Award: Best Foreign Actress: Marilyn Monroe (won). *Tagline:* Some countries have a medal for Everything.

On June 29, 1956, in a civil ceremony in White Plains, New York, Marilyn Monroe married for the third and last time. Her husband was world-renowned playwright and Pulitzer Prize winner Arthur Miller. Two days later, they married again, this time in a traditional Jewish ceremony (Monroe converted to Judaism for Miller). Within two weeks, the newlyweds flew to London to begin work on Laurence Olivier's *The Prince and the Showgirl*.

It was a crowded honeymoon.

Monroe's business partner Milton Greene, her acting coach Paula Strasberg and secretary Hedda Rosten accompanied the pair. Along with the "oil and vinegar" relationship that developed between Monroe and Olivier, Miller was left to pick up the pieces. Acting as mediator between his wife and the cast and crew who were constantly waiting for her to show up on set, as well as coddling Monroe's fragile emotional state throughout the filming, it was a tough job.

Parkside House was a stately residence of a dozen rooms that was about an hour from London and an hour's drive from the studio. Hidden away on a country path called Wick Lane, there were several acres of manicured gardens with a gate that opened onto Windsor Park. The newlyweds had their own private sanctuary there. But behind closed doors, the honeymoon phase wore off quickly.

With a flourishing career of his own to nurture, Miller found himself being dragged

Title card for *The Prince and the Showgirl* (1957).

down with the weight of his wife's personal and professional insecurities. Miller's work took a backseat. Within weeks of their marriage, Miller realized that maintaining a functioning Marilyn Monroe was a full-time job, and a damn near impossible job.

Shortly before filming began, Olivier was hit with the "oh, by the way..." bombshell announcement that Monroe's acting coach Paula Strasberg would be accompanying her on set. Though he was less than thrilled with his leading lady wanting her acting coach with her at all times, Olivier reluctantly accepted the situation, hoping that if Monroe felt secure in her environment, then he, as the director, would get the best out of her.

In an effort to bolster his mood and confidence, Olivier contacted two of Monroe's previous directors, Billy Wilder and Joshua Logan. Both cheerfully commiserated with Olivier, telling him that working with Monroe was hell, but that he would be getting a pleasant surprise when it was all over (Olivier, p. 172).

Logan told Olivier that Monroe was unlike every other actress. "Don't tell her exactly how to read a line," he advised. "Let her work it out some way herself no matter how long it takes." Logan blamed Olivier for the problems he had with Monroe during the production because Olivier failed to heed his advice (Rosenfeld, Megan. "Joshua Logan Steps Into Another Role—As Teacher"). He specifically told Olivier never to get bombastic or remotely demanding in tone. Logan assured Olivier that if he followed that advice, he'd get the performance he desired, and maybe even a performance that would surprise him. Olivier either didn't listen to Logan's advice or Monroe rubbed him the wrong way from day one and he was simply unable to toe the line to appease her. The angrier Olivier got, the more insecure Monroe became. She was terrified to come to set, and she often didn't, which only served to further stoke Olivier's rage.

Louis Berg of the *Los Angeles Times* (April 28, 1957) reported that a unique coat of arms for the fictional Carpathian country was cleverly created by the film's production designer, Roger Furse. The shield carried a representation of a mountain (Mon) and a deer (Roe). The writer of the original play *The Sleeping Prince*, Terence Rattigan was represented as three rodents (rat-again). Olivier was there as an olive tree, and Warner Brothers was symbolized by a double-headed eagle and gold checks (money).

The multi-award winning 2011 film *My Week with Marilyn*, starring Michelle Williams as Marilyn Monroe, is based on the diary entries of Colin Clark, third assistant director on *The Prince and the Showgirl*. The behind-the-scenes drama that plagued this much-hyped British production is legendary. To think that a film about "the making of the film" was even conceived as entertainment in the first place, especially so many years later, is confirmation that the clash of cultures, personalities and egos was perhaps even more riveting than the production itself.

On February 9, 1956, Olivier traveled to Manhattan for a press conference with Monroe at the Plaza Hotel. They announced their plans to star together in the film that would be based on Rattigan's *The Sleeping Prince*. It was an exciting time for Monroe. After negotiating her new contract with Fox, an additional clause allowed her the freedom to develop her own projects away from the studio. *The Prince and the Showgirl* would be the first (and only) independent production for her newly formed Marilyn Monroe Productions. It would also be her first (and only) film that was shot outside America. Olivier agreed to reprise his stage role, but only if he could also produce and direct the film. As the president of the company, Monroe negotiated the film rights to the play, as well as financial backing and a distribution deal with Warner Brothers. Her company's vice-president (and secondary shareholder), photographer Milton Greene, served as executive producer. Aside from her salary, Monroe would also receive a ten percent share in the film's profits. In creating her own production company, she reclaimed her rights to choose what she wanted to do, when she wanted to do it, whom she wanted to do it with, and how much money she'd get for her trouble. As with most aspects of Monroe's life, it was good while it lasted, but it didn't last long.

The anticipation of the "All-American Girl" and "The Great Shakespearean Thespian" appearing together for a press conference to announce their upcoming film created quite an atmosphere. They were, quite literally, "The Prince" and "The Showgirl." Close to 200 reporters and photographers showed up to witness the event. As the questions came, as if on cue, Monroe's black spaghetti strap on her figure-hugging dress snapped. As she reacted to retain her modesty, the gallery of witnesses went wild. It was one of Hollywood's earliest and most talked-about "wardrobe malfunctions." While the cameras flashed to capture the mishap, the American media went as far to accuse Monroe of staging the scene. She denied the claims. In an art-imitating-life moment, during the opening scenes of the film, we see Olivier as the Prince Regent backstage, visiting the cast of *The Coconut Girl*, the play that Monroe, as Elsie Marina, is starring in. As the Prince Regent makes his way along the line of actors, he gets to the end of the line and encounters a very nervous Elsie. As she respectfully curtsies to his highness, the strap on her gown snaps. Whether the real-life strap snap was purposeful or otherwise, the onscreen duplication was a testament to Monroe's sense of humor and her ability to laugh at herself, despite the criticism of the press.

Now 30 years old, Monroe was desperate to shake off some of her sex symbol image and be recognized for her body of work, not just her body. She was hopeful that her professional association with the director, producer and star, Olivier, would give her worldwide reverence as a "serious actress."

Likewise, Olivier had his own agenda. Now almost 50 years old, and a veteran of both stage and screen, Olivier was recognized for his contribution to the arts, knighted by his country, bestowed with countless awards and respected by his peers. He was married to Vivien Leigh, who played the part of The Showgirl in the London stage play. It was as though Olivier had lived for half a century and done it all.

In Hollywood years, age was against him. Olivier was desperate to successfully return to film as a mature actor. His celluloid career had taken a back seat to his theater work, but *The Prince and the Showgirl* was the beginning of a new chapter in his already impressive résumé. While Monroe had her own motives, Olivier did too, for it would be *his* association with the ever-popular "Hollywood It Girl," that would inevitably give him a chance at a reignited film career. With the foundations of the production being set on what Monroe and Olivier could do for each other's professional futures, it's not surprising that the production itself got lost within the ulterior motives of its stars.

Monroe idolized Olivier. He was an intellectual actor, a legend. And like any red-blooded male, Olivier was initially taken with Monroe's beauty; however, he never gave her much credit for anything more than just another Hollywood blonde. While most members of the cast were veterans of the stage, "professional thespians" so to speak, and one-time colleagues of Olivier, this much-hyped "movie star" from America had come from a whole other world, and it didn't take long for Monroe to feel patronized when in Olivier's company. It set the mood for the rest of the production.

When Olivier viewed the first rushes and complained to Monroe that her teeth appeared yellowed (and they are) on film, he suggested that she clean them with baking soda and lemon juice in an effort to naturally whiten them. Monroe was insulted and furious at the claim, and this early confrontation only served to bring her already shattered confidence down to a whole new low. Monroe had never been confident in her abilities as an actress, but her appearance was rarely questioned. Her looks were her mainstay. Olivier had taken a swipe at her looks *and* her talent. Monroe held a grudge. Olivier would pay for those opinions and outbursts ... for the entire production.

Vera Day recalled a moment when Olivier was setting up camera angles and he "politely" told Monroe that he was unable to see her in the position she was standing in. She immediately retorted, "Oh well, if you can't see me, I will go home," and she left the set, leaving the cast and crew open-mouthed at what just happened (Morgan, p. 250).

Monroe's fragility was obvious, but Dame Sybil Thorndike genuinely liked her and respected her for who she was and what she had achieved in front of a camera and with little training. Thorndike often took it upon herself to take Olivier aside to reason with him or explain ways of getting around Monroe's emotional complexities in order to get the best out of her, but the damage was already done. Sir Laurence Olivier, and the pedestal Marilyn

Monroe had placed him on, had come crashing to the ground with a thud. Likewise, Olivier's initial infatuation with Monroe was quickly replaced with feelings of frustration, anger and disappointment.

The Prince and the Showgirl is a whimsical Cinderella-like tale about the Prince Regent of Carpathia (Olivier) and Elsie Marina, aka The Showgirl (Monroe). In London to attend the 1911 coronation of King George V, the Prince Regent spends a night at the theater. After going backstage to congratulate the cast of *The Coconut Girl*, he takes a liking to Elsie, a beautiful showgirl. He sends her a note later that evening, inviting her to the Embassy for supper. A nervous Elsie thinks he must have mistaken her for someone else, but she proceeds to get ready for the party all the same. The rest of the film takes place over the course of several days, but except for the morning when she groggily emerges from her bedroom wrapped in the bedspread with the coat of arms strategically placed on her derriere, Elsie wears the same white evening dress, day and night, in every scene.

Upon arrival at the Embassy, Elsie realizes it is an intimate party—for two! Realizing the Prince Regent has ulterior motives, she prepares to leave, but the prince's well-meaning servant Northbrook (Richard Wattis) tries his best to convince her to stay. He assures her that he'll personally interrupt the supper before the Prince Regent makes any romantic moves. Using the excuse that her aunt has been taken to hospital, it will give her the perfect excuse to leave immediately. Not convinced, Elsie quickly makes her way to the front door. As the doors are opened for her to leave, Elsie is viewed from behind. She then drops below camera to curtsy, thus revealing the arrival of the Prince Regent. Alas, Elsie has no choice but to turn around and go through with the date.

The stuffy Prince Regent pays little attention to Elsie during their dinner. His constant telephone interruptions annoy Elsie, but she amuses herself by talking to herself, drinking champagne and serving her own food. Eventually the Prince Regent gives Elsie his full attention. As he attempts to make a pass at her, a drunk and giggly Elsie refuses his advances. After being told that he should be more romantic, the Prince Regent goes into seduction-overdrive, ordering his servants to perfume the room, dim the lights and play the violin outside the door. They eventually kiss, but the alcohol takes hold and Elsie collapses. A frustrated Prince Regent summons his servants to take her to a spare room to sleep it off.

When Elsie wakes the following morning, the Prince Regent is less than interested in her staying around. However, his righteous, almost deaf mother-in-law (the mother of his deceased wife), the Queen Dowager (Thorndike), takes a liking to her and she asks her to replace her lady-in-waiting for the coronation. The Prince Regent begrudgingly complies with his mother-in-law's wishes. Elsie attends the coronation and in a humorous *My Fair Lady*–like fashion, as she's driven through the streets in the royal carriage, she loses her composure, as she waves and shouts to her excited friends. A stern look from the Prince Regent silences her. But he is actually amused at her spontaneous behavior, and his seemingly immovable frown ever so slightly transforms into a sly smile.

With Jack Cardiff behind the camera, it's no surprise that many of the scenes are breathtakingly orchestrated. The coronation scene is a fine example. It's set to music and entirely told through Elsie's emotions, without words. Over the course of several days, we see Elsie's vivacious personality gradually chip away at the Prince Regent's emotionless dictatorial demeanor.

Once the coronation is over, the Prince Regent plans on sending Elsie back to the theater. However, the Prince Regent's 16-year-old son King Nicolas (Jeremy Spenser) steps in and invites her to be his date at the coronation ball that evening.

Prior to the coronation, Elsie overhears a telephone conversation in which Nicolas plots to overthrow his father. Nicolas pleads with her not to tell and, to his relief, she promises she'll keep his secret. At the ball, Elsie convinces Nicolas to support his father, but Nicolas has a few conditions before signing the agreement. In just a couple days, her mediation between father and son mends their rocky relationship.

The rigid Prince Regent does everything in his power to bury his feelings for Elsie, but he finally gives into his love for her. In doing so, his relationship with his son and his staff is transformed. He is a new man. After they profess their love for each other, a newly rejuvenated Prince Regent begins to make plans for Elsie to return home to Carpathia with him.

Though she's in love with him, Elsie declines his offer. She tells him that she still has eighteen months left on her theater contract and she must see it through. The Prince Regent has eighteen months of political obligations to fulfill, after which his son will reign in his place. In a year and a half, both would be free to pursue their relationship further. But both dejectedly admit that anything can happen in eighteen months.

The Prince Regent and Elsie leave the embassy and go their own ways. That's the end of the fairy tale ... or is it? While the implication is their time apart will be temporary, there's also a sense of sadness that that their time together was a momentary romance between two people that could never be together: a Prince ... and a Showgirl.

During the supper scene, as the Prince Regent makes his telephone calls and ignores Elsie, she amuses herself with food and champagne. It took two days of shooting, thirty-four takes and twenty jars of caviar for her to get the scene right. Olivier suggested she mime the eating, but just as she insisted that the onscreen champagne not be replaced with the usual apple juice, she ate the caviar and drank the alcohol. As filming dragged on, it didn't help matters that she was bloated ... and drunk! Throughout the production, her drinking increased, as did her sleeping pill intake. When she wasn't sleeping, she was either irrational or hysterical.

Jean Kent, who appeared alongside Monroe in two brief scenes, said, "I think poor Larry [Olivier] must have aged at least 15 years during the making of that film.... [Monroe] never arrived on time, never said a line the same way twice, seemed completely unable to hit her marks on the set, and couldn't and wouldn't do anything at all without consulting her acting coach, Paula Strasberg, whose presence was clearly resented by Larry Olivier" ("'Grubby' Marilyn Monroe made Laurence Olivier 'age fifteen years' during filming," *The Telegraph,* January 24, 2013).

Two weeks into filming, Miller flew back to New York to visit with his children. Claiming she was sick, Monroe refused to work while Miller was away. While her initial illness was feigned, soon after she found out that she was pregnant. However, by late August, just a few weeks along, she miscarried. Miller was still in New York.

On August 1, 1957, an ectopic pregnancy was terminated, and she would suffer yet another miscarriage while married to Miller. While those three pregnancy losses were reported in the media, it's more than likely there were others that went unmentioned. Monroe's inability to bear a child only deepened her depression. Her sadness at being motherless was very real, but her ability to take care of a baby also seemed unrealistic. She could barely take care of herself.

Three weeks into filming, Olivier's wife Vivien Leigh also miscarried. Like Monroe, Leigh had mental health issues to contend with. Olivier has been accused of being unsympathetic to Monroe's emotional problems, but in all fairness, his own reality was less than ideal. Olivier was dealing with a neurotic wife and an equally neurotic leading lady.

Monroe's emotional state was elevated further when she "accidentally" read an uncomplimentary entry about herself in her husband's notebook. It's been suggested that Miller had written that he sometimes felt embarrassed by her behavior in front of his friends (*Vanity Fair,* November 2010). Exactly what Miller wrote isn't known but the possibilities range from his notes being general musings about his disappointment in his wife's erratic behavior during the production of *The Prince and the Showgirl*, to comparing her to his ex-wife — to calling her a whore. Whatever it was, Monroe was devastated by the discovery. Miller tried to squirm his way out of the hairy situation by telling his distressed wife it was just a writer's ramblings and nothing more. Monroe knew better. She was deeply affected by her husband's wavering loyalty and disappointment in her, and their marriage. She never got over it.

A critical husband, a critical leading man–director, the weight of the success or failure of her latest film on her shoulders and the emotional and physical pain of another miscarriage. On top of her usual array of anxieties and insecurities, Monroe was at her breaking point. When Joshua Logan visited the set, he was greeted with the front side of Monroe's dressing room door! Still holding a grudge over the *Bus Stop* (1956) scene that was cut, the scene that *she* thought would have made her performance Oscar-worthy, she flatly refused to see him. Paula Strasberg coddled and cosseted her to the nth degree, but even her ever-present protective cocoon was losing its effect. New York–based Freudian psychoanalyst Margaret Hohenberg made an emergency flight to London to counsel Monroe and later Anna Freud, daughter of Sigmund Freud, also treated her.

On the recommendation of Milton Greene, Monroe had been having regular sessions with Dr. Hohenberg since 1955, but she stopped seeing her by early 1957, following her break-up with Greene. Monroe's lifelong interest in psychotherapy was catapulted to an obsessive level when she moved to New York and became a student at the Actors Studio and its teaching philosophy known as the Method. Her teachers, Lee and Paula Strasberg, encouraged their students to use Freudian introspection to better develop the emotions of the characters they'd portray. As a result, in a move to better herself as an actress, Monroe dredged up her troubled past on an almost daily basis. The intense therapy did nothing but enforce her lack of self-esteem and cause her anxieties and depressive state to worsen.

The theory behind the Method style is to talk out a scene and search for the character's motivation. Serious Method actors will lose themselves completely, taking on the persona of their character, even after "cut" is called. Others will live their character, both on set and away, until a production is over. This intense form of preparation was totally opposite to Olivier's style of acting. He knew his character. He read the script. He learned his lines. He'd rehearse the scene, shoot it and move on. Olivier's classic approach clashed with Monroe's style of analytical preparation. He didn't get it. He didn't get her. He felt suffocated and out of control. Despite the fact that Olivier directed *The Prince and the Showgirl,* he was duly directed by Monroe's cluster of controlling cronies. It would be over a decade before Olivier felt ready to direct another film (*Three Sisters* in 1970).

Years later, Olivier was obviously still wounded by the traumatic experience. "I've never been so glad when anything was over," he said. "[Monroe] was thoroughly ill-mannered. Always late. And terribly rude. It was utterly humiliating. Being a star and an actress is not necessarily the same thing" ("Moods of an Idol," *Sydney Morning Herald*, May 25, 1980).

Cinematographer Jack Cardiff confirmed the fact that Olivier's bitterness towards Monroe never waned. Olivier often referred to her as the "bitch" who lacked talent and sex appeal. Cardiff said that Olivier went out of his way to antagonize Monroe during production, even allowing or encouraging his wife Vivien Leigh on the set to observe Monroe playing the role that Leigh had played on stage. Leigh's presence terrified an already insecure Monroe, but Olivier reveled in making her squirm any chance he could get. In doing so, Olivier made the shoot far worse than it should have been. While Monroe initially acknowledged Olivier's status as a great actor, he refused to acknowledge her status as an actress, let alone a world-famous sex symbol. There was no mutual respect, and any hero-worship that Monroe felt for Olivier was snuffed out by his arrogance and intolerance of her very existence. Early on, right before a scene, Olivier barked his directorial instructions at Monroe, then sarcastically snapped, "Try and be sexy." She felt humiliated and she never forgave him for the cruel jibe. Cardiff said:

> Marilyn had this ghastly obsession with method acting and was always searching for some inner meaning with everything, but Larry would only explain the simple facts of the scene. I think she resented him. She used to call him "Mr. Sir," because he had been knighted [Hastings, "'Try to Be Sexy': How Larry Olivier Set Out to Humiliate Monroe"].

Cardiff waited around for Monroe as much as anyone else, and while he completely understood Olivier's frustrations, he remained loyal to Monroe to the very end, insisting that her lateness had nothing to do with arrogance. She was shy. She was nervous. Olivier brought the worst of her fears out in her and she brought the worst of his fears out in him. It was a personality clash with a dash of cultural differences thrown in for good measure.

A few months before her death, Cardiff met with Monroe in a hotel room. He remembered her being this sad, lonely figure sitting in a large room. One dim light lit the space and she wore dark glasses. They had a drink and they sat side by side on a settee to talk. She told him what had been going on in her life. It wasn't good.

Cardiff died on April 22, 2009, at 94. Right to the very end, his opinion as to how Monroe died never changed. He strongly believed she was killed because she knew too much. President Kennedy told her a lot of stories about the 1961 CIA-backed invasion of Cuba, and when he found out that she had written the information down in her diary, he wanted her to hand it over. Cardiff said, "[The murder theory] makes sense to me because she had the diary" (Hastings, "'Try to Be Sexy': How Larry Olivier Set Out to Humiliate Monroe").

On the evening of October 11, after a long day of filming, Monroe played the part of the dutiful wife of the genius playwright and they attended the opening of Miller's play *A View from the Bridge* at the Comedy Theatre. Leaving from the Oliviers' home, Monroe and Miller arrived with Olivier and Leigh and they were met with massive crowds outside the stage door of the theater. For the first time in a long time, Monroe was personable and in high spirits. When the play was over, she and Miller took to the stage to take a bow and they met with cast and crew backstage. The evening could not have gone better. To the outside world, the Millers and the Oliviers were the best of friends who were collaborating on *The Prince and the Showgirl* and supporting each other's work. The façade was convincing. The following day, filming continued. For the rest of the production, Monroe was either late or sick—or both.

Before returning to the United States, Monroe and Miller were invited to attend a Royal Film Performance at the Empire Theatre in Leicester Square, London. Other stars in attendance that October 29 included Victor Mature, Joan Crawford, Brigitte Bardot, Anita Ekberg, Arlene Dahl and Norman Wisdom, all of whom, along with Marilyn, were presented to Queen Elizabeth and her sister, Princess Margaret. Monroe wore a gold lamé gown with topaz straps and a gold cape. Long white gloves, a white handbag and two-inch heels completed her ensemble. As the queen came down the line to greet her, Monroe's curtsy was flawless. They chatted for several minutes and as the queen moved on to other guests, Princess Margaret took over the conversation. Monroe recommended she see her husband's play *A View from the Bridge*.

November 16, 1956, was Monroe's last official day on set. Before leaving she profusely apologized to the cast and crew for her lateness and the too-many sick days that caused delays. She seemed sincere. Even the most ardent Monroe haters found themselves forgiving her, or feeling sorry for her. With filming complete, the production was only eleven days over schedule, a triumph in itself considering the numerous problems that arose. But Olivier had no sense of relief. He was utterly exhausted and less than satisfied with the accomplishment, or lack thereof. He openly admitted to "feelings of vague disquiet" (Olivier, p. 174). Unlike other directors before him, Olivier felt that he had failed to get Monroe's best performance out of her. He had suffered through Monroe's many moods and paranoia. He had come too far and worked too hard to be dissatisfied with the final result.

So, he came up with a plan.

Olivier invited Monroe and Arthur Miller to a private screening. He asked that they watch the film through, and when it finished to come and see him. Little did they know that their reaction was crucial to the film staying untouched—or not. Olivier patiently waited for the screening to be over. He was quite willing to put his own feelings of discontentment aside if Monroe and Miller were happy with the final result. They weren't. Both agreed there was room for improvement, though with filming already wrapped they asked Olivier what could be done to improve a film that was finished.

Olivier's speech began.

He said that he would dedicate two days to re-shoots, but only if Monroe agreed to *his* terms. No matter what their personal and professional differences were, the one thing they both wanted was for *The Prince and The Showgirl* to have a successful outcome. And they both agreed the film in its current state would not achieve that goal. If the re-shoots were to go ahead, Olivier told Monroe that she would need to undertake to contribute to a better atmosphere between the two of them, discipline herself to absolute punctuality, and accept his word when he passed something as okay and not insist on take after take more than was necessary. They had literally crossed the finish line, the film was done, but in agreeing to go back a few steps for the good of the film, Olivier felt empowered for the first time since the *Prince and the Showgirl* circus came to town. "For once," he said, "I had the other side by the short and curlies, and they knew they had to agree" (Olivier, p. 175).

While Olivier was initially buoyed by the chance of a do-over, the euphoria ended on the first day of shooting. In the scene of the first meeting between the Regent and Elsie, Olivier said they spent the entire morning trying to inject a scintillating spirit into the scene to give it "the sparkle needed to make a lively start to a picture from which a great deal would be expected" (Olivier, p. 175).

Olivier explained what was needed in more ways than he could have imagined. Monroe just wasn't getting it, at least not until she searched for the answer from her guru, Paula Strasberg. "Honey, just think of Coca-Cola and Frank Sinatra!" said Strasberg (Coleman, p. 269). Olivier was beside himself. At a loss to even decipher what *that* meant in relation to the scene that he had repeatedly tried to explain to her on a literal level, he was amazed and confused that it was Strasberg's bizarre explanation that got them the money shot. As much as he tried to understand it, how it came to be didn't matter any more. It was over. The fact was, he got the shot and the film would be all the better for it.

Australian-born Jocelyn Rickards was new to the film industry, an assistant to Roger Furse on the sets and men's costumes for *The Prince and the Showgirl*. She described the experience as "like being an observer at a civil war. Olivier and Monroe did not get on, and both stars had rival entourages of sickening sycophants" (Jocelyn Rickards papers).

As Monroe and Miller prepared to leave London, Olivier said that it had been agreed upon by all parties that no feelings of animosity should, or would, be publicly displayed at the airport. The eyes of the press, and the world, were upon them. The film's success depended on the public believing that everyone was the best of friends. A carefully orchestrated plan was put in place. A plan that would surely debunk the vicious rumors of there being major conflicts between the two stars throughout the course of the production. Olivier had set up his own camera crew to take photos of Monroe and Miller with himself and Vivien Leigh at the airport. Both couples lovingly hugged, kissed and waved goodbye to each other. All the right shots were taken. Monroe and Miller boarded their plane. The film was complete, and the publicity charade was achieved with great success ... or so Olivier thought at the time. Later he admitted that the phony public display of affection fooled no one. The newspapers called it "an absurd show" (Olivier, p. 175).

Not surprisingly, the press book for the production builds up the "natural rapport" between the two stars: "It has been said that Olivier and Monroe are the new Bogart and Bacall, Boyer and Bergman. They are being called the happiest couple in the happiest comedy of the year."

Despite the enormous conflict surrounding the making of the film, Monroe's charming, comedic performance in *The Prince and the Showgirl* is one of the best of her career, and most critics agreed. Philip K. Scheuer reviewed the film in the *Los Angeles Times* (May 19, 1957):

> Miss Monroe's role is again a natural ... she is a showgirl playing a showgirl, and in the moments during which she seems self-conscious it is thoroughly possible that the showgirl would be. The limitations of Marilyn the actress may also be those of Elsie, the part; Olivier has certainly done what he could with both.

Bosley Crowther of the *New York Times* (June 14, 1957) wasn't as kind. He wrote:

> Sir Laurence is kept pretty much a stuffed-shirt, wearing a monocle and speaking in Teutonic accents that are unpleasant and hard to understand. And Miss Monroe mainly has to giggle, wiggle, breathe deeply and flirt. She does not make the showgirl a person, simply another of her

pretty oddities... [T]he main trouble with *The Prince and the Showgirl*, when you come right down to it, is that both characters are essentially dull.

Reviews were mixed, but the onscreen rapport between Monroe and Olivier is something to behold. To know their effortless performances took such an effort to capture, it somehow makes the film all the more magical. Though Monroe was bypassed for an Oscar nod (she was never nominated for an Academy Award), she was recognized for her exceptional work in *The Prince and the Showgirl* with the Italian David Di Donatello Prize for the Best Foreign Actress of 1958, as well as France's Crystal Star Award (March 1959) for Best Foreign Actress. Both awards are the European equivalent of an Oscar. *The Prince and the Showgirl* was the twelfth highest grossing film of the year.

In his 1982 autobiography *Confessions of an Actor*, Olivier remembers a night at the home of some unnamed Hollywood friends. At the time, some twenty-five years had passed since *The Prince and The Showgirl* was made. Knowing how painful the experience was for him, as a bit of a lark, and to watch him squirm, Olivier's sadistic hosts ran the film for their guests on their library projector. From that experience, Olivier gained a whole new perspective, maybe even a warm appreciation of the film. Even more surprising, he was kind toward Monroe's performance, saying:

> I was a bit embarrassed as I didn't know how long it might be before the joke would begin to get a bit tired; however, the picture ran through, much to my surprise. At the finish, everyone was clamorous in their praises. I was as good as could be, and Marilyn! Marilyn was quite wonderful, the best of all. So. What do you know? [Olivier, p. 176].

After returning from the stresses of England, the Millers rented a cottage in Amagansett, Long Island, New York. It was an attempt to reconnect as a couple and save a flailing marriage. Though Monroe still suffered with anxiety and insomnia, the pressures of being away from a film set helped her mood considerably. Miller was able to begin writing again. One of his short stories, "Please Don't Kill Anything," was written during their stay and inspired by his wife's love of animals.

Throughout the course of 1956, Marilyn Monroe Productions was already in serious trouble. Miller was meddling in his wife's business arrangements, and Monroe began to distrust Milton Greene's motives. By April of 1957, the partnership that led to a groundbreaking deal was gone. Monroe and Greene parted ways.

Greene was more than just a photographer, he was a friend, confidante, business partner, possible lover, and he created an image of Monroe on film that few could match. She was, for any photographer, the perfect subject. But Greene knew her best angles, how she should be lit, how her hair and makeup should look, and he used that knowledge from his still sessions to further accentuate her beauty for the moving image. Greene and his wife Amy were yet another couple who opened the doors of their home to her. Their secluded Connecticut retreat was as much hers as it was theirs. It was the sanctity of a conventional home that Monroe had craved all her life.

Throughout her life, she weaved her way in and out of many lives. When she was in, she was really "in" but when she was done, she walked away and moved on with no looking back. While Monroe's behavior could have easily caused many of her peers to abandon her, she was the one who usually left these professional and personal relationships. The Greenes would be no exception. "We had our own life," Amy Greene said later. "We were not living through her. She was living through us" ("Monroe Felt Greene Was Assuming Too Much Control," *Sunday Times Magazine*, July 22, 2001).

Certainly, when Monroe married Miller, the dynamics of Monroe's relationship with Greene changed. Greene had stuck his neck out on more than one occasion, not only to save Monroe from herself, but also to protect her best interests. Though married, he was probably in love with her, as most men were, and when Miller started taking control of her life, Greene felt slighted. Before Miller, Greene was a big part of her life, and he wasn't willing or able to take a step back to make room for another man, even if it was her husband. The two men were at loggerheads during the shooting of *The Prince and the Showgirl*, and Monroe was in the middle. It did nothing to help her anxieties that two of the most important men in her life couldn't stand each other. She was the prize, and neither of them wanted to share. She had to choose. Monroe eventually believed that Greene had gotten too possessive and was even making deals behind her back.

Supposedly, Greene had attempted to set up a British subsidiary of Marilyn Monroe Productions and Monroe suspected Greene had shopped for antiques during his stay in London, shipping them home behind her back and billing his purchases to the production company. Certainly, Miller fed much of Monroe's paranoia about Greene. It's debatable as to whether or not Greene's actions were deliberately deceptive, or if his decision to not involve her in the day-to-day dealings of the company was his way of being protective of Monroe's delicate state of mind.

When Greene arrived at the offices of Miller's lawyers to end his contract, everyone in Monroe's camp expected it to cost dearly. Greene asked for the $100,000 that he initially invested. "That's all you want?" asked a perplexed Miller. "Take more," whispered Monroe. "No," said Milton, as his wife Amy Greene recalled. "Let me be the only one in your life never to take more" ("Monroe Felt Greene Was Assuming Too Much Control," *Sunday Times Magazine*, July 22, 2001). Although Marilyn Monroe Productions continued to function as a company, it remained operable for accounting purposes only. *The Prince and the Showgirl* was its only independent production.

Monroe wouldn't be seen in another film for two years. Her star power was questioned and whispers of a "comeback" emerged. But she never really went away. She was always there, perfecting her art at the Actors Studio in New York and playing the real life role of "wife" to Miller.

When the June 1958 *Photoplay* magazine conducted a popularity poll, twenty-five top stars were named. Debbie Reynolds, Natalie Wood, Joanne Woodward and Diane Varsi were a few of the names on the list; Monroe was nowhere to be seen. Most of her fan letters asked the same question, "Why don't you make more pictures?" The public wanted to see her, but toward what would be the end of her career, Monroe insisted on quality over quantity. In order to recoup, she needed a certain amount of rest between productions.

By 1959, Monroe made her long-awaited return to the big screen in the Billy Wilder directed comedy smash hit, *Some Like It Hot*. The production was fraught with problems, most of which were due to Monroe's delicate mental and physical health, her habitual tardiness, her inability to remember her lines, and the close-knit circle of enablers who turned a blind eye to her behavior. Her increasing dependence on doctor-prescribed medication was the root of all of the above issues. However, the final results were nothing short of brilliant: Monroe was not only back, she was better than ever.

Some Like It Hot (1959)

Marilyn Monroe appeared as Sugar Kane Kowalczyk. United Artists. 120 minutes. Working Titles: *Fanfares of Love* and *Not Tonight Josephine! Director:* Billy Wilder. Producers: I.A.L. Diamond, Doane Harrison and Billy Wilder. *Screenplay:* Billy Wilder and I.A.L. Diamond. Story: Robert Thoeren and Michael Logan. *Original Music:* Adolph Deutsch. *Cinematography:* Charles Lang, Jr. *Costume Design:* Orry-Kelly (for Marilyn Monroe) and Bert Henrikson. *Production Dates:* August 4 to November 6, 1958. *Filming Locations:* Hotel del Coronado, Coronado, California. *Release Date:* March 29, 1959. *Genre:* Comedy. Black and White. Salaries: Marilyn Monroe: $100,000 plus ten percent of the gross over $4 million. Tony Curtis and Jack Lemmon: $100,000 plus five percent of the gross over $2 million. Billy Wilder (for producing, directing and writing): $200,000 plus 17.5 percent of the gross above double the negative cost, rising to 20 percent after the film broke even. *Production Cost:* $2.883 million ($500,000 over budget). *Domestic Box Office Receipts:* $7.5 million; $5.25 million (worldwide). *Other Cast:* Tony Curtis (Joe), Jack Lemmon (Jerry), George Raft (Spats Colombo), Pat O'Brien (Detective Mulligan), Joe E. Brown (Osgood Fielding III), Nehemiah Persoff (Little Bonaparte), Joan Shawlee (Sweet Sue), Billy Gray (Sig Poliakoff), George E. Stone (Toothpick Charlie), Dave Barry (Beinstock). *Soundtrack:* "Runnin' Wild" by A.H. Gibbs, Joe Grey and Leo Wood. Performed by Marilyn Monroe. "Sugar Blues" by Clyde McCoy. Performed by Clyde McCoy and His Sugar Blues Orchestra. "Down Among the Sheltering Palms" by A.H. Gibbs, Joe Grey and Leo Wood. "Randolph Street Rag" by Adolph Deutsch. "I Wanna Be Loved by You" by Bert Kalmar, Herbert Wood and Harry Ruby. Performed by Marilyn Monroe. "Park Avenue Fantasy (Stairway to the Stars)" by Matty Malneck and Frank Signorelli. "I'm Through With Love" by Gus Kahn, Matty Malneck and Jay Livingston, Performed by Marilyn Monroe. "Sweet Georgia Brown" by Ben Bernie, Maceo Pinkard and Kenneth Casey. "By the Beautiful Sea" by Harry Carroll and Harold Atteridge. "Some Like It Hot" by Matty Malneck and I.A.L. Diamond. "La Cumparsita" by Gerardo Matos Rodriguez. *Awards:* 1959 Grammy Awards (USA): Best Soundtrack Album, Original Cast, Motion Picture or Television (nominated). 1960 Academy Awards: Best Costume Design (b&w): Orry-Kelly (won); Best Actor in a Leading Role: Jack Lemmon (nominated); Best Art Direction-Set Direction (b&w): Ted Haworth and Edward G. Boyle (nominated); Best Cinematography (b&w): Charles Lang (nominated); Best Director: Billy Wilder (nominated); Best Writing, Screenplay Based on Material from Another Medium: Billy Wilder and I.A.L. Diamond (nominated). 1960 BAFTA Awards: Best Foreign Actor: Jack Lemmon (won); Best Film from any Source: Billy Wilder (nominated). 1960 Directors Guild of America (DGA Award): Outstanding Directorial Achievement in Motion Pictures: Billy Wilder (nominated). 1960 Golden Globes (USA): Best Motion Picture; Comedy (won). Best Motion Picture Actor (Musical/Comedy): Jack Lemmon (won). Best Motion Picture Actress (Musical/Comedy): Marilyn Monroe (won). 1960 Laurel Awards: Top Female Comedy Performance (Golden Laurel Award): Marilyn Monroe (2nd place). Top Male Comedy Performance (Golden Laurel Award): Jack Lemmon (2nd place). Top Comedy (Golden Laurel Award; 3rd place). 1960—Writers Guild of America (WGA Award; screen): Best Written American Comedy: Billy Wilder and I.A.L. Diamond (won). 1989—National Film Preservation Board (USA): National Film Registry (Award). 2000—PGA Awards: PGA Hall of Fame; Motion Pictures: Billy Wilder (won). 2000—The American Film Institute (AFI) honored *Some Like It Hot* as the funniest film of all time. *Some Like It Hot* won an Academy Award for Best Costume Design/Black and White (Orry-Kelly). It also received nominations for Best Actor (Jack Lemmon); Best Art Direction (Ted Haworth and Edward G. Boyle); Best Cinematography/Black and White (Charles Lang); Best Director (Billy Wilder); and Best Screenplay (Billy Wilder and I.A.L. Diamond). *Taglines:* The movie too HOT for words!; Marilyn Monroe and her bosom companions.

"I want the world to know," said director Billy Wilder, "that Marilyn is not only on time, she is three hours early." It was her first day of shooting on *Some Like It Hot* and Monroe wasn't due on set until the afternoon. Wilder's announcement to the press seemed promising. In hindsight, it was the kiss of death. (Thomas, "Billy Wilder Finds Marilyn Reports Fantastically Early").

Wilder and his frequent writing partner I.A.L. Diamond loosely based *Some Like It Hot* on the 1935 French production *Fanfare d'Amour*, written by Robert Thoeren and Michael Logan. A German remake, *Fanfaren der Liebe* (1951), was directed by Kurt Hoffman. The gangster plotline didn't exist in the French or German production, but American censors were far stricter than their foreign counterparts so Wilder and Diamond needed a valid reason for their male leads to cross dress.

Joe (Tony Curtis) and Jerry (Jack Lemmon) witness Chicago's Saint Valentine's Day massacre of 1929. When "Spats" Colombo (George Raft) and his band of gangsters spot them, they escape, but they're marked men. So, they leave town—as women. Dressing in drag, Joe becomes "Josephine" and Jerry becomes "Daphne." Boarding a train to Florida, they join an all-girl band and meet the delectable blonde Sugar (Monroe), the band's singer and ukulele player. She takes a liking to "Josephine" and "Daphne" and never suspects her new girlfriends are anything but girls. "Josephine" and "Daphne" do their darnedest to keep up their feminine masquerade while lusting over Sugar at the same time. Once in Florida, Joe comes up with an idea of donning a secondary disguise and an heir to Shell Oil, Junior, is born. Doing his best impersonation of Cary Grant, Junior knows everything that attracts Sugar and manipulates himself into her life. As believable as "Josephine" was to Sugar, so is Junior. She falls for his charms, but Joe has to keep up the double disguise, which leads to more laughs. In the meantime, Osgood Fielding III (Joe E. Brown), a real-life millionaire, takes a shine to Daphne. The laughs continue when "Daphne" falls for Osgood. Joe has to remind Jerry that he's a man, but tells him to play along until he can woo Sugar with his Junior disguise. When Osgood invites "Daphne" to his yacht, Joe tells Jerry to keep him ashore so he can pretend the yacht is his and romance Sugar. While on board the yacht, Junior tells Sugar that no woman can arouse him, and she sets a plan in motion to prove him wrong. The scenes between Sugar and Junior on board the yacht are intercut with scenes of Osgood and "Daphne" dancing and enjoying their own idea of romance. When Osgood proposes to "Daphne," he accepts! Realizing he's got himself into a pickle, he tells Joe that he'll confess to his true identity after they're married, and he'll benefit financially from Osgood's millions following the annulment.

As if the boys aren't in enough trouble, a conference for Friends of Italian Opera sees the Chicago gangsters arrive at the same Florida hotel. Recognizing Joe and Jerry, they attempt to chase them down. More gangsters are killed and Jerry and Joe once again have front row seats to the slayings. Escaping to the safety of the yacht, Jerry and Joe reveal their true identities to Sugar and Osgood. Joe tells Sugar who he really is, and she tells him she loves him regardless. Jerry as "Daphne" has trouble revealing the truth to Osgood, knowing that he'd be throwing away his chance of becoming the "wife" of a millionaire; he dances around the confession with a number of excuses that do nothing to put a smitten Osgood off going through with the ceremony. When Jerry removes his wig and shouts, "I'm a man!" an unfazed Osgood responds with, "Well, nobody's perfect."

The *Some Like It Hot* script wasn't finished until four days before shooting was finished (*New York Times*, January 24, 1960). In coming up with the now-famous last line spoken by Joe E. Brown, Wilder and Diamond were struggling to find something that would fit. In the

The three "girls" (Tony Curtis, Marilyn Monroe and Jack Lemmon) in a promotional still for Billy Wilder's *Some Like It Hot* (1959).

course of conversation, Diamond said, "Nobody's perfect." Wilder's ears pricked up. He thought the line *could* work and he sent it to the mimeograph department, but only so they'd have something down on paper. It was temporary, until they came up with something better. They never found another line, and they didn't need one. From beginning to end, Wilder and Diamond wrote one of the best scripts in film history, and their words were brought to life by one of the best ensemble casts in film history, making *Some Like It Hot* a proverbial "lightning in a bottle" moment for everyone involved. The Writers Guild of America has ranked *Some Like It Hot* number nine on the list of the ten best screenplays ever written.

There was something in almost every scene that would raise the eyebrows of the censors. With two men dressed as women, both of them beating off male admirers, the taboo topic of homosexuality is explored, and that's just the tip of the iceberg. Monroe as Sugar Kane Kowalczyk climbing into the same train berth as Jack Lemmon, even though he's dressed as "Daphne," the open consumption of alcohol, gambling, racketeering, provocative costumes, a smoldering scene between Monroe and Curtis after he confesses to being impotent and she makes it her mission to arouse him, band member's unplanned pregnancy—the list goes on and on. The script would never have been approved. And that's why Billy Wilder didn't ask for it to be. It was a $2.8 million gamble (coming in $500,000 over-budget due to Monroe's antics) to make a film without script approval, and *then* submit it to the Production Code Administration for their endorsement. Information contained in the *Some Like It Hot* file in the MPAA/PCA Collection at the AMPAS Library, has correspondence dated March 5, 1959, from the Very Reverend Monsignor Thomas F. Little of the National Catholic Legion of Decency. He said *Some Like It Hot* had:

> Screen material elements that are judged to be seriously offensive to Christian and traditional standards of morality and decency... The subject matter of "transvestism" naturally leads to complications; in this film there seemed to us clear inference of homosexuality and lesbianism. The dialogue was not only "double entendre" but outright smut. The offense in costuming was obvious.

The Legion of Decency gave the film a "condemned" rating and did their darnedest to sway Geoffrey Shurlock, head of the PCA, into doing the same thing. In a response letter dated March 18, 1959, he wrote:

> So far there is simply no adverse reaction at all; nothing but praise for it as a hilariously funny movie. I am not suggesting, of course, that there are not dangers connected with a story of this type. But girls dressed as men, and occasionally men dressed as women for proper plot purposes, has been standard theatrical fare as far back as *As You Like It* and *Twelfth Night*... We of course are not defending the two exaggerated costumes worn by the leading lady.

Though many sources claim the film still *wasn't* approved and was subsequently released without the MPAA seal of approval, the MPAA/PCA Collection at the AMPAS Library proves this to be untrue. The *Some Like It Hot* file contains a PCA certificate, dated February 10, 1959. It was released with PCA approval, which it only got by the skin of its teeth. Though it was almost a decade before filmmakers were completely unrestricted in the type of themes and content included in a film, soon after *Some Like It Hot* was released, a classification system was suggested as a future replacement to the archaic Hays Code. (Mondello, "Remembering Hollywood's Hays Code, 40 Years On").

By the mid–1950s the Legion of Decency had an inflated sense of its power in controlling the choices of religious filmgoers and their recreational activities outside the church. Steering Catholics away from films because of its prudish classification system was a thing of the past and little to no attention was paid to the ratings handed down (Curtis and Vieira, *Some Like It Hot, Me, Marilyn and the Movie*, p. 207, p. 208).

Right around the release of *Some Like It Hot,* it was apparent that a Hollywood uprising had begun and the censors were well aware of the about-face. As they gradually loosened the reins on what was and what wasn't acceptable, directors like Wilder, Alfred Hitchcock and Otto Preminger actively rebelled against the system. But many filmmakers (and studios) still adhered to the rigidity of the censorship guidelines, purely out of fear.

Public rejection and theaters flat-out refusing to play a film with controversial content were legitimate concerns, but the risks of stepping outside the box and into a world of unrestricted artistry proved to be a brave and successful move. Films that rebelled against the moral censorship code rules usually gained critical acclaim, box office success and industry awards. Additionally, the American Film Institute honored *Some Like It Hot* as the funniest movie of *all time*.

A. H. Weiler of the *New York Times* (March 30, 1959) wrote:

> As the band's somewhat simple singer-ukulele player, Miss Monroe, whose figure simply cannot be overlooked, contributes more assets than the obvious ones to this madcap romp... [She] proves to be the epitome of a dumb blonde and a talented comedienne... *Some Like It Hot* does cool off considerably now and again, but Mr. Wilder and his carefree clowns keep it crackling and funny most of the time.

Monroe had the right to approve every still picture of her shot on the set of her films, and she took the job seriously. Luke Yankee, son of Monroe's *Bus Stop* (1956) co-star Eileen Heckart, said:

> Mama said she'd never seen anyone go through a photographer's proof sheet with more speed and dexterity than Marilyn Monroe. She would sit in her trailer with a grease pencil and mark 200 photos in about a minute—and she was always right. Marilyn knew the camera better than anyone—and she knew every contour and angle of her own face.

She also had the option to close the set to visitors when she was working. It was a privilege given to few stars. The second day of work on *Some Like It Hot*, it was an open set. When word spread that Monroe was working on the lot, producers, directors and actors from other sets crowded the sound stage to watch. Maureen Stapleton and Montgomery Clift left the set of their film *Lonelyhearts* (1958) to witness a bit of Monroe magic. "I could watch Marilyn all day," said Stapleton. "She's wonderful." Clift initially wandered over "just for a look," but he remained for an hour (Hyams, "Marilyn Is Back!: She's The Same Old Marilyn—Tardy, Temperamental and Terrific").

Though Monroe's Fox contract stated that all of her films be shot in color, *Some Like It Hot* was an independent production for United Artists. Personally, she felt she photographed better in color and she was against shooting the film in black and white. However, the heavy drag makeup that Tony Curtis and Jack Lemmon were wearing throughout much of the film took on a sickly green tint when photographed in color. Wilder showed Monroe the color test shots to prove it. Only then did she agree to film it in black and white. That was just one of many hurdles in what would be a marathon race. Her frequent late arrivals to set and her memory lapses with the simplest of lines were pushing her director and co-stars to the brink of insanity. Jack Lemmon said:

> You might do forty takes with Marilyn, or you might do one, and [Wilder's] gonna print the one that's best for her. I figured that out fairly early and made up my mind, if I let this get to me, it's going to hurt my performance. But it was easier for me, especially in the second half, because I'm off with a rose in my mouth doing tangos with Joe E. Brown, while Tony [Curtis] has those long scenes with Marilyn [Curtis and Paris, p. 161].

Certainly, Curtis was frustrated with Monroe's behavior too, so much so that when a reporter asked him what it was like making love to Marilyn Monroe, he came back with, "It was like kissing Hitler." It was a stupid answer to a stupid question. Yet that comment has taken on a life of its own, circulating for decades and analyzed to death. In just about any interview that Curtis did post–*Some Like it Hot*, he was asked what he meant by *that* comment. It was sarcasm, plain and simple. Later in life he admitted to saying it, but for years, Curtis denied he even said it at all.

In the scene where Monroe knocks on the hotel room door and Lemmon and Curtis throw on their wigs before she enters, her line was, "It's me, Sugar." Instead, she'd come out with lines such as, "Sugar, it's me" and "It's Sugar, me." Thirty takes included these types of variations on the correct three words.

"Where's that bourbon?" was yet another three-word line she had trouble with. After being dumped by Curtis in his second disguise as the Cary Grant–inspired Shell Oil heir Junior, a depressed Sugar stumbles into Curtis and Lemmon's room, looking for some bourbon to ease her heartbreak. "Where's the whiskey?" "Where's the bottle?" "Where's the bon bon?" were all variations on the scripted "Where's that bourbon?" line.

Lemmon said he never saw a director come up with so many different ways to help her play the scene. She'd apologize and walk out the door, shaking her hands and taking deep breaths in an attempt to relax herself. Standing in the room in full makeup, wearing high heels and with their legs and feet aching, Lemmon and Curtis waited and waited for her to get it right. They passed the time by putting a ten-dollar wager on how many takes it'd go to. Lemmon forgot who won the bet but he recalled it was eventually printed somewhere around take 48. Other sources claim it was closer to 59 takes, and only after Wilder taped the correct line into every drawer of the dresser. He originally taped it into the drawer that she was supposed to open, but then she forgot which drawer it was in! In the end, Wilder didn't care which drawer it was in, any one of them would do, so long as she said the correct line and they could all just move on.

As Monroe searches through the dresser drawers, she does say, "Where's that bourbon?" but she has her back to the camera, which leads many to speculate about whether or not she did eventually get it. It's possible Wilder gave up and just had the line dubbed in post-production (www.dvdjournal.com).

For years, Wilder spoke freely about his frustration with Monroe's behavior on set. In fact, his public criticism about her lack of professionalism sparked a telegram war between himself and Monroe's then husband, Arthur Miller. In a February 11, 1959, telegram to Wilder, Miller wrote, in part, "…you are an unjust man and a cruel one." On the same day, Wilder shot back with, "The company pampered her, coddled her and acceded to all her whims. The only one who showed a lack of consideration was Marilyn."

The following day (February 12, 1959), Miller wrote:

> [T]he simple truth is that whatever the circumstances she did her job and did it superbly, while your published remarks create the contrary impression without mitigation. That is what is unfair … it was your job as director not to reject her approach because it was unfamiliar to you, but in the light of the results you could see every day on the screen, you should have realized that her way to working was valid for her, completely serious and not a self-indulgence … that you lost sight of this is your failure and the basic reason for my protest at the injustice not only toward her as my wife, but as the kind of artist one does not come on every day in the week" [Billy Wilder papers].

Wilder responded with his usual sharp wit and a pinch of sarcasm:

I hereby acknowledge that good wife Marilyn is a unique personality and I am the Beast of Belsen. But in the immortal words of Joe E. Brown, "Nobody is perfect" [Curtis and Vieira, *Some Like It Hot, Me, Marilyn and the Movie*, p. 206].

Without doubt, during the filming of *Some Like It Hot,* Monroe was in the midst of a personal crisis. Emotionally and physically, she was the worst she'd ever been. She was also pregnant with Miller's child. Despite her condition, she continued to consume alcohol and take potent drugs to help her sleep and ease her anxiety. It was a recipe for disaster.

Monroe's body shape noticeably changes from scene to scene in *Some Like It Hot.* By the end of the film she's pouring herself into dresses that certainly aren't suited to a woman in her first trimester of pregnancy. There was no plot explanation as to why Sugar was so obviously gaining weight. A few weeks after filming wrapped, at three months along, Monroe suffered her third miscarriage. Miller blamed the stress of the production and Wilder for the loss. Monroe blamed herself. Had she taken her doctor's warnings about the harm the drugs and alcohol would do to her developing child, the outcome might well have been very different, thus steering her own life in a more positive direction. With each miscarriage, her own state of mind worsened. Shortly before discovering she was pregnant, Monroe overdosed on sleeping pills, but she was found in time by her acting coach, Paula Strasberg, and hospitalized for the weekend. Typically, the public relations department released a statement saying that she was suffering from "exhaustion."

When location shooting moved to San Diego for a month, Miller chose not to accompany his wife. The Millers certainly had their share of marital problems, but without her husband by her side, Monroe floundered. And when she floundered she usually took too many pills. Upon hearing of the overdose, Miller rushed to be with her. There was no suicide attempt. The only attempt going on was an attempt at attention. She got her way. Throughout the back-and-forth battles with Wilder, Miller staunchly supported his wife, even when she was so obviously in the wrong.

Wilder eventually apologized for his public and private outbursts toward Monroe and she was encouraged to reciprocate and bury the hatchet, so to speak. Following a recording session for the *Some Like It Hot* soundtrack album, she phoned Wilder's home. However, the apology didn't quite go as planned. Wilder's wife Audrey answered and said that her husband was out. "Well, when you see him, will you give him a message from me?" Monroe asked. "Please tell him to go fuck himself." She paused for a moment, then ended the call with, "And my warmest personal regards to you, Audrey" (Curtis and Barry, p. 162). Audrey Wilder said that her switch in tone was as if a demon had momentarily possessed her. After Wilder heard about the phone call, he philosophically stated, "She is a very great actress. Better Marilyn late than most of the others on time" (Wilder and Horton, p. 25).

Over the years, Wilder's memories and reflections of working with Marilyn Monroe ranged from hatred to admiration. He once said that shooting a scene with Marilyn "was like going to the dentist. During the hours you were there, it was hell. But afterward, it was wonderful" (*Reno Evening Gazette*, June 22, 1970).

When asked if he would ever make a picture with Monroe again, Wilder quipped, "In the United States, I'd hate it. In Paris, it might not be so bad—while we were waiting, we could all take painting lessons on the side" (Wilder and Horton, p. 25). Wilder's glib comments were entertaining in their own right. He said what he felt and he rarely filtered his comments to avoid insulting someone, even if it was Marilyn Monroe. However, following Monroe's death, Wilder confessed that the often nerve-wracking ordeal of coddling a performance out of her was worth every gray hair. "Maybe she was tough to work with. Maybe she wasn't even an actress. But it was worth a week's torment to get those three luminous minutes on the screen" (*Tri City Herald*, August 6, 1962).

Some Like It Hot was a box office sensation. Aside from Monroe's $100,000 salary, her ten percent cut of box office receipts over $4 million made the film the biggest payday of her career. Additionally, many critics raved that it was Monroe's best performance to date. *Variety* (February 24, 1959) wrote:

> It's a wacky, clever, farcical comedy that starts off like a firecracker and keeps on throwing off lively sparks till the very end... Marilyn has never looked better. Her performance as Sugar, the fuzzy blonde who likes saxophone players "and men with glasses," has a deliciously naïve quality. She's a comedienne with that combination of sex appeal and timing that just can't be beat. If, at the time of the filming she was pregnant, and the tight dresses she's asked to wear just don't fit very well, never mind. This gal can take it, and so can the audience.

Throughout her career, Monroe was notorious for her mood swings, her lateness and for struggling with her lines. On all three counts, *Some Like It Hot* was no exception. However, there were also days on the film where she'd get a scene line perfect in one or two takes. In his 1993 autobiography, Tony Curtis wrote that he found it odd that Monroe could have such trouble with one simple line, yet she could pull off a long scene, such as the one in the train berth with Jack Lemmon and the other girls, on the first take. It was hit or miss with her (Curtis and Paris, p. 167).

Obviously, Monroe's ability to work, and work well, was entirely dependent on whether or not she was under the influence of drugs or alcohol. Her increased consumption of both substances were to help her sleep, and they were also used to escape the realities of what her life had become. Losing yet another baby shortly after the filming of *Some Like It Hot* did nothing to ease her depression and insecurities about ever becoming a mother. It was the one role she was desperate to play, but as it happened, motherhood eluded her.

Following the completion of *The Seven Year Itch,* Wilder swore up and down that he would never, *ever* work with her again. No doubt, there was a love-hate relationship between Wilder and Monroe. They both publicly ridiculed each other, but they also appreciated each other's good qualities. They brought out the worst in each other, but they also brought out the best. Their two film collaborations proved it. Following Monroe's death, Wilder explained why he decided to work with her one more time:

> When you got her to the studio on a good day, she was remarkable. She had a quality that no one else ever had on the screen, except Garbo. No one. She was a kind of real image, beyond mere photography. She looked on the screen as if you could reach out and touch her [Curtis and Vieira, *Some Like It Hot, Me, Marilyn and the Movie*, p. 27, p. 28].

Some Like it Hot was the third highest grossing film of 1959.

Let's Make Love (1960)

Marilyn Monroe appeared as Amanda Dell. Twentieth Century–Fox. 119 minutes. *Alternate Titles: The Millionaire* and *The Billionaire*. *Director:* George Cukor. *Producer:* Jerry Wald. *Writer:* Norman Krasna. Additional Material: Hal Kanter. *Original Music:* Lionel Newman. *Cinematography:* Daniel L. Fapp. *Costume Design:* Dorothy Jeakins. *Production Dates:* Early January to March 6, 1960, April 11 to mid–June 1960. *Production Cost:* $3.585 million. Box Office Receipts: $4.5 million. *Release Date:* September 8, 1960. *Genre:* Comedy-Musical-Romance. Color and CinemaScope. *Other Cast:* Yves Montand (Jean-Marc Clement/Alexander Dumas), Tony Randall (Alexander Coffman), Frankie Vaughan (Tony Danton), Wilfrid Hyde-White (George Welch), David Burns (Oliver Burton), Michael David (Dave Kerry), Mara Lynn (Lily Nyles), Dennis King, Jr. (Abe Miller), Joe Besser (Charlie Lamont). *Soundtrack:* "Let's Make Love": Written by Jimmy Van Heusen and Sammy Cahn. Performed by Marilyn Monroe (with chorus) and reprised by Yves Montand. "Hey You with the Crazy Eyes": Written by Jimmy Van Heusen and Sammy Cahn. Performed by Frankie Vaughan. "Specialization": Written by Jimmy Van Heusen and Sammy Cahn. Performed by Marilyn Monroe. "Incurably Romantic": Written by Jimmy Van Heusen and Sammy Cahn. Performed by Frankie Vaughan and Marilyn Monroe, and reprised by Yves Montand and Marilyn Monroe. "Give Me the Simple Life": Written by Rube Bloom and Harry Ruby. "Sing Me the Song That Sells": Written by Jimmy Van Heusen and Sammy Cahn. "Cool It Baby": Written by Carroll Coates. "My Heart Belongs to Daddy": Written by Cole Porter. Performed by Marilyn Monroe. *Awards:* 1961 Academy Awards: Best Music, Scoring of a Musical Picture: Lionel Newman and Earle Hagen (nominated). 1961 BAFTA Awards: Best Film from any Source: George Cukor (nominated); Best Foreign Actor: Yves Montand (nominated). 1961 Golden Globes (USA): Best Motion Picture: Musical (nominated). 1961 Laurel Awards (Golden Laurel):Top Musical (3rd place). 1961 Writers Guild of America (WGA Award, screen): Best Written American Musical: Norman Krasna and Hal Kanter (nominated). *Taglines:* MARILYN MONROE and YVES MONTAND the French entertainment sensation! Doing what they do best in *Let's Make Love*.

When Monroe and her husband Arthur Miller, together with Yves Montand and his Oscar-winning actress wife Simone Signoret, took adjoining rooms at the Beverly Hills Hotel for the imminent shooting of Monroe and Montand's latest feature *Let's Make Love*, Miller and Signoret couldn't have known how literally their spouses would take the film's title.

Montand and Signoret had been married since 1951. Montand was an Italian-born Frenchman, stereotypically European in his views on marriage and infidelity. Monroe and Miller had been married since 1956 and their relationship was on shaky ground. Montand felt it was his right to stray and Monroe was unhappily married to a staid, intellectually brilliant man who adored her, yet at the same time lacked the ability to romance her in the traditional way.

Montand's affairs were tolerated by his wife, and his fling with Monroe was no exception. However, this one wasn't like the others. For Signoret, her husband's affair with Monroe was much harder to bear because they were friends, or so she thought. It was a two-sided betrayal. Likewise, Montand and Miller were also friends. Montand would later express his regret for betraying his friend by bedding his wife. It was a secondary consequence to a fling that would have otherwise been another notch on his belt and nothing more.

The search for the male lead in *Let's Make Love* was a nightmare. Yul Brynner, Cary Grant, Charlton Heston, Rock Hudson and Jimmy Stewart were all approached, and all had different reasons for not signing on. Gregory Peck did sign the contract but after

Title card for *Let's Make Love* (1960).

Miller toiled with the script to bring Monroe's role to the forefront, Peck was no longer interested. While the script changes were said to have displeased Peck, he claimed it was a scheduling problem that caused him to pull out. According to Miller biographer Martin Gottfried:

> [Monroe] pressured Arthur into revising the script and by the time he was through, having added plot motivation and what he called "humor of character" as well as material for her, Gregory Peck withdrew because of the diminished size of *his* role. That was as sensible a sequence of events as there would be during the making of this picture [Gottfried, p. 325].

Producer Jerry Wald revealed that *Let's Make Love* was originally written for Yul Brynner. He was to play a Greek industrialist, but he had real-life wife problems and he backed out. The script was then rewritten for Peck. He approved Monroe as his co-star and when George Cukor was signed to direct the film, everything appeared to be on track. However, when Monroe's part was expanded, Peck was furious. Peck's exit was surprising because his contract was a generous one that included ten percent of the gross, which would have guaranteed him about a million dollars in salary.

Wald pursued Cary Grant for the role, but he had a previous film commitment. Charlton Heston was next in line, but he demanded a $250,000 guarantee against 7.5 percent of the profits. Monroe was getting $100,000 for her part, so Heston was nixed too. Monroe suggested Rock Hudson, and Wald agreed that he'd be a good fit though it meant borrowing him from Universal-International. While Hudson was willing to do the film, his studio wasn't willing to let him.

Jimmy Stewart was committed to the Air Force reserve and was unavailable. With everyone else signed up, the production was losing $15,000 a day while the search for the male lead continued. Yves Montand was their saving grace (*The Press-Courier,* August 12, 1960). While his agents insisted on a holdout until his salary was equal to Monroe's, his eventual $100,000 fee was a huge salary for an unknown foreign actor. Both Miller and Monroe felt that Montand could pull off the lead role. He barely spoke English, but he fit the role of a French billionaire perfectly. Montand was charming, good-looking, and he could sing and dance. The language barrier was a minor hiccup, or so they thought at the time. Montand got the part and he took lessons in English before shooting began, but even he admitted he failed to completely trust his acting coach and ended up memorizing his lines rather than thoroughly learning the English language. Several reviews made reference to Montand's heavy French accent being so hard to understand that his humor failed to come through.

The film as a whole got mixed reviews, mostly leaning towards the positive, and Monroe's performance as the Cinderella-like actress who captures the heart of the billionaire was generally praised, save for the *New York Times* (September 9, 1960):

> [N]ot much is happening with a rather untidy Miss Monroe. She is fumbling with things on the sidelines, batting her eyes and sighing songs. The old Monroe dynamism is lacking in the things she is given to do by the cliché-clogged script…

The Pittsburgh Press (August 29, 1960) praised Monroe's performance, albeit in a backhanded way:

> It is Marilyn's show and the others are merely supporting players. That bland, childish expression on her face, her tiny gestures and wee intakes of breath when rhapsodizing over trifles, her general air of complete innocence—all add up to a portrayal that's amusing. Her director George Cukor deserves a citation.

The Southeast Missourian (March 19, 1961) gave the film and its stars a glowing review. Under the headline "Monroe & Montand: Double Dynamite!" it read in part:

> Termed by preview audiences as hotter than *Some Like It Hot,* the internationally renowned MM turns in the best performance of her star-studded career. Yves Montand, the toast of Paree and acclaimed as France's greatest entertainment export, makes his first American movie appearance and is a shoo-in for dozens more offers. Undoubtedly *Let's Make Love* is the entertainment treat of the year. The biggest and best cast, the funniest story yet, music that can't be beat … in short, a winner all the way.

If Monroe's screen time was enhanced, obviously the critics' reviews prove that it only served to improve the overall film. Her acting, singing and dancing are naturally captivating, and though some contemporary articles mention her excess weight in a multitude of costumes and outfits, she looks stunning throughout. A hint of a slight tummy bulge was nothing unusual for Monroe, especially in later years, and while her rounded tummy is on display in certain scenes here, she is far from heavy and still slighter in frame than she appeared in the latter part of *Some Like It Hot.*

Montand holds his own as the playboy billionaire Jean-Marc Clement. His performance is witty and charming, and despite his accent sometimes being a little hard on the ears, certainly his role is equal to hers. In viewing the completed film, it's somewhat baffling to concur Gregory Peck's opinion that his role in the revised script was of lesser importance.

Monroe's Amanda is a woman eerily similar to herself, which is no doubt due to Arthur Miller's script revisions. Miller wrote Monroe's *Let's Make Love* character (as he would also do on *The Misfits*), but he seemed to have a hard time differentiating between his wife's off-screen personality and the fictional characters she was portraying. When it came to his wife, Miller walked a fine line between "reel-ism" and realism. As a result, Amanda and Roslyn (*The Misfits*) had an undeniable vulnerability and ease about them because in both instances, Monroe is essentially playing herself.

Amanda is an actress-singer-dancer starring in a financially shaky off–Broadway production. She failed to finish high school, but she's an avid student and lover of history and she's determined to better herself. When she's not rehearsing, she's attending night school to earn her high school diploma. In between rehearsals, she knits, though not very well, to keep her hands busy. She's sexy yet innocent.

A chance meeting between Amanda and billionaire Jean-Marc Clement (Montand) happens when he and his publicity director Alexander Coffman (Tony Randall) attend the rehearsals of the off–Broadway play. After learning that the play depicts him and his womanizing ways in an unfavorable manner, Clement decides to see the imminent public humiliation for himself. In a dimly lit theater, he gets more than he bargained for when the beautiful Amanda slides down a pole, scantily clad in sheer black pantyhose and a knitted sweater. He's mesmerized as she suggestively coos, "My name is—Lolita ... and ... ahhhh...I'm not supposed to ... play—with boys!" before beginning her sexy "My Heart Belongs to Daddy" song-and-dance routine.

The role of Clement has yet to be cast, so when he's mistaken for one of the actors who are there to try out for the role, he reluctantly plays along. He sees the opportunity as an interesting experiment and a chance to get closer to Amanda.

Clement easily gets the part as himself. Taking the name Alexander Dumas, he proceeds to fumble his way through song-and-dance numbers, all the while competing for Amanda's attention and affection with the likes of the smooth, good-looking and much younger Tony Danton (Frankie Vaughan).

As a playboy billionaire, for years Clement has wined and dined a multitude of women with his charm and his money. For the first time in his life, he's truly in love—and for the first time in his life, he has to really work to get the girl. Though he's tempted to reveal his true identity to win Amanda's heart, he stoically keeps up the farce, pretending to be the low-income actor who is merely playing the part of the rich man, in the hope that Amanda will love him for himself first, before his money. After declaring his love for her, Clement reveals his identity to Amanda but she runs away, spooked into thinking he's gone crazy. The last part of the film is dedicated to making her believe that he is the real Jean-Marc Clement, and of course he gets the girl. After a passionate final scene kiss in the elevator of Clement's New York building, Amanda ponders whether or not she still needs to get her high school diploma.

As usual, Monroe shines when she's on the screen. Montand is believable as the debonair, billionaire playboy and Wilfrid Hyde-White is brilliant as Clement's dry-witted mentor, George. Veteran comic Joe Besser has a small role as a joke writer and Milton Berle, Bing

Crosby and Gene Kelly make cleverly scripted cameo appearances as themselves. All three are in on the plan to woo Amanda, and they're beckoned for and paid handsomely by Clement to privately tutor him in being funny and to learn to sing and dance. Clement is a willing but inherently bad student, which only serves to set their screen time up for a very amusing subplot, more so given that Montand was a multi-talented showman in real life and a sellout performer in his native France.

Montand's wife, French actress Simone Signoret, gave a dignified response to the swirling rumors that Monroe was having an affair with her husband:

> If Marilyn is in love with my husband it proves she has good taste, for I am in love with him too. Marilyn Monroe is a warm, delightful person. I lived with her for three months [*New York Journal-American*, November 14, 1960].

By all reports Montand's affair with Monroe was brief; perhaps she felt it was something more than a fling, but no matter what happened between them, he would always return to his wife, as all good European husbands do. After filming was completed, he angered Monroe by publicly declaring that she had "a schoolgirl crush" on him. Later he claimed that he had been misquoted (*Spokane Daily Chronicle*, November 14, 1960).

By the end of July 1987, Montand was back at the Beverly Hills Hotel to promote his latest film, *Jean de Florette*. In an interview he covered a broad range of topics, including an insight into what went on during the filming of *Let's Make Love*. Almost three decades had passed and both his wife and his lover were dead. Although he was a little more forthcoming than he had been in times past, he was still reserved about his fling with Monroe. Describing it as a "secret and a beautiful thing," he elaborated a little further, but stopped short of revealing details of their romance. He also spoke of his fear of saying yes to a role that required him to speak English, a language that he didn't know. It seems that his insecurities and Monroe's insecurities collided as one and when their respective partners left town due to a Screen Actors Guild strike (March 7 to April 11, 1960), they found solace in each other. Montand said:

> I had to learn all of my lines by heart. I had no connection to my own language. [Monroe] was so afraid of shooting, every moment afraid… We helped each other… I couldn't speak a word of English, so I stay in my rich bungalow which looks like a gold jail and I don't go outside because I feel like an imbecile. And she was here and we worked together, etc., etc., etc., but I don't want to talk about that [*The Evening News*, July 24, 1987].

In the film's pressbook, Montand gives his opinion of Monroe and her abilities as an actress:

> Marilyn is aware that her technique is not as experienced or as perfect as some. For this reason she is never satisfied with her work, but persists in doing it over and over until she is fairly content that she has given the best that is in her. To anyone who has worked as long in the show business as I have, this may be a trifle wearing at times. But because it is for the good of the picture, one cannot carp at such… Marilyn is a generous player, she gives all the time. If her skill is in any way limited, her heart is always right.

By early February of 1960, the usual production cracks were beginning to show. Monroe was late, or sick, and production was held up waiting for her to arrive to set or be well enough to work. *The Sun* (February 18, 1960) reported that two sets of actors were told to stand by for duty. If Monroe was present and available to work, her scenes were shot; if she was absent, scenes without her were filmed. Tony Randall was said to have reported for work day after day without performing at all. One day he took an extended nap and on another day his first scene wasn't shot until 5 p.m.

A couple of months later, Randall spoke out about the persistent rumors surrounding Monroe's nervous state and constant tardiness. When asked by reporter Richard Gehman if she was "difficult," Randall shook his head and said:

> I haven't found her that way. She was sick when the picture started—flu. A doctor gave her a prescription that caused some kind of allergic condition; a kind of nerve paralysis…[then] she came back to work, and nobody works harder. She's in here at six o'clock—well, seven, sometimes all set to go, day in and day out [Gehman, "The Big M," *The Milwaukee Sentinel*, May 1, 1960].

Less than two years following Monroe's death, Randall spoke out about her insecurities, not just as an actress but as a person. His words were sympathetic:

> Often in a scene, she'd absolutely panic, break into a cold sweat, forget her lines right in the middle of a sentence and run off in tears. It wasn't temperament, it wasn't anything but plain ordinary fear, a complete lack of confidence, an inability to convince herself that she had any talent at all. Marilyn could hardly look at you in the eye, it was as if she was afraid to because she thought you felt she was something of a freak and that you were so much better than she was. It destroyed the poor girl [*Pittsburgh-Post Gazette*, March 31, 1964].

Decades later, Randall's memories had soured: All he remembered was that Monroe was late to set and he was tired of waiting for her to be ready. On March 11, 2000, he said, "Marilyn Monroe was no fun to work with. She would report to work around 5:00 in the evening. You've been in makeup since 8:30 in the morning waiting for her. That ceases to be amusing after about a week" (www.houstontheatre.com).

When Associated Press staff writer Bob Thomas, asked Monroe why there had been so many delays in filming, she said:

> Oh, it hasn't been going so badly. We started with Mr. Gregory Peck, but then Mr. Peck made other arrangements. So we had to start all over again with Yves Montand. I was a little sick in the early part of the picture, but I've been all right lately. Then there was the strike… We were so lucky to get Mr. Montand, who is a brilliant actor, a great singer, and fine dancer and very, very romantic. And I am so lucky to be with George Cukor, a brilliant director I've always wanted to work with.

While *Let's Make Love* was originally slated for an 83-day shooting schedule, from pre-production to its conclusion it took six months to complete. The delays weren't all Monroe's fault. The merry-go-round of finding an available (and Monroe-approved) male lead, and the lengthy writers' and actors' strike, contributed to the overtime. Time is money, especially on a film set, and *Let's Make Love* was no exception. As filming was delayed, then restarted, the production ran into a scheduling conflict with a Japanese concert date that Montand was contractually obligated to fill. The studio couldn't let him go, and the studio paid them his fee in full: $120,000. Director George Cukor said that in return for the payoff, Montand had to commit to making another film in 1963. Frankie Vaughan was equally unfortunate. While other actors got weekly salaries, the delays meant additional money, but Vaughan was working for a flat fee. As filming dragged on and on, he was turning down engagements in England because he was committed for the run of the film. Unlike Montand, he hadn't booked his services in advance so the studio wasn't obligated to pay off his unattended gigs.

While Randall and Wilfrid Hyde-White were frustrated with the seemingly endless production, they managed to keep a sense of humor about the situation. In his "Hollywood" column (*Meridien-Journal,* May 26, 1960), Associated Press staff writer Bob Thomas wrote of a conversation they had while driving toward the *Let's Make Love* set one day.

> RANDALL (worriedly): Oh dear, I have one line today, I think. Something like, "What a life!"
> HYDE-WHITE (soothingly): Cheer up, old boy. If you need help with it, call me.
> RANDALL: Do you have any lines today?
> HYDE-WHITE: Heavens, no. I haven't had a line in a fortnight.

Hyde-White was one of the few co-stars throughout the course of Monroe's career who was thankful to her for holding up production. On the last day of shooting, he kissed Monroe on the cheek and said, "Thank you, my dear, for the longest and most remunerative contract I've ever had" (Buskin, *Blonde Heat: The Sizzling Screen Career of Marilyn Monroe*, p. 229)

Even this late into Monroe's career, and even with so many successful films under her belt, her insecurities ran deep. During one scene, Monroe's character is sitting off to one side and doing homework for a night school course she is taking. She is making notations in a book. After the scene was shot, Monroe went back to her dressing room. She left the notebook where she had been sitting and someone in the cast looked across at the open page. She was making real notes and they were all to herself.

What am I afraid of?

Why am I so afraid?

Do I think I can act?

I know I can act, but I am afraid.

I am afraid and I should not be and I must not be (Gehman, "The Big M," *The Milwaukee Sentinel*, May 1, 1960).

Cukor said that he and Monroe came to an agreement that she should only work when she felt she was ready to begin. But he still became frustrated at shooting a film by Monroe's clock. And producer Jerry Wald let loose with the understatement of the decade when he said:

> [Monroe] is not punctual. But I'm not sad about it. I can get a dozen beautiful blondes who will show up in makeup at 4 a.m. promptly each morning. But they are not Marilyn Monroe. Marilyn doesn't come cheap but she's nice to have around when the grosses are counted [*Gadsden Times*, July 17, 1960].

It was unfavorably reviewed upon its original release but when viewed today, *Let's Make Love* is a charmingly natural film with ease of flow and some white-hot song-and-dance numbers. Monroe's fling with Montand buoyed their onscreen chemistry, but the repercussions from their adulterous indiscretions continued long after filming had stopped. Although Montand had strayed from his marriage before, his affair with Monroe deeply affected Signoret. And Monroe felt intense guilt over betraying the trust of her friend. While Signoret was devastated, embarrassed and emotionally bruised from the infidelity, following Monroe's death she said, "[Monroe] will never know how much I didn't hate her" (Burnside, "Monroe, Miller, Montand, Signoret: When Golden Couples Meet," *The Independent,* February 22, 2011).

Montand and Signoret's marriage was anything but ideal; however, it lasted for over three decades, until Signoret's death on September 30, 1985. She was 64 years old. Yves Montand died on November 9, 1991. He was 70 years old.

The Misfits
(1961)

Marilyn Monroe appeared as Roslyn Taber. Seven Arts Productions and United Artists. 124 minutes. *Director:* John Huston. *Producer:* Frank E. Taylor. *Writer:* Arthur Miller. *Original Music:* Alex North. *Cinematography:* Russell Metty. *Costume Design:* Jean Louis (for Marilyn Monroe). *Production Dates:* July 18 to November 4, 1960. *Filming Locations:* Dayton, Nevada (rodeo scenes), Los Angeles, California, Mapes Casino, Reno, Nevada, Misfits Flat, Stagecoach, Nevada, (horse-roping scenes), Pyramid Lake, Pyramid Lake Indian Reservation, Nevada, Quail Canyon, Reno, Nevada. Production Costs: $4 million. *Domestic Box Office Receipts:* $4.1 million. Marilyn Monroe's salary: $300,000, plus ten percent of the film's profits. *Release Date:* January 31, 1961 (world premiere in Reno, Nevada). *Other Cast:* Clark Gable (Gay Langland), Montgomery Clift (Perce Howland), Thelma Ritter (Isabelle Steers), Eli Wallach (Guido), James Barton (Fletcher's Grandfather), Kevin McCarthy (Raymond Taber), Estelle Winwood (Church Lady). *Awards:* 1961 Golden Globe Award (presented March 5, 1962): "World Film Favorite,": Marilyn Monroe (won). Directors Guild of America (DGA Award): Outstanding Directorial Achievement in Motion Pictures: John Huston (nominated). 1993—Genesis Awards: Feature Film—Classic (won). *Taglines:* It shouts and sings with life … explodes with love!'; "SMASHING" thru the Excitement Barrier!

It was long, arduous, full of conflict and filmed in such stifling temperatures that, for many involved, it really did feel like hell. When *The Misfits* finished shooting, Clark Gable reportedly said, "Christ, I'm glad this picture's finished. [Monroe] damn near gave me a heart attack" (Riese and Hitchens, *The Unabridged Marilyn: Her Life from A to Z*, p. 168). Little did he realize how eerily prophetic those words were.

How many of the problems associated with this seemingly cursed production were the fault of Marilyn Monroe? Quite a few. However, it's unfair to blame the shocking and unexpected death of "The King of Hollywood" on her too. Though certainly, at the time, *that* was the implication. Monroe could be blamed for many things, but not that one.

In 1956, Arthur Miller traveled to Nevada to obtain a divorce from his wife, Mary. While there, he wrote about the cowboys (and the women) in the area, the hardened mustangers who made a living by rounding up the desert's wild horses. Many of Nevada's residents were there temporarily, obtaining quickie divorces and going back to their lives elsewhere, just as Miller was doing. Others made Nevada a permanent home because they didn't fit into conventional living any place else. And so Miller's short story, aptly titled "The Misfits," was written. It was published in *Esquire* magazine in 1957 and Miller would later adapt it into a screenplay (his first) of the same name. As a love letter to his wife, he would create one of the best characters of her career. That said, her name was merely changed for the sake of the story. Roslyn *was* Marilyn. The role was written for her, but it also *was* her.

Miller's cousin, Morton Miller, once recalled seeing Monroe's reaction to the body of a dog on the side of the road. The animal had obviously been hit by a car. It affected her deeply. Shutting her eyes, covering her face with her hands, she shrieked. She was, Miller conceded, "over the top about animals, children, old people. She could be fierce about protecting them. She would get absolutely outraged that somebody had killed a fish. Although she ate fish, she didn't want to see them murdered" (Bigsby, p. 593). Monroe also found gardening therapeutic. In a December 1960 interview with Jon Whitcomb of *Cosmopolitan* magazine she said:

The Misfits (1961)

The Misfits (1961) was fraught with problems from start to finish. Montgomery Clift and Monroe (pictured here) had their full shares of inner demons, but Clift managed to rise above his issues. As a result, he pulled off one of the best performances of his career. Both on and off the set, Monroe's personal problems affected the film in a myriad of ways. It was a miracle the film was completed at all. Drawing on her own personal problems, Monroe's performance as Roslyn is arguably one of the rawest and realest versions of her true self ever put on film.

> I try to grow things. Flowers and vegetables both. I have a green thumb. I can even plant things without roots. I just transplant them and they grow. I planted some seeds, nasturtiums, I think, when they come up, you're supposed to thin them out. What a pity, I thought, to throw out these little growing things, so I pulled them up and transplanted them very carefully; they had been so close together some didn't even have roots. Arthur [Miller] said, "That's impossible, they can't live." But, all of them did. And it says on the cover of the seed packages that you can't transplant them!

Miller never denied the similarities between Roslyn and his wife, saying, "It really didn't start out that way when I was writing the screenplay, but [Monroe] has such a strong personality I just couldn't escape it" (Johnson, "Hollywood Today," *Ocala Star-Banner*).

In 1960, Miller would return to Nevada, with Monroe, for the filming of *The Misfits*. By this time, the honeymoon was well and truly over. Monroe and Miller were barely talking and on the verge of divorce. Monroe was a pill-popping time bomb and the production was plagued with one problem after another.

Ten years after Monroe's death, in an interview with Earl Wilson for a Cleveland, Ohio, newspaper, the *Plain Dealer* (August 6, 1972), John Huston reflected on Marilyn Monroe's acting abilities. Like others before him, he seemed astonished at her depth of talent and her ability to get a printable scene, especially because he witnessed her mood swings, dysfunction and self-destruction first hand. Professionally speaking, Huston was in a better position than most to see the heartbreaking disintegration of life and talent: He had directed Monroe in the very beginning of her career. But the fresh-faced starlet who burst onto the world's stage in *The Asphalt Jungle* was about to star in her last completed film, again directed by Huston. On location in the middle of the Nevada desert, now in her mid-thirties, Monroe was a drug-addled icon with a reputation of being unreliable and unstable. Before the stresses of filming had even begun, she was on the verge of another divorce, teetering on the edge of a nervous breakdown and mixing pills and alcohol in potentially lethal doses. Huston said:

> Marilyn came up with things from some mysterious, inexplicable source ... she would reach down and discover something in some cavern within herself that was strange and extraordinary and kind of universal ... as an actress, she was about 12 years old, but she always astonished me at what she could do.

In *The Misfits*, Monroe's Roslyn is an emotionally delicate, newly divorced beauty who vies for the love and friendship of three men, Gay Langland (Clark Gable), Perce Howland (Montgomery Clift) and Guido (Eli Wallach). She falls in love with Gay but is conflicted in her feelings for him and the other two men after discovering they hunt wild horses to sell for slaughter. As the audience, we follow these complicated characters, all of them broken in their own way, all of them afraid to trust, yet all of them desperate to cling to each other and find their own place in the world, both alone and together.

The Misfits came in at half a million dollars over the estimated budget and forty days over schedule. Its total cost of around $4 million was an extraordinary amount at the time. Gable's contract assured him $750,000, plus $48,000 a week overtime and ten percent of the gross. He was always on time and ready to go, and despite his own problems, Montgomery Clift knew his lines inside out. Monroe's tardiness, including a two-week hospital stay following a complete breakdown, along with director John Huston's increasing gambling debt, contributed to the entire production being temporarily shut down. The out-of-control schedule bolstered Gable's salary to one million dollars, *before* a percentage of the gross. With a deal like that, Gable had every reason to thank Monroe for her lateness, not complain about it.

At the time, it was an unprecedented amount of money for an actor to earn on a single film, but at fifty-nine years old, Gable was close to retiring from pictures. Unlike many of his peers, whose poor film roles or lack of box-office appeal towards the tail end of their careers saw their star power fizzle, Gable was determined to end his illustrious Hollywood run on a high note both creatively and financially.

The ensemble cast of Gable, Monroe, Wallach, Clift, Thelma Ritter and Kevin McCarthy made *The Misfits* the most expensive black and white film to date, and that was before the delays. As it turned out, the film would be Gable's swan song. It would also be Marilyn Monroe's last film, or last *completed* film, since the ill-fated *Something's Got to Give* (1962) was never finished due to her death.

Gable's character challenges his advancing age by seeking new challenges. Clift's character is a lonely thrill seeker, Wallach is a widowed pilot with confidence issues. Ritter is a likable divorcée whose only flowers come from her ex-husband, on the anniversary of their divorce. Monroe is a beautiful divorcée, insecure and disillusioned with life. No matter how far she goes down life's road, she always ends back up at the beginning, lost and alone.

Huston knew Monroe's reputation for being late to set. According to his memoirs, he tried accommodating her from the very beginning. He changed the daily call to set from 9 a.m. to 10 a.m.. It made no difference at all. Huston wrote that Monroe would show up later and later, sometimes not appearing until three or four in the afternoon. In his autobiography *The Good, the Bad, and Me: In My Anecdotage*, Eli Wallach wrote that Gable "had one ironbound clause in his contract—at 5 p.m. no matter where he was in a scene, he'd leave the set, waving a polite good-bye as he drove away" (Wallach, p. 223).

So Huston's leading man stopped work at five sharp (though he started as early as required) and his leading lady very often showed up an hour or two before Gable was scheduled to leave for the day. Considering many of their scenes were together, it gave little time to get what he needed to on film. And because Monroe was in most of the scenes, everyone had to wait for her.

In one scene where Wallach was supposed to stand in front of Monroe's character's house and call up to her, he played the scene to an empty window because she was still yet to arrive on set. Huston shot Monroe's response when she got to set and everything was assembled in the editing room. That said, Wallach's solo window scene was an exception; few scenes could be shot around her so Monroe's delays were everyone's delays. And she even managed to delay the film *before* any shooting began.

In order to avoid the scorching Nevada heat, Huston wanted to start shooting in April. However, Monroe was still working on *Let's Make Love*. The film had already run months over schedule and thousands over budget. The 33-day Screen Actors Guild strike against the major film studios, Fox included, had further delayed its production, and the negative publicity from Monroe's affair with her leading man Yves Montand and his subsequent "love her and leave her" approach to their controversial and highly publicized affair, had given her already shaky confidence a severe beating.

Once again she felt used, and in turn she used potent tranquilizers to make it all go away. There was nothing discreet about their romance. The papers were all over it. Of course, Montand initially blew it off as nothing. Monroe was mortified, not only because of his blasé attitude, but also because her public reputation was at stake. She was a married woman. He was a married man. They had both betrayed spouses, and friends. Arthur Miller and Simone Signoret were the innocent victims and they played the roles of the cheated spouses with their heads held high. Their united dignity only served to make Monroe and Montand look worse.

By the time *Let's Make Love* was finished, *The Misfits* was already way behind schedule. Monroe was incapable of going from one film to the other without sufficient rest and recuperation in between, so by the time she was ready to go back to work, *The Misfits* had a start date of July 18. It was now the middle of summer. The northern Nevada desert heat was at its worst and with shooting days well over 100 degrees, it was exactly the situation Huston set out to avoid.

As usual, Paula Strasberg was Monroe's constant shadow, and she even dressed as such: an all-black outfit, complete with black hat and black parasol and a large black purse. She and Monroe would converse about how to play a scene as if no one else was around, or knew what they were doing, Huston included. Over the years Strasberg had been given a number of nicknames from various cast and crew members, and not just the usual derogatory ones because of her overbearing nature. Her mourning-like clothing choices gave her the nicknames "The Black Bat," "The Lady in Black" and "The Spider," and on *The Misfits* she was given the moniker "Black Bart." Unlike most directors who butted heads with Strasberg, Huston worked her to his advantage. He was the director, the captain of the ship, but he let Strasberg think she was co-captain, and that was where previous directors went wrong. Huston's tactics empowered Strasberg and calmed Monroe. Though he hated Strasberg as much as anyone else, by pretending to value her presence on set, it was the difference between getting Monroe to perform and getting the film completed. The alternative was to pack up and go home with an incomplete mess. The latter wasn't an option, but it was a very real possibility if the Strasberg-Monroe collaborative demands weren't met. Huston played the game to his advantage while Strasberg and Monroe felt they were controlling the film. It was a win-win situation.

While Monroe felt she needed Strasberg on set with her at all times, it seems that Strasberg's presence made her second-guess and doubt her performance more than ever. Monroe looked past Huston and gave the usual side glance to Strasberg for approval following a take. If she or Monroe felt another one was needed, Huston didn't argue, he duly obliged. Wallach said, "What Paula and Marilyn seemed not to know was that Huston had final say in the editing" (Wallach, p. 221).

Huston was all praise for Gable because he was a complete professional and a pleasure to be around. He never uttered a word of complaint against Monroe, no matter how late she showed up to set. Like Huston, Gable knew how to work her insecurities in order to get the best out of her. She idolized him and he knew that too. Wallach wrote, "Whenever she would finally arrive on set, Gable would hug her and compliment her on the work she had done in earlier scenes with him. Marilyn told me that she was happiest working with him" (Wallach, p. 225).

Wallach recalled one morning when Monroe was only a few hours late, which was early for her. She ran up and threw her arms around Gable and said, "Oh, forgive me. I'm so sorry I'm late." Gable smiled and said, "No hurry, honey" (Wallach, p. 222). Gable's pandering put Monroe in a good mood, and when she was in a good mood, it helped everyone.

During production, Monroe was taking pills to sleep, pills to wake up, pills to calm down. She'd take 300 mg of Nembutal in the evening, three times the normal dose, and she would poke holes in the capsules with a pin to make them work faster. She was a full-blown addict. Sometimes she was unable to function at all, at other times she was surprisingly functional. Despite appearing vacant and troubled, when it came time for her to shoot a scene, it was as if a switch was thrown. She drew upon her own demons and gave the perfect performance that was needed for her character. There were still times when she forgot simple lines and would suddenly stop mid-scene because she "lost her motivation," but when it all came together *The Misfits* was as raw and as real as Monroe had ever been on screen. Every inch of Hollywood manufacturing was stripped away. She spoke in her own voice, ditched the darkened mole on her left cheek and abandoned the "little girl lost" persona.

Huston felt that Roslyn was a personal portrait of Marilyn, by Miller. "It's all truth—not fact—but truth," he said (Johnson, Erskine, "*Misfits* Stresses More Mood Than Thought"). And that was the film's overall vibe: It was all about mood, and truth, and the profound flaws in each of the characters involved in the story, flaws that very much mirrored their real-life selves.

Personally, Monroe was on the brink of collapse, but professionally, she had evolved into what she had strived so hard to be: a serious actress. Certainly, being the wife of one of America's greatest playwrights helped, yet there would be no happy ending, on any level. Following filming, Monroe's marriage to Miller would end … and her life would end soon after. At that point in time, despite what she had achieved, Monroe was far too broken to ever realize what she had become, or what she would become in the decades to follow. Huston said:

> I was very disturbed by her actions and appearance … when she was herself, though, she could be marvelously effective… She would go deep down within herself and find it and bring it up into consciousness. But maybe that's what all truly good acting consists of. It was profoundly sad to see what was happening to her… [Huston, p. 287].

Huston was obviously very concerned for his film, *and* for his fragile leading lady. It was no secret that Monroe's marriage was crumbling; she and Miller were living in separate hotels while on location and she was acrimonious to him on set. Miller was still legally her husband and in a last-ditch effort to get Monroe some help, Huston pleaded with him to get her off the drugs, warning him that if he didn't, "she'll be in an institution in two or three years—or dead!" His words were prophetic, but Huston's lecture was nothing that Miller didn't know himself. And, with their marriage all but over, Miller was, as Huston described it, "at the end of his rope" (Huston, p. 288).

As Monroe's drug intake increased, her moods became more and more irrational. It wasn't beyond her to be outright vindictive and have spontaneous outbursts of anger, but that side of her wasn't her true self. Still, it was this Jekyll and Hyde drug-induced state that everyone on the production was forced to deal with. When she did come to set, it was anyone's guess as to how she would act and react, or if she was even capable of either.

Huston witnessed Miller's humiliation on more than one occasion, not only by his wife but also by her entourage of enablers, including Strasberg, who bullied him to gain favors with her. It was a pack mentality, led by Monroe, the woman he adored and wrote *The Misfits* for. It was heartbreaking to watch, not just the breakdown of a marriage, but the breakdown of an actress who seemed beyond help, or beyond wanting help. Monroe's behavior towards Miller was little thanks for his belief in her, not only as his wife, but as a serious actress. Without doubt, the role of Roslyn Taber was one of the meatiest characters of Monroe's career, and for that, she had Miller to thank.

Miller was steely-faced at the best of times. He's often been accurately described as Lincoln-esque in his appearance and character. Even when he was supposedly happy, Miller gave off a forced smirk that looked difficult to muster. Miller's demeanor never changed, not even with the torment of his humiliation.

The final nail in the coffin, so to speak, was after a long day of shooting in the stifling desert heat. It was evening and Huston was about to drive to his hotel. The accommodation was miles from the set. As Houston looked back, he saw Miller, standing alone. Huston was the last ride out of there. Everyone else was gone. The place was deserted. Monroe and her entourage had purposefully ditched him and if Huston hadn't spotted Miller when he did, he would have been stranded out there all night.

While Huston was sympathetic to Monroe's problems, the side of her that came out when the drugs took hold was *not* her, and it wasn't pretty. She was in the midst of a serious, long-term addiction and she needed help. Everyone knew it, and many had tried to help her. She said and did things that made it harder to discount her actions as that of a sick person; instead she evoked the persona of a cold-hearted, selfish, irrational bitch. Certainly Miller had his own personality faults. As a writer, all of his feelings flowed through his pen. As a man, and the husband of a woman who needed constant reassurances, he was incapable of satisfying her needs.

Huston felt for him and the position he was in. Working with Monroe was a dose of Miller's every day life. It was anything but easy. Huston said, "[M]y sympathies were more and more with him" (Huston, p. 287).

Huston wasn't in the best of health either. Decades of smoking had caused emphysema, and like everyone else he found the intense heat intolerable. He often fell asleep during takes, mainly because he was up all night drinking and gambling. Huston was on location in a gambling mecca and he took full advantage of the situation. A night wouldn't go by without him visiting Reno's casinos, usually Harrah's Club or the Maples Hotel, and he often lost more than he won. In the film, Huston has a cameo as a gambler in a blackjack scene. For authenticity purposes, he insisted on using his own money to place actual bets in the scene. In reality, he lost thousands during the course of the production—upwards of $50,000. While United Artists gave the casinos an advanced credit for the entire cast and crew, Huston managed to run way over the stipend with his own bets. When the president of United Artists, Max Youngstein, arrived to inform Huston that funds for *The Misfits* had all but dried up, production ceased. Huston made sure the blame was laid on Monroe's shoulders, not his. Huston eventually took a $25,000 advance on his next film, *Freud*, to cover his debts. Towards the end of August, producer Frank Taylor informed the cast and crew that Monroe had been hospitalized (she flew back to Los Angeles on August 27) for an emotional breakdown and production would be shut down until she was well enough to return. While Monroe *was* certainly in dire need of medical intervention, Huston used her condition to mask the production's financial failings, *his* failings. Monroe was, once again, the vulnerable target to deflect attention from the real issue at hand.

After her breakdown and subsequent hiatus from the film, a quick detox of sorts, Huston visited Monroe in the hospital. Her brightened demeanor gave him hope. She was enthusiastic, lucid, and apologetic for her behavior, and more importantly, she was aware of the effects the drugs had on her emotional and physical being. On her return to Reno she was met with open arms, and the cast and crew were cautiously optimistic that the hospital stay had worked wonders. With too many dollars and too much time already lost, there was a film to finish—and fast. A couple of days of a newly revived Marilyn Monroe brought hope. Then the cycle of doom began all over again.

Huston visited her suite one Sunday afternoon, hoping to get a sense of what the week ahead would bring for her, which really meant what it would bring for the production as a whole. One wonders what he was thinking, since the Marilyn Monroe he was dealing with at that time was an hour-by-hour proposition. After Monroe opened the door, that realization hit him square in the face. Huston said she greeted him "euphorically" and then "went into a kind of trance." He was shocked by her appearance. She was unkempt, dirty and she was wearing "a short nightgown which wasn't any cleaner than the rest of her" (Huston, p. 289). This was the Marilyn Monroe he had to work with now. She was a shell of her worst self, if that was even possible.

While it was a relief that the film was done, the drama was far from over. Two days after filming finished, Clark Gable had a heart attack and was hospitalized in a critical condition. Many reports suggest that the endless hours of waiting for Monroe to show up in the desert heat had caused his heart attack. While it certainly didn't help, his crash dieting to get into shape for the film, along with decades of heavy drinking and smoking, had all contributed to his condition. Before filming even began, Gable failed the physical exam required by the production's insurance company. His doctor ordered him to bed for two weeks, told him to immediately stop drinking and smoking and prescribed pills to lower his escalating blood pressure. He obeyed orders, passed the next examination "and went straight home to celebrate with a cigar and brandy" (Harris, p. 369).

It's long been suggested that Gable did his own stunts, wrangling horses to the ground and exerting himself beyond anything a man of his age and physical condition could handle. Huston debunked these rumors in his 1994 biography *An Open Book*, saying: "Towards the end of the film there was a contest between Clark and the stallion the cowboys had captured. It looked like rough work, and it was, but it was the stunt men that were thrown around, not Clark" (Huston, p. 290).

Perhaps Huston was just covering his own ass. Montgomery Clift biographer Patricia Bosworth claims that many blamed Gable's death on Huston because he was the one who goaded Gable into roping the wild horses without using a double.

Following his hospitalization, Gable seemed to be making a steady improvement, but ten days after his first heart attack, a second heart attack took his life. Gable passed away on November 16, 1960. He was fifty-nine years old and just four months away from becoming a father to his only son, John Clark Gable. Gable's pregnant wife Kay had become friendly with Marilyn throughout the production of *The Misfits*, but an interview with Louella O. Parsons shortly after her husband's death changed everything. She said:

> It wasn't the physical exertion that killed him. It was the horrible tension, the eternal waiting, waiting, waiting. He waited around forever, for everybody. He'd get so angry that he'd just go ahead and do anything to keep occupied [Harris, *Clark Gable: A Biography*, p. 378–379].

For Monroe, the combination of her separation from Arthur Miller, mixed reviews for *The Misfits* and the unexpected death of Clark Gable, her idol, the make-believe father she dreamed about since she was a little girl, was devastating. And any suggestion that his pregnant widow felt that it was *her* actions that had contributed to his premature death was incomprehensible.

Monroe's depression grew deeper so her psychiatrist Marianne Kris recommended hospitalization. On February 7, 1961, under the patient name Mary Miller, Monroe was admitted to the Payne Whitney Psychiatric Hospital in New York City. *The Lewiston Daily Sun* (February 10, 1961) ran the headline, "Some Concerned Over Marilyn: Nature of Her Illness Brings Conflicting Reports." A statement released on her behalf by an unidentified spokesman said:

> Marilyn Monroe was admitted to New York Hospital ... for a period of rest and recuperation following a very arduous year in which she completed two films in rapid succession [*Let's Make Love* and *The Misfits*] and in which she has had to face marital problems. Both films required considerable physical exertion and she had no time in which to rest...

Placed in the security wing, Monroe grew frantic at the primitive conditions. Desperate, she wrote a two-page letter to Lee and Paula Strasberg. They were powerless to do anything so they contacted the one person they knew would do something, Joe DiMaggio. When the hospital told him they'd need the permission of Dr. Kris to release her, DiMaggio threatened to take down the hospital stone by stone if they didn't let her out. After several days of a hellish confinement, she was released into DiMaggio's care. He was Monroe's knight in shining armor. He got her out when no one else could. Once she was transferred to Columbia University Hospital she wrote a lengthy letter to Dr. Greenson about the lack of empathy and archaic cell-like conditions at Payne Whitney. It was the beginning of a renewed relationship between Monroe and DiMaggio. After undergoing his own therapy to deal with anger issues, the same anger issues that ended their marriage, he was a changed man. Monroe was her usual insecure self and she needed protecting from the world and from herself. After Payne Whitney, DiMaggio had proven himself to be the one person she could always rely upon, and the romance between the baseballer and the blonde bombshell began all over again.

During Monroe's hospitalization, Kay Gable wrote frequently to her. While Monroe's condition worsened because of Clark Gable's death and the guilt she felt for her behavior during production, it appears Kay felt her own sense of guilt for lashing out in her grief and giving a quote to Louella O. Parsons that implied that Monroe was responsible for her husband's death. Following the birth of Clark's son, Kay wrote a three-page letter to Monroe, friendly in tone, thanking her for the "beautiful plant" she sent to the hospital following the birth of her son. She also says, "I miss Clark each day..." and on the last page she says, "It would be so pleasant if you could spend some time with us, bring Joe [DiMaggio] too if you wish." She ended the letter with "Love, Kay." That May, Monroe attended the christening of John Clark, putting the hostility rumors to rest once and for all.

World-renowned Monroe collector Greg Schreiner spoke of Monroe's generosity; he also further confirmed Clark Gable's loyalty and respect for her during the production:

> One night during the making of *The Misfits*, the company went to the Cal-Neva Lodge to see Frank Sinatra. Unbeknownst to anyone, Marilyn picked up the entire check. Everyone thought the evening was on Frank. There was talk of rewriting the last scene of the film but Marilyn loved this scene and hated changing it. Clark Gable had the final say and put his foot down. There would be no more rewrites. Marilyn was grateful to Clark for standing behind her.

Clark Gable saw a rough cut of *The Misfits* before his death. He was exceedingly proud of the film and felt his performance was the best of his career. Not surprisingly, massive crowds turned out to witness the King of Hollywood give his final performance. But even with the publicity of Gable's death propelling the film's hype, *The Misfits* didn't resonate with 1960 audiences, or critics for that matter.

The film cost around $4 million to make and it equaled its cost in domestic box office returns. Though it was considered a bomb in its day, over time, *The Misfits* has developed into a modern-day classic. The film has since made a healthy profit via home video sales.

It was one of the most harrowing films ever shot, taking a toll on everyone involved. Gable felt too ill to attend the wrap party and Monroe and Miller took separate planes home. *The Misfits* was the epitome of a cursed film.

On November 11, 1960, Monroe publicly announced her separation from Miller. By January 20, 1961, a quickie Mexican divorce was granted. Monroe reflected on her relationship breakdown with Miller:

> I want to find someone to love me—ugliness and beauty and all. But people see only the glamour and fall in love with that, and then when they see the ugly side they run away. That's what Arthur has done.... I wanted some calmness, some steadiness, in my life, and for a time I had that with Arthur. That was a nice time. And then we lost it [Rennel, "She Was a Sex Symbol and He Was an Aloof Intellectual. Why Did Marilyn Monroe Marry a Misfit?"]

On July 23, 1966, the night of Montgomery Clift's death, *The Misfits* was scheduled to be shown on television. When Clift's live-in secretary-nurse-companion Lorenzo James entered Clift's bedroom around 1 a.m. to say goodnight, he asked him if he wanted to watch the film before going to sleep. "Absolutely not!" Clift shouted back. Those were the last words he spoke to James, and most probably anyone.

At 6 a.m., James went back to Clift's bedroom to wake him. His bedroom door was locked. It was never locked. After repeatedly knocking and shouting with no response, James unsuccessfully tried to break the door down. Frantic, he eventually entered through a window after climbing a ladder that he had found in the garden. Once inside, his worst fears were realized. Montgomery Clift was dead. He was forty-five years old.

The Medical Examiner's official report stated that he found Clift's body "lying face up in bed, glasses on, no clothes on. Right arm flexed. Both fists clenched. No evidence of trauma. Rigor present. Underclothes and pants scattered about on floor of bedroom. Liquor cabinet in bedroom. No empty bottles lying about. No notes, weapons, etc." An autopsy performed by Dr. Michael Baden, associate medical examiner, concluded there was no evidence of foul play or suicide. Cause of death was noted as a heart attack that was brought on by "occlusive coronary artery disease" (Bosworth, *Montgomery Clift: A Biography*, p. 411-p. 412).

Without doubt, Clift was a tortured soul. His inner conflict relating to his own homosexuality made him prone to periods of moodiness, as well as reckless and neurotic behavior. Throughout his life, he entered into casual sexual liaisons with both men and women. Aside from a myriad of health problems, including hypothyroidism, varicose veins, intestinal ailments and cataracts, he had become addicted to pills and booze to ease the physical and emotional pain following a May 12, 1956, serious car accident that left him with permanent facial injuries. During the filming of *Raintree Country* (1957) with Elizabeth Taylor, Clift attended a party at Taylor's house. In the early hours of the morning, just moments after he left, and only a quarter of a mile down the hill from Taylor's house, Clift lost control of his car and slammed into a telephone pole. Taylor ran down the hill to find the steering column folded in on itself, impacting into Clift's face from forehead to chin. His teeth had been knocked out and several were lodged in his throat. Taylor got them out, one by one. He was alive, and surprisingly lucid. Taylor stayed eerily calm, covering Clift's mangled, bloody face with her silk scarf to protect him from the photographers who had reached the scene prior to the ambulance. She threatened that she'd have them banned from every studio in town if they dared to take one photo of Clift. She cradled his head in her lap and protected his dignity for close to an hour because the ambulance got lost on the way to the accident scene. Traveling with him to the hospital, Taylor held Clift's hand. Describing his increasingly worsening condition, she said:

> By the time we reached the hospital, his head was so swollen that it was almost as wide as his shoulders. His eyes by then had disappeared. His cheeks were level with his nose. It was like a gigantic red soccer ball [Walker, *Elizabeth: The Life of Elizabeth Taylor*, p. 169].

Despite agonizing reconstructive surgery, Clift's face was permanently scarred. A severed nerve caused paralysis throughout his left cheek. His mouth was twisted. His nose was crooked. His speech was affected, and his back injury caused him constant pain. He also suffered with impairment of vision and balance (Capua, *Montgomery Clift: A Bibliography*, p. 143).

For an actor whose craft is all about beauty, emotion and expression, Clift's injuries were the cruelest of all life's blows. Yet, despite the obvious challenges facing his professional future, he continued acting and he did it well. Some say, even better than ever. However, behind the scenes, Clift was on a path to self-destruction. Uppers and downers were used to get through each day and alcohol was a prominent fixture in his life. Mentally and physically, he was a broken man.

Though half of Clift's film career came *after* the car accident, his irrational and unpredictable behavior caused many of Hollywood's major studios to avoid hiring him. He was no longer the Hollywood "pretty boy": No amount of trick lighting or makeup was good enough to mask the cruel reminder of the night he almost died. Audiences flocked to see Clift's post-accident pictures. At first, it was mostly out of a macabre curiosity, but he rose above the public's fascination with his new face, proving he still had "it" by earning himself a well-deserved 1962 Best Supporting Actor nomination for his role in *Judgment at Nuremburg* (1961).

Clift lived for a decade after that near-fatal car crash, but because of his chronic substance abuse, his post-accident years have long been referred to as the "longest suicide in Hollywood history." Ironically, during filming on *The Misfits*, Monroe described Clift as "the only person I know who is in worse shape than I am" (Ferguson, p. 74).

Soon after the breakdown of his relationship with Monroe, Miller married Austrian-born photographer Inge Morath. She was one of the contracted still photographers working for the world-renowned photo agency Magnum, and she was assigned to *The Misfits* for the duration of the shoot. Ironically, many of the hauntingly candid shots of Monroe that were captured during the production were taken by Morath.

Miller and Morath had two children together, Rebecca (born 1962) and Daniel (born 1966); Daniel was born with Down syndrome. Despite Morath's strong maternal desire to keep her son within the family unit, at Miller's insistence the baby was institutionalized almost immediately after his birth. He was rarely talked about and Miller refused to visit him. Miller's autobiography *Timebends: A Life* was over 600 pages in length yet Daniel wasn't mentioned. If there was ever a time to "write" his wrongs, face the truth and acknowledge his youngest child to the world before his death, that was the time. He chose not to. Writer Francine du Plessix Gray said:

A publicity photo for *The Misfits* (1961). Front row: Montgomery Clift, Marilyn Monroe, Clark Gable; behind them, Eli Wallach and director John Huston. At the very back is writer and soon-to-be ex-husband of Marilyn Monroe, Arthur Miller. *The Misfits* was Clark Gable's last film, and Marilyn Monroe's last completed film.

Inge told me that she went to see him almost every Sunday and that [Arthur] never wanted to see him. Once he was placed in Southbury [the Connecticut Institution for retarded children], many friends heard nothing more about Daniel [Andrews, "Arthur Miller's Missing Act"].

If there is any defense for Miller's reasoning, Down syndrome wasn't properly understood at the time. Upon the advice of family doctors, most Down syndrome children were locked away in institutions for life. Those radical parents who went against medical advice and insisted on keeping their disabled children at home were a rarity.

Soon after meeting on the set of *The Crucible* (1996), an adaptation of Miller's play of the same name, Rebecca Miller married actor Daniel Day-Lewis. Day-Lewis made a conscious effort to get to know his brother-in-law, who by this time was living in a supported living program with a roommate. He was a functioning adult with a disability. He worked, he socialized, he was an advocate for human rights and he even competed in the Special Olympics in four events (skiing, cycling, track and bowling). It's said that Day-Lewis encouraged Arthur Miller to get to know his son, which he eventually did, albeit on a limited level. But Daniel never looked to Arthur as his father because Arthur never gave Daniel a chance to be his son. By the time he made an attempt at a half-hearted connection, Daniel was almost thirty years old.

Miller's final play, *Finishing the Picture*, opened on October 5, 2004, at the Goodman Theatre in Chicago. It was loosely based on the filming of *The Misfits*. Set in Reno, the play had as its female lead Kitty, a drug-addicted movie star whose inability to function has put her latest film over budget and behind schedule. Once again, Kitty *is* Marilyn Monroe. The two meddlesome acting coaches are no doubt meant to be Lee and Paula Strasberg and the long-suffering screenwriter husband Paul is a representation of Miller. Right to the very end of his life, decades after his divorce from Monroe, Miller still drew on his experiences with her for his work.

Finishing the Picture closed on November 7, 2004, and 89-year-old Miller died three months later. To the surprise of many, his will left provisions for his disabled son, Daniel. The will's inclusion of Daniel as an equal beneficiary, along with his sister Rebecca and half-siblings Jane and Robert, was perhaps the most important piece of writing that Arthur Miller had ever done. Though it was a gesture that more than likely cleared his deathbed conscience from decades of guilt and denial, Miller finally acknowledged his youngest son: the happy, loving, very well-adjusted "misfit" that was his own flesh and blood.

Another Miller play with a character based on Monroe was *After the Fall* [1964]. The character of Quentin [obviously Miller] is a Jewish intellectual from New York, and Maggie is a suicidal blonde who resembles Monroe in every possible way. *After the Fall* is a posthumous re-telling of their complicated relationship, unfiltered, simply because Monroe was no longer around to be offended by its content. The transparently autobiographical play was criticized for being too raw, especially since the public was still reeling from Monroe's death not long before the play's January 23, 1964, opening. Miller seemed oblivious to these emotions and the public and critical reactions shocked him. Howard Taubman of the *New York Times* [February 2, 1964] wrote, "[H]as not Mr. Miller exceeded the bounds of good taste and decency in revealing so much of his life with Marilyn Monroe? For, of course, there is almost no pretense that Maggie, [the] generous-hearted, childlike enchantress and sick, self-destructive creature, is anything but the late, beautiful, tormented film star, or that Quentin is anyone but the author. Had Mr. Miller the right to go this far?" While much of a writer's work is drawn from personal experiences in some way, *After the Fall* is self-analytical and self-serving. The script is better suited to a psychiatrist's couch, not a stage. Likewise, the aforementioned character Kitty in Miller's final play *Finishing the Picture* was clearly based on Monroe's deteriorating mental and physical condition, along with the many issues that surrounded the making of *The Misfits*.

Something's Got to Give (1962)

Marilyn Monroe appeared as Ellen Wagstaff Arden. Twentieth Century–Fox. *Director:* George Cukor. *Producer:* Henry T. Weinstein. Based on the 1940 screenplay *My Favorite Wife* by Bella and Sam Spewack. *Screenplay:* Nunnally Johnson and Walter Bernstein. *Original Music:* Johnny Mercer. *Cinematography:* Franz Planer and Leo Tover. *Costume Design:* Jean Louis. *Production Dates:* April 23 to June 8, 1962 (production was officially shut down on June 11, 1962). *Production Cost:* $2.3 million (the unfinished movie was never released). *Release Date:* June 1, 2001 (reconstructed version with surviving footage). *Other Cast:* Dean Martin (Nick Arden), Cyd Charisse (Bianca Russell Arden), Tom Tryon (Steven Burkett aka Adam), Alexandra Heilweil (Lita Arden), Robert Christopher Morley (Timmy Arden), Wally Cox (Shoe Salesman), Phil Silvers (Johnson), John McGiver (The Judge), Grady Sutton (The Judge's Clerk), Eloise Hardt (Miss Worth), Steve Allen (Psychiatrist). *Soundtrack:* "Something's Gotta Give": Written by Johnny Mercer. Instrumental version by Ray Anthony and his Orchestra. Vocal version performed by Frank Sinatra.

Something's Got to Give, a remake of the popular 1940 comedy *My Favorite Wife* starring Cary Grant, Randolph Scott and Irene Dunne, starred Marilyn Monroe as Dean Martin's long-lost, thought to be dead wife Ellen. It was a modern, edgy, sophisticated role that had the potential to reinvent her career and her image. But it wasn't to be. Monroe died before her last film was ever completed. She was fired, then rehired on *her* terms at a higher salary and a change in director. George Cukor was out, Jean Negulesco was in. Filming of *Something's Got to Give* was scheduled to restart in late October 1962, but on August 5, 1962, Monroe was found dead in her bed. At a cost of $2 million plus, there wasn't enough footage to piece it together into anything releasable. *Something's Got to Give* was quite literally a dead loss.

It's very apparent that Fox's issues with *Something's Got to Give* had little to do with Monroe, and everything to do with the out-of-control budget on *Cleopatra* (which cost over $45 million). Fox was well aware that she often got sick, she was always late, she forgot her lines and most of her films ran over time and over budget.

At the time, Fox was in a financial freefall. The bigwigs were scrambling to save the studio from bankruptcy, to save face and to regain some sort of control. Since *Cleopatra* was being filmed overseas, they wielded the axe closer to home.

Something's Got to Give was shut down and Fox blamed Marilyn. Publicly accused of unprofessional behavior, she was ridiculed and dragged into a media "he said-she said" before being sued by the studio for the production's losses. Over the years she'd made millions for Fox as a contract player, and for the bulk of that time she was paid a low salary. It meant nothing.

Upon viewing the existing raw footage from the *Something's Got to Give* shoot, it's interesting to see how poised Monroe looks throughout. Even when she muffs a line, she takes it in her stride and she's calm and professional about starting over. She doesn't look depressed or troubled.

As an example of how misused she was when she did show up for work: A fifteen-second scene of her film dog "Tippy" greeting her as she returns home took an entire day to shoot, and none of the delays were her fault. Watching just six minutes of this one day's worth of footage is enough to make you realize how much time was wasted. There's a trainer constantly trying to get the dog to "speak" and "act" with Monroe. George Cukor (the set was an authentic reproduction of his actual home) is heard in the background, directing the scene as she repeatedly interacts with the dog and recites her lines without incident. She laughs a lot and appears happy, composed and in good spirits, all despite the fact that the dog isn't being cooperative. Monroe remains cheerful as the dog is repeatedly positioned and directed to "speak, speak—*speak*!" While the dog does bark on cue several times, it's inconceivable to think that this fifteen-second sequence couldn't have been pieced together in the editing room. Incidentally, the dog's name in the film is "Tippy," in memory of Monroe's beloved childhood pet that was shot by a neighbor during her time with Ida and Albert Bolender.

Following an airplane crash, Ellen is believed to have been lost at sea. After five years, she's presumed dead. One day, she returns home to her husband Nick (Dean Martin) and two young children Lita (Alexandra Heilweil) and Timmy (Robert Christopher Morley), after being stranded on a deserted island the whole time with a handsome stud, Steven, aka Adam (Tom Tryon). But Nick has moved on with his life and has just married Bianca (Cyd Charisse). As it happens, Ellen comes home on the same day that her husband and his new wife return from their honeymoon.

Nick does his best to keep Ellen's real identity from his new bride. Their children don't remember her although they instantly take a liking to her, and Ellen plays along until Nick feels ready to reveal all. Adopting a foreign accent and going by the name Ingrid Tic, Monroe's acting is natural and charming to watch.

When Nick finds out that Ellen went by the name of Eve to Steven's island name of Adam, he starts to doubt his first wife's fidelity and grows increasingly jealous. Ellen cons a nerdy shoe salesman (Wally Cox) into pretending that he was her island companion.

Monroe's final day of work on *Something's Got to Give* was June 1, 1962, her 36th birthday. A week later, Fox fired her. The studio sued Marilyn Monroe Productions for half a million dollars (it was later increased to $750,000) due to "willful violation of contract." It was announced that Lee Remick was hired to replace her, but only after Kim Novak and Shirley MacLaine turned the role down. Remick was fitted with Monroe's costume and was even photographed with director George Cukor. But Dean Martin's contract gave him leading lady approval, and with what appeared to be a stroke of loyalty not often seen in Hollywood, Martin alerted studio executives to the fine print in his contract. He flatly refused to work with anyone but Marilyn Monroe. His allegiance with her was payback for her initial request to cast him as her leading man. In a statement, Martin said:

> I have the greatest respect for Miss Lee Remick and her talent and all the other actresses who were considered for the role, but I signed to do the picture with Marilyn Monroe and I will do it with no one else ["Martin Follows Marilyn Monroe in Film Walkout," *Lewiston Morning Tribune,* June 10, 1962].

Martin's agent Mort Viner said that his client just wanted out of the film, *period*. Though it appeared Martin was being loyal to Monroe, in reality, he just didn't want to reshoot his scenes with another actress, especially on a film that wasn't showing much promise (Taraborrelli, p. 448). Martin's stance may have been self-serving, but in Monroe's eyes, he was just about the only person in her life who was willing to put his career on the line for her. In reality, the film was all over the place. Monroe's performance, what little they had, didn't seem usable, and Martin was staring down the barrel of a box office bomb.

Monroe was absent often and shooting was way behind schedule as a result. She claimed she was too sick to work (and many days she was), but she still mustered enough energy to fly to New York for President Kennedy's birthday celebration. While permission for Monroe to sing at the May 19, 1962, Presidential Birthday Gala was granted when contracts for the film were signed, acute sinusitis, high fevers and a chronic virus (conditions few believed were as bad as she made them out to be) had all caused costly production delays preceding the event. Given the circumstances, the studio changed their minds at the last minute. She went anyway. Fox hit her with a breach of contract notice when she arrived in New York. From that point on, she fully expected to be fired from the film.

A snapshot of Marilyn Monroe on the set of her last film, the uncompleted *Something's Got to Give* (1962). The production was problematic from the very beginning. Monroe was hired, fired and re-hired (because co-star Dean Martin refused to work with anyone else). She died before filming could resume. Four decades later, fragments of the film were masterfully pieced together into a comprehensible 37-minute short that showcased Monroe's beauty and acting talents to perfection.

The publicity that was generated from her appearance at the Presidential Birthday Gala should have been used to promote the upcoming film; instead, the studio punished her for it. Ironically, her perpetual lateness was a planned in-joke of sorts and it was a theme throughout the entire night. She was always going to perform towards the end of the show. Contrary to popular belief, she arrived on time, and following Lawford's introduction of, "Mr. President, the late Marilyn Monroe..." she sang "Happy Birthday, Mr. President" exactly the way she had rehearsed it.

The Jean Louis–designed, flesh-colored, rhinestone-encrusted "nude dress" that Monroe wore to the Gala was sold in 1999 for $1.3 million. Monroe paid $12,000 for it. She wore nothing underneath and she was sewn into it prior to the performance. Following her sensual, breathy performance of "Happy Birthday, Mr. President," Kennedy jokingly thanked her by saying, "I can now retire from politics after having had 'Happy Birthday' sung to me in such a sweet, wholesome way."

In five weeks of shooting on *Something's Got to Give,* Monroe had showed up for work a dozen times. While the production filmed around her as best they could, they eventually reached a standstill and there was nothing left to shoot. They needed her and she wasn't available.

To be fair, Monroe wasn't the only actress running the studio into the red at the time. In fact, in comparison to what Elizabeth Taylor was costing the studio on the extravagant historical epic *Cleopatra* (1963), the production delays and budget blowouts on *Something's Got to Give* was mere pocket change.

It was no secret that Taylor was having a passionate affair with her co-star, Richard Burton. The film had extensive delays, mainly due to Taylor's ill health which ended up causing a shift in location from London to Rome to speed her recovery. Taylor was treated like the queen she was portraying on screen. Back home, Monroe was being set up for a fall that even she didn't see coming, at least not until it was too late.

With an initial budget of $2 million, *Cleopatra* ended up costing the studio over *$45 million* to complete. Taylor's salary was an unprecedented one million dollars alone. In comparison, Monroe's salary for *Something's Got to Give* was $100,000. Cukor's salary was around $300,000 and Dean Martin's salary was also $300,000, plus a share of the film's profits.

When adjusted for inflation, *Cleopatra* is *still* the most expensive motion picture ever produced. It was so costly it almost bankrupted the studio. Tensions were high, nerves were frayed, funds were low, and it's clear that *Something's Got to Give* and Marilyn Monroe were the scapegoats for some very anxious studio executives who felt they were spinning out of control with both productions. The lesser of the two films had to go.

Not surprisingly, Monroe was insanely jealous of Elizabeth Taylor, not just because of her much higher salary, but because of the pandering from the studio and the publicity that she was getting at the time. Fox gave Taylor concessions that Monroe could never get away with, and her subsequent firing proved that fact. Monroe hatched a plan to shift the focus back to her. The infamous pool scene in the unfinished film was supposed to imply that Ellen was taking a late night skinny dip. Of course, she would be wearing a flesh-colored bathing suit to retain her modesty, but the "implication" of nudity was there.

Though it was a closed set, Monroe allowed photographers to stay, including twenty-three year old rookie Lawrence Schiller. Monroe had already made up her mind. She may have been getting into the pool with a bathing suit on, but she was definitely coming out without it. She let Schiller in on her plan, but she made him promise that if she came out of the pool with nothing on, that his photos would only appear on magazine covers that *didn't* have Elizabeth Taylor anywhere in the same issue. Her plan worked. Monroe's image from that shoot appeared on magazine covers in over thirty countries.

Though this was the first time she was so exposed, Monroe had done several bedroom scenes where she insisted on being naked underneath the sheets. Had *Something's Got to Give* been completed and released as planned, Monroe would have been the first A-list actress in the sound era to appear nude on film. (Jayne Mansfield ended up taking the prize in the

1963 sex romp *Promises! Promises!*) Not surprisingly, news of the controversial scene made Monroe a hot interview topic. She said:

> I had been wearing the [swim] suit, but it concealed too much ... and it would have looked wrong on the screen ... the set was closed, all except members of the crew who were very sweet. I told them to close their eyes or turn their back, and I think they all did... I was a little embarrassed by the fact I don't swim very well. I only dog-paddle but I'm buoyant and I can float ... there was a lifeguard on the set to help me out if I needed him, but I'm not sure it would have worked. He had his eyes closed too ["Marilyn Goes Swimming in Her 'Birthday' Suit," *The Press-Courier*, May 26, 1962].

Monroe's impromptu nude scene and photo session caused a sensation. She regained the spotlight, but once again she had to use her body to do it. Her recent gall bladder surgery caused her to lose twenty-five pounds. She was the thinnest she had ever been, but Schiller remembered her to be insecure and angry about resorting to such a cheap stunt. "It's still about nudity," she said. "Is that all I'm good for?" she demanded of Schiller. "I'd like to show that I can get publicity without using my ass or getting fired from a picture," she continued ("The Lost Marilyn Monroe Nudes: Outtakes from Her Last On-Set Shoot Revealed in June's V.F."). As it turned out, she used her ass *and* she got fired!

When Dean Martin showed up to set on May 22 with a cold, Monroe balked at working with him for fear that she'd catch it. Martin was off for a couple of days and the time was spent shooting the nude pool scene. By May 25, Martin was well enough to return to work. Monroe had an ear infection but she battled through, playing the part of the Swedish Nanny to perfection. By the weekend, she was bedridden and too sick to return to work on Monday. She reappeared on Tuesday, and she and Martin shot the poolside confrontation scene. Wednesday was a holiday (Memorial Day) and Thursday, Monroe spent the day filming the shoe store scenes with Wally Cox.

June 1, 1962, was Monroe's 36th birthday. It was a work day and George Cukor insisted that if Monroe showed, they were going to work. Any form of celebrating would be reserved for later. The scene consisted of Ellen introducing the fake Adam to Nick. The nerdy shoe store clerk does his best to convince a suspicious Nick of his time with Ellen on the island. In the last scene Monroe filmed that day, she called Nick down from the stairs to ask if he was interested in meeting Adam. With a rare full day of filming in the can, at 6 p.m. her stand-in Evelyn Moriarty presented her with a sheet cake and a card. World-renowned Marilyn Monroe collector Greg Schreiner, who developed a friendship with Evelyn Moriarty, said:

> Evelyn Moriarty worked with Marilyn on *Let's Make Love, The Misfits* and *Something's Got to Give*. She always told me that the woman written about in print was many times not the Marilyn she knew. Her Marilyn was very real, kind, down to earth and caring. Evelyn had to be careful not to admire something of Marilyn's or the next day it would appear at her doorstep. The Marilyn Evelyn knew was very shy and a perfectionist. Everything about her had to be absolutely the best. She never saw the temperament that people talked about. She was never demanding or asked for special treatment. To relieve tensions, as she left the dressing room she would always begin shaking her hands and wrists. She suffered from chronic nerves and would become so tense and apprehensive that she would literally run for her dressing room and throw up. Evelyn was responsible for organizing Marilyn's last birthday party [which] took place on the set of *Something's Got to Give*. The studio gave her a grand total of $15 to spend. Evelyn bought a cake and chipped in the money for the rest of the things needed.

Dean Martin and Monroe's publicist Pat Newcomb bought champagne and George Cukor gifted her with two Mexican figurines, a swan and a bull. The "birthday festivities" ended in less than half an hour and Monroe left the set for the last time. She was determined not to go back, not until things changed—drastically. That evening, a Muscular Dystrophy Association charity event at Dodger Stadium served as her very last public appearance. On Monday, June 4, Monroe called in sick. Before filming wrapped for the day, Dean Martin's patience came to a screeching halt and *he* walked off the set. The following evening, Monroe was threatened with a half-million dollar lawsuit if she didn't return to work post haste. On June 7, she was officially fired.

On June 11, the cast and crew of *Something's Got to Give* were suspended. And if things weren't messy enough already, they were about to get far worse. Martin's refusal to work with another co-star caused Cyd Charisse to sue him for $14,000 in lost earnings. Fox increased its lawsuit against Monroe, raising it to $750,000. The studio initially filed suit against Martin for $500,000, but by June 19, Martin's hold-out for Marilyn Monroe's return was the catalyst for the studio to lay the blame for the film on his shoulders. On the grounds that Martin had verbally promised to consider a replacement for Monroe, then declined in "bad faith" to do so, the action sought the film's costs to date, plus an additional million dollars in "exemplary damages." In total, both he and his company, Claude Productions, were sued for a whopping $3,339,000. A week later, and on the grounds of "false, fraudulent and misleading statements," Martin countersued through his production company for $6,885,000 (Tosches, p. 344). Both lawsuits went nowhere.

Following her dismissal, Monroe went back to the medium she was most comfortable with: still photography. She engineered her own publicity campaign and set out to show Fox that she was still viable, still popular and still a bankable star. Her photo sessions with Bert Stern for *Vogue* and George Barris for *Cosmopolitan* turned out to be some of the most beautiful, soulfully revealing images ever taken of her. Around the same time, Richard Merryman interviewed her at length for *Life* magazine. This revealing interview, her last, appeared in the August 3, 1962 issue of the iconic publication.

The crew of *Something's Got to Give* placed a sarcastic ad in *Variety* "thanking" her for putting them out of work. Monroe responded, saying, "Please believe me. It was not my doing. I so looked forward to working with you" (Summers, p. 370).

According to producer, Henry T. Weinstein: "During the 32 days that the picture was in production, Marilyn showed 12 days, and during those 12 days, managed only four days' work. The most she could deliver was a page and a half of script per day compared with three to four pages from other actors" (Shearer, "Who Really Runs Hollywood?").

There had been much hoopla in the press about Monroe's firing, Martin's refusal to work with anyone else, the studio suing both Monroe and Martin, and Martin countersuing the studio. Near the end of July, Monroe agreed to meet with Fox studio executives to discuss the future of *Something's Got to Give*.

After all the years she had given to Fox and all the money she'd made for them (over $60 million), it is somewhat baffling that they would fire her because she was acting exactly how she'd always acted. She was tardy, paranoid, she had trouble with her lines, she was often ill, and most productions she worked on ran behind time and cost more money than initially expected. The more she was pushed, the more she would pull away. If she wasn't coddled to perform, she wouldn't, or *couldn't* perform. Tensions on the set of *Something's Got to Give* were not conducive to Monroe's delicate persona. The production was doomed from day one.

Extensive rewrites on the *Something's Got to Give* screenplay were undertaken by Nunnally Johnson. When he left prior to filming, several other writers were hired to tweak the story and much of Johnson's vision was filtered out. As new script pages were distributed to cast and crew, different colored pages would identify the newly revised story and ensure everyone was literally on the same page. While Monroe initially received the newly revised colored pages like everyone else, to avoid confusing her, the studio started sending her rewrites on white paper. Even when she was sick and couldn't work, she studied her lines with Paula Strasberg, but with the replacement pages coming in white, upon revision, her lines were often different which only served to confuse her further.

History proves that Monroe was difficult to work with. But at the end of the day, her films at their very least broke even, and at their very best made a bundle. While Fox tried to replace her, she was irreplaceable. Once again, when it came to Monroe, Fox's stubbornness, lack of compassion and disloyalty would cost them.

On August 1, 1962, Monroe was not only rehired, she was signed to a one million dollar, two-picture deal. Her salary for *Something's Got to Give* was dramatically increased to $250,000 (two and a half times her original amount), her script suggestions were noted, she would receive $750,000 for an additional film, and at Monroe's request, director George Cukor was let go in favor of her *How to Marry a Millionaire* director Jean Negulesco. All lawsuits were dropped. The only request from the studio was that Monroe would keep Paula Strasberg off the set. She agreed. With all parties in agreement, the production was scheduled to restart in the latter half of October 1962, following the completion of Dean Martin's nightclub tour. Monroe was now in the catbird seat. For the first time since filming began, she was truly happy. But it wasn't to be. Just four days after Marilyn Monroe was rehired—she was dead.

In late January of 1962, Monroe had purchased her very first house, a modest Mexican-style hacienda at 12305 Fifth Helena Drive in Brentwood. The house was in need of renovating, but it was a task Monroe was willing and excited to do in order to make the place her own. At the time of her death, renovations were well underway. Ironically, four paved tiles at the entrance of the house showed a crest with the prophetic words "Cursum Perficio" written underneath—Latin for "Here Endeth the Chase" or "My Journey Ends Here."

A couple of months after Monroe's death, George Cukor returned from a European trip. Everywhere he went, people of all walks of life asked him about Monroe. He said:

> They were having a Marilyn season in Beirut. In Paris I learned there was an epidemic of suicides and attempted suicides after her death. I'm not sure I pleased people with my answers to their questions. She was a girl fraught with crises. There was a crisis every day of her life, and perhaps one night was more critical than others [Hopper, "Europeans Are Curious About Marilyn Monroe: Quiz Director"].

Over nine hours of *Something's Got to Give* footage was locked away in Fox vaults for four decades. Not all of it featured Monroe; in fact, a lot of it didn't because on many days they shot around her absences. Still, the remaining footage was eventually edited down to 37 minutes and featured in the 2001 documentary *Marilyn Monroe: The Final Days*. Its executive producer Kevin Burns said that it was editor Tori Rodman's job to undertake the enormous task of surgically editing the fragments of Monroe's uneven performance into a cohesive story. There were a lot of flubbed lines and unusable scenes. Initially, Burns felt that piecing together Monroe's few usable scenes would be an impossible undertaking. However, it was done, and done well. What we're left with is a brief glimpse into what might have been. Burns concludes, "[W]hen you see what exists [in *Something's Got to Give*], [Monroe] looks fabulous. She looks smart and strong and luminous. And in some ways, it is the best acting I have ever seen her do" (King, "Marilyn Monroe's Last Film Work Resurrected for New Documentary").

Following Monroe's death, Fox salvaged the sets for *Something's Got to Give* and the film was recast with Doris Day and James Garner in the lead roles. Polly Bergen, Thelma Ritter, Don Knotts and Chuck Connors made up the supporting cast and Michael Gordon directed the film. The script essentially matched that of *Something's Got to Give*, and the newly titled *Move Over, Darling* was released on Christmas Day, 1963.

At a cost of $3.35 million, the film grossed about $6 million domestically, making it one of the most successful films of that year. That said, there were some things that only Monroe could do; in other words, don't expect to see a nude pool scene in *Move Over, Darling* featuring Doris Day. The box office success of *Move Over, Darling* proves that had *Something's Got to Give* been completed and released, it too would have been a successful production, despite its inflated costs.

For years and for various reasons, Monroe teetered between the fine line of life and death. She was a unique talent, a timeless beauty, a tortured soul, but she was also a ticking time bomb, coddled and prodded along from film to film. For the last decade of her life, any one of her films could easily have been her last. There was always something about Monroe that created a sense that her time on this earth was short. That was the key element that drew people to her then, and five decades after her death, it's the key element that *still* draws people to her. Without doubt, Monroe will be studied, revered and rediscovered for generations to come. Gone too soon but forever alive via her films and thousands of photographs, Marilyn Monroe is a perpetual being.

In hindsight, it's somewhat ironic that Monroe's final film was titled *Something's Got to Give*. For many years, it was clear to many who knew her, both professionally and personally, that something *had* to give, at least eventually.

On August 5, 1962, at just thirty-six years old—it finally did.

In Monroe's final print interview, she refers to her position in the world in past tense. She said, "Fame *was* a special burden, which I might as well state here and now. I don't mind being burdened with being glamorous... But what goes with it can be a burden..." ("Hollywood Shocked by Marilyn's Death," August 6, 1962).

Arthur Miller once said, "I took [Marilyn Monroe] as a serious actress before I ever met her. I think she's an adroit comedienne, but I also think that she might turn into the greatest tragic actress that can be imagined" (Ricci, Conway, p. 14). Miller's prediction was correct, but in no way did he ever mean the word "tragic" in the literal sense. It just happened to turn out that way.

Extra Parts ... and Missed Opportunities

The Shocking Miss Pilgrim (1947)

While this production is often noted for marking Marilyn Monroe's film debut, she's not actually seen on screen. The sound of her voice saying "Hello" on the other end of a phone was the extent of her work and her scene as a telephone operator was cut from the final print.

Twentieth Century–Fox. 85 minutes. *Directors:* George Seaton, Edmund Goulding (uncredited), John M. Stahl (uncredited). *Producer:* William Perlberg. *Writer:* George Seaton. *Original Music:* David Raksin. *Cinematography:* Leon Shamroy. Costumes: Orry-Kelly. *Production Dates:* November 1945 to February 1946. Release Dates: January 4, 1947 (USA), February 11, 1947 (New York City, New York, USA). *Production Cost:* $2.595 million. *Domestic Box Office Receipts:* $2.734 million. *Genre:* Comedy-Musical-Romance. Color: Technicolor. *Other Cast:* Betty Grable (Cynthia Pilgrim), Dick Haymes (John Pritchard), Anne Revere (Alice Pritchard), Allyn Joslyn (Leander Woolsley), Gene Lockhart (Saxon), Elizabeth Patterson (Catherine Dennison), Elisabeth Risdon (Mrs. Prichard), Arthur Shields (Michael), Charles Kemper (Herbert Jothan), Roy Roberts (Mr. Foster).

Mother Wore Tights (1947)

This Walter Lang–directed Betty Grable-Dan Dailey musical has long been rumored to include Monroe as an extra. While there are plenty of scenes with extras throughout the film, her on-screen appearance remains unconfirmed. The one solid connection that she has with the film is that her Technicolor, silent screen test (July 19, 1946) was filmed on the *Mother Wore Tights* set. Monroe was instructed to walk across the room, sit down, light a cigarette, put it out and leave. She was then told to walk upstage, look out a window, sit down again, walk downstage and exit the camera frame. Her first studio contract resulted from this screen test.

Green Grass of Wyoming
(1948)

This Louis King–directed horse-themed film starred Peggy Cummins, Charles Coburn, Lloyd Nolan and Burl Ives. Monroe is rumored to have been an extra.

Sitting Pretty
(1948)

Clifton Webb stars as Mr. Belvedere, ingenious babysitter to the three young sons of Mr. and Mrs. King (Robert Young and Maureen O'Hara). Monroe doesn't appear in the film but there are *Life* magazine photographs of her on the set, sitting on a couch with Clifton Webb and Laurette Luez (she's not in the final film either). Seated between the two beauties, Webb holds a massive box of chocolates on his lap as all three indulge. Many biographers have speculated whether or not the photographs were from a deleted scene, but they appear to have been nothing more than photos of a set visit (Webb and Monroe were friends) that was captured by photographer Loomis Dean. None of the shots featuring Monroe ever appeared in *Life* to promote the film and there's no reason to believe that Monroe was ever a part of the production since Fox had already dropped her contract.

You Were Meant for Me
(1948)

This Lloyd Bacon–directed musical starred Jeanne Crain and Dan Dailey. Monroe is rumored to be an extra in the crowd scenes.

Riders of the Whistling Pines
(1949)

In this Gene Autry western for Columbia Pictures, Marilyn Monroe appears several times in a rather unconventional way: A photo of crop-dusting pilot Joe Lucas's (Jimmy Lloyd) late wife is a studio publicity portrait of Monroe. The photo is shown as a full screen shot several times throughout the film. When Joe asks Gene Autry to sing a song for his lost love, Autry sings "Hair of Gold" to the photo of Monroe. The photo is last seen on the control panel of Joe's aircraft; she then goes down with him and the plane, but not before he salutes her first.

Royal Triton Gasoline TV commercial
(1950)

Monroe appeared in her only television commercial in 1950 for Royal Triton Gasoline. She is seen at the wheel of a convertible, then we see the back of the car and four very willing men pushing it into the gas station. She's out of gas. "This is the first car I ever owned," she says. "I call her Cynthia. She's going to have the best care a car ever had." She then turns to the gas station attendant and says, "Put Royal Triton in Cynthia's little tummy." "Right, lady," says the gas station attendant. Monroe then turns to the camera in closeup and sexily purrs, "Cynthia will just love that Royal Triton."

Screen Test
(December 10, 1950)

Monroe made a screen test with Richard Conte for the role of a gangster's moll in the film *Cold Shoulder*. Conte was earmarked to star in the Fox production along with Victor Mature. Monroe's drama coach Natasha Lytess helped her study for the part. The screen test lasted a little over a minute and she wore the familiar sweater dress previously seen in *The Fireball* (1950), *All About Eve* (1950) and *Home Town Story* (1951). While Monroe looks the part in her screen test, her acting is melodramatic and she gives the impression that she's trying too hard to impress. That said, she was soon re-signed to a new, long-term Fox contract. Most likely it was her standout performances in *The Asphalt Jungle* (1950) and *All About Eve* that convinced Zanuck to give her a second chance. Despite Louella O. Parsons running the headline "Marilyn Monroe Gets First Starring Role in *Cold Shoulder*," the film was never made (*The Deseret News*, July 19, 1950).

Born Yesterday
(1950)

This George Cukor–directed classic gave Judy Holliday a 1951 Best Actress Golden Globe (Musical-Comedy) as well as a 1951 Oscar for Best Actress in a Leading Role. Holliday had starred in the original Broadway stage version (1642 performances) for almost four years (February 4, 1946 to December 31, 1949), so it was hard to see anyone taking the screen role away from her, least of all a relative newcomer like Marilyn Monroe. Monroe tested for the lead role of Billie Dawn during her tenure with Columbia. The writer of *Born Yesterday*, Garson Kanin, said that Columbia boss Harry Cohn refused to take the six steps from his desk to the projection room to look at her test, despite reports from many that Monroe's performance was "excellent" (www.immortalmarilyn.com).

Meet Me After the Show (1951)

This Richard Sale–directed musical starred Betty Grable, Macdonald Carey, Rory Calhoun and Eddie Albert. In a 1993 interview, Carey confirmed Monroe's appearance in the film: "Richard Sale always used Marilyn, and she was with me in *Meet Me After the Show*. She was sort of an extra in some of the scenes, which I remember because she had a very pretty body and face" (Buskin, *Blonde Heat: The Sizzling Screen Career of Marilyn Monroe*, p. 29).

Across the Wide Missouri (1951)

Marilyn Monroe was on location near Durango, Colorado (where *A Ticket to Tomahawk* had been filmed), when this movie was made. When a major battle scene between the mountain men and the Native American was scheduled to take place near Andrews Lake, a local standby laborer, Mickey Hogan, had his work cut out for him: Since the topsoil around the lake was made up of peat moss, it was highly flammable. The majority of the crew and many of the spectators were smokers, which made a fire a very real possibility. It was Hogan's job to travel on horseback armed with a fire extinguisher, putting out smoldering hot spots that were starting up. Monroe was bored so she asked if she could join Hogan on his fire hunts. She was given a horse and a fire extinguisher and off they went. Hogan remembered her joining him two or three times: "She didn't have anything to do [so] she just enjoyed riding and doing something" (Peel, "Durango's Brief Brush with Marilyn"). *Across the Wide Missouri* was an MGM western starring Clark Gable, Ricardo Montalban, John Hodiak and Adolphe Menjou. Monroe's work on this film was solely behind the scenes ... as an assistant standby laborer!

Wait Till the Sun Shines, Nellie (1952)

When Marilyn tested for a part in this feature, editor Barbara McLean told its director Henry King, "That girl's going to be a big star." King replied, "Well, I haven't got time to wait." McLean said, "I'd sure take her if I was directing the picture" (Staggs, p. 94). Unfortunately for Monroe, McLean wasn't directing the picture. King saw no place for her in the film.

1953

This year was big for Marilyn Monroe films that were talked about but never made. The *Los Angeles Times* (January 29, 1953) announced that she would be the female lead opposite Tyrone Power in a Fox film titled *Princess of the Nile*, to be produced by Leonard

Goldstein. Monroe was slated to play a dual role as the princess and as a dancer in a café in Memphis during the Crusades in the 13th century. Power would meet her as he's passing through to Asia Minor. It was to be shot in 3D and Technicolor. *Princess of the Nile* was released in 1954 with Debra Paget, Jeffrey Hunter, and Michael Rennie as the main stars. Additional films mentioned for Monroe in the same article were *The Lady or the Tiger* and *Form Divine*. One role that Monroe was desperate to play was Nefer (eventually played by Bella Darvi, the mistress of Darryl Zanuck) in the epic drama *The Egyptian* (1954). However, Zanuck wasn't interested in what parts *she* wanted to do, he was only interested in what parts *he* wanted her to do. Zanuck assigned her a role in a lowly B-musical, *The Girl in Pink Tights* aka *Pink Tights* with Frank Sinatra. Sinatra was slated to receive $5,000 a week. Monroe had initially said she'd consider the role if the studio could get Gene Kelly as her co-star. Monroe was no stranger to studio suspensions (which meant no work, no pay), and on January 25, 1954, she was again suspended for failing to show up to start shooting *The Girl in Pink Tights*. The studio released this statement: "If Miss Monroe's failure to appear is based on her desire to approve scripts, the studio wishes to point out that the outstanding success of her previous vehicles is evidence enough of the studio's ability to select stories for her" ("*Pink Tights* Irk Marilyn," *Pittsburgh Post-Gazette*, January 26, 1954). Monroe had already unsuccessfully tried to renegotiate her contract with Zanuck. Disillusioned with the studio's casting and script choices, Monroe refused to do the film until she read the script. Zanuck ordered her to report for work on the first day of shooting (December 15, 1953, then extended to January 25, 1954). Without knowledge of the screenplay, Monroe stood her ground: no script, no work.

Charles Feldman of Famous Artists was trying to renegotiate Monroe's Fox contract, and in the meantime, she and new husband Joe DiMaggio flew to Japan for the opening of the 1954 baseball season. For the first time in a long time, DiMaggio wasn't the center of attention. He was now Mr. Marilyn Monroe, and it was a role he never got used to. Soon after their arrival, Monroe revealed in a press conference that she would be traveling to Korea to entertain troops stationed there. DiMaggio disapproved of the trip, mostly because he despised the thought of his wife being ogled by thousands of sexually frustrated soldiers. Monroe was voted the most popular pin-up for soldiers during the Korean War, and she was going to take the opportunity to thank them for the honor, whether her husband liked it or not. From February 16 to 19, 1954, Monroe performed ten shows over four days, for 100,000 soldiers. Some walked miles to see her. Despite the subzero temperatures she insisted on wearing a skintight dress with spaghetti straps, and nothing underneath. She contracted pneumonia and returned to Japan with a 104-degree temperature, but despite her illness, she described the Korea trip as one of the greatest moments of her life. Upon her return to Hollywood, she was still on suspension. When Fox did send her the script, it was as bad as she suspected, and to make matters worse Natasha Lytess criticized her treatment of the studio and insisted that Monroe take the part. It was the beginning of the end of their relationship. DiMaggio despised Lytess, so it wasn't going to take much to tip Monroe against her. Lytess may have felt Monroe's allegiance crumbling, and this was her way of trying to get Fox on her side in case Monroe dispensed with her services.

The Girl in Pink Tights would have put Monroe in the role of Jenny, a schoolteacher turned saloon dancer. Sheree North was initially touted as her replacement, but then the film was permanently shelved. North ended up playing Monroe's mother Gladys Baker in the 1980 TV movie *Marilyn: The Untold Story,* based on Monroe's life.

The Jack Benny Show (September 13, 1953)

Monroe made her debut television appearance in a comedic skit with Jack Benny on his first episode of the 1953 season, "The Honolulu Trip." Monroe appears in a dream sequence after Benny imagines her on a cruise with him. The long-running gag that Benny is cheap and that he doesn't age a day past 39 years of age is incorporated into the skit. Later, and with Monroe in on the gag, he makes fun of his box office failure *The Horn Blows at Midnight* (1945). The scene played out as follows:

JB: Marilyn, Marilyn, why did you walk away from me? Why, why did you wanna leave me?
MM: Because I can't trust myself with you.
JB: What?
MM: You're so strong and I'm so weak. And when you look at me with those big blue eyes…I just…I just…
JB: I understand.
MM: In the picture, all I wanted was money and diamonds. But now, for the first time, I realize that all I really want—is you!
JB: Marilyn…
ANNOUNCER: Dream on, Mr. Benny, dream on.
JB: Marilyn, Marilyn—I'm mad about you.
MM: I'm mad about you, too, Jack. Jack, Jack. Will you do something wonderful for me? It would make me very happy.
JB: Well, of course, Marilyn. I'd do anything—anything—for you. What is it?
MM: Well, in my next picture, there's going to be so many love scenes, I want *you* for my leading man!
JB: Oh, Marilyn, I'd, I'd love to be your leading man.
MM: Good! Now, if we can only get permission from Darryl Zanuck.
JB: Why? Who did Mr. Zanuck have in mind?
MM: Himself.
JB: Gee, Marilyn. I, I just can't get over—just the both of us, here, all alone on the Loreline.
MM: Yes, Jack. I never dreamed it could happen to I.
JB: Neither did me.
MM: (sighs).
JB: Marilyn, why, why are you sighing?
MM: I was just thinking, Jack, how generous you are. Just so we could be alone on this trip, you chartered the Loreline for $600,000!
JB: I did?
ANNOUNCER: If that doesn't wake him up, nothing will!
JB: Marilyn, Marilyn—I know this is sudden, but—will you, will you marry me?
MM: Marry you? But look at the difference in our ages!
JB: Well, there isn't much difference Marilyn—you're 25 and I'm 39.
MM: Yes, but what about 25 years from now? When I'm 50 and you're 39?
JB: Gee, I never thought of that…
ANNOUNCER: I did!
JB: You shut up!
JB: Marilyn, Marilyn—will you, will you have dinner with me tonight?
MM: I'd love to, Jack. Thanks ever so.
JB: At eight o'clock?
MM: All right, but I'd better be going now. [Monroe now sings "Bye, Bye Baby" to a swooning Benny, before a kiss goodbye.]

MM: My, that's strange.
JB: What's strange?
MM: I'm crazy about you. But that kiss didn't affect me at all!
JB: That's funny...I'm a wreck!
MM: See you later, Jack.
JB: Don't forget. Marilyn, don't forget dinner tonight.
MM: I won't.
JB: At eight o'clock.
CHUBBY BLONDE IN MONROE'S PLACE: I'll remember.
JB: Marilyn—come back here a minute. Please come back. Marilyn—give me one more kiss before you go.
The chubby blonde throws Benny back into her arms and kisses him passionately.
JB: Hey, wait a minute! You're not Marilyn Monroe!
CHUBBY BLONDE: Well, you ain't no Errol Flynn!
JB (bewildered): Gee, I was so sure I was ... talking to Marilyn Monroe.
ANNOUNCER: Ahh, yes, the sea plays many mental tricks as you're gently lulled in the cradle of tranquility, but there's nothing as soothing and restful as a Pacific cruise back from the tropical islands of enchantment.

Monroe looked radiant and happy throughout the segment. Despite her history of flubbing lines, she not only got through the eight-minute skit with Benny, her timing was perfect. At the end of the segment, Benny brings Monroe on stage with him. Before she appears, he thanks "20th Century–Fox, for allowing me to dream about Marilyn Monroe."

JB: Marilyn, umm, this is your first, first appearance in television, isn't it?
MM: Yes it is, Jack.
JB: Well, I'm quite flattered that you made your first appearance on my show, I really am.
MM: Thank you.
JB: Just wonderful to have you. Have you a picture that's coming out pretty soon, a new picture? I mean we've seen *Gentlemen Prefer Blondes*, another one, a new one?
MM: Yes. It's called *How to Marry a Millionaire*. It's also in CinemaScope.
JB: Oh it is, in CinemaScope too.
MM: Yes.
JB: You know, I, umm, I made a picture once, ummm [audience laughter]...*The Horn Blows at Midnight*. And I believe if *that* had been made in CinemaScope it would have been a huge success.
MM: Well, you know, CinemaScope is very complicated. In order to put the big screen in all the theaters, they have to take out a lot of seats.
JB: Well, in my picture, they could have taken out all of the seats!
MM: Jack.
JB: What?
MM: I don't know why you're always panning *The Horn Blows at Midnight*. I saw it.
JB: You did?
MM: Yes.
JB: And you don't know why I'm panning it? Did you like it?
MM: No.
JB: Well, thanks ever so! [Benny and Monroe laugh, he kisses her hand and says, "So long, goodbye, Marilyn," as she dashes off stage.]

Monroe received a brand new black Cadillac as payment for her appearance on *The Jack Benny Show*. Despite the success of her debut television appearance, her lack of confidence made appearing on live TV terrifying for her. Aside from her April 8, 1955, interview on Edward R. Murrow's *Person to Person* TV show at the home of photographer Milton Greene and his wife Amy, *Jack Benny* was her only live television appearance.

1954

A Twentieth Century–Fox memo housed at the Margaret Herrick Library (among the Charles Brackett papers) from writer-producer Charles Brackett to studio executive Darryl F. Zanuck confirms a proposed biopic on the life of actress Marion Davies, with Monroe in the lead role, to be written and directed by Billy Wilder. Additionally, the *Los Angeles Times* (June 21, 1954) mentioned other movies that were to have featured Monroe: *The Lady and the Lumberjack* with Alan Ladd, *Jewel of Bengai* and the Western, *The Gun and the Cross*.

1955

Following the success of *Gentlemen Prefer Blondes* (1953), *The Hollywood Reporter* wrote in December 1954 that Monroe and Jane Russell were going to team-up again in *How to Be Very, Very Popular* (1955). Monroe turned down the opportunity because she was unhappy with the script. The film was recast with Sheree North in Monroe's would-have-been role of Curly and Betty Grable in Russell's would-have-been role of Stormy Tornado. The film was a flop.

Australian Tour (1955)

During her Hollywood hiatus, Monroe was offered $200,000 to fly to Australia for a twenty-five-day tour of the country to headline her own stage show. According to *Variety* (August 17, 1955), the exorbitant offer was proposed by Lee Gordon. Although it was the most money she would have *ever* earned for less than a month of work, it still wasn't enough to lure her Down Under.

The Girl in the Red Velvet Swing (1955)

This Richard Fleischer–directed feature starred Ray Milland, Joan Collins and Farley Granger. Monroe refused to play a role and was suspended by the studio.

Guys and Dolls (1955)

Monroe told columnist Earl Wilson that she was very interested in the part of Miss Adelaide but the role went to Vivian Blaine, who also played the part on Broadway.

The Barker
(1955)

Edwin Schallert of the *Los Angeles Times* (July 15, 1955) reported that Arthur Landau had recently purchased the stage rights to a musical version of *The Barker*. A deal was being sought with Monroe as the star, but only if Fox would permit her to be loaned. George Sidney was reportedly approached to direct.

The Smiling Rebel
(1955)

The *Los Angeles Times* (December 6, 1955) reported that representatives for Monroe were interested in a Civil War story by Hermett Kane about a woman spy.

1956

According to a Louella O. Parsons column in the *Milwaukee Sentinel* (October 9, 1956), Monroe and Jayne Mansfield were competing for the female lead in *Kind Sir*, the Norman Krasna adaptation of his own play which starred Mary Martin and Charles Boyer. Clark Gable was being hotly pursued as the leading man. *Kind Sir* ended up being the working title for *Indiscreet* (1958). The lead roles were played by Ingrid Bergman and Cary Grant.

1956

Monroe adored Jean Harlow and during her early Hollywood career, newspapers often described Monroe as "the new Harlow." As early as mid–1954, Monroe was touted as the only actress that producers wanted for a movie featuring Harlow as a character, saying, "[T]hey will settle for no one else." A bonus for her and a percentage for Fox was offered to secure the services of Monroe (*Youngstown Vindicator*, June 4, 1954). Fox later had the idea of filming the story of Harlow's life themselves. According to *Variety* (June 1956), Fox producer Buddy Adler "took the wraps off the studio's long projected plan to biopic Harlow with Marilyn Monroe playing the late screen star." Arthur Miller convinced Monroe that playing her idol would do nothing to advance her career. Despite being the first star ever to be approved for the biopic by Harlow's mother, Monroe rejected the role at her husband's suggestion. Following her divorce from Miller, and with the project still in limbo, Monroe was once again slated to take on the role of her idol. This time tragedy intervened. At 4 p.m. August 5, 1962, the day her body was discovered, Monroe had an appointment set up with Hollywood columnist Sidney Skolsky and Jean Harlow's mother, about *The Jean Harlow Story*, a film in which she was set to star. Two movies on the life of Harlow were made a few years later.

The Revolt of Mamie Stover (1956)

This Raoul Walsh directed feature was another Monroe reject though she never read the script. It was based on the William Bradford Huie novel of the same name. Jane Russell stepped in to take the role of Mamie, a wartime prostitute chased out of San Francisco by the law. Traveling to Honolulu to start a new life, she tries her best to turn over a new leaf but her shady past keeps catching up with her.

Baby Doll (1956)

Monroe asked director Elia Kazan to cast her in the title role of Baby Doll Meighan but he rejected her because she was "too old." Carroll Baker, a few years younger than Monroe, got the part. Kazan avoided casting Monroe because of her neuroses. In his autobiography, he revealed that he considered her a "good comedienne, but not much more" (Banner, *Marilyn: The Passion and The Paradox*, p. 291). She may have lost the part in the film, but she was still associated with it in some way. Marilyn Monroe proved she bore no grudges towards Kazan for casting Baker: On December 4, 1956, she was an usherette at the *Baby Doll* benefit for the Actors Studio.

Forty Guns (1957)

Director Samuel Fuller said that Monroe wanted Barbara Stanwyck's role of the tough rancher Jessica Drummond in his CinemaScope western, with a touch of film noir. Stanwyck plays the no-nonsense feminine leader of a gang of forty crooks, each of them toting a gun, hence the title. It's hard to imagine Monroe in the role, but Fuller said, "Marilyn Monroe wanted so badly to play it" (Smith, *Starring Miss Barbara Stanwyck*, p. 263).

Will Success Spoil Rock Hunter (1957)

On December 15, 1955, *Stars and Stripes* reported that 20th Century–Fox was interested in buying the rights to George Axelrod's Broadway sensation (October 13, 1955 to November 3, 1956, 444 performances) for a screen adaptation with Monroe in contention to play a character that would essentially be a satire of herself. When Fox did buy the film rights, Jayne Mansfield reprised her stage role of Rita Marlowe, the sexy Stay-Put lipstick girl, opposite Tony Randall as the lowly advertising man Rockwell P. Hunter, in one of his funniest celluloid performances.

The Midwife of Pont Clary

Director, Jean Negulesco wrote to Monroe at the Bel Air Hotel on July 14, 1958; with the letter he sends flowers and inquires about her throat. The gist of the letter is about the book *The Midwife of Pont Clary*. He encloses a copy for her to read, writes enthusiastically of the story and says, "*The Midwife of Pont Clary* is fundamentally sex... I have quite an exciting idea for the treatment of the story... I would like to sit down and talk to you about it... Please give this book to Arthur [Miller] to read." Negulesco obviously wanted Monroe for the lead. The film was never made.

The Brothers Karamazov (1958)

For almost a decade, Monroe was desperate to play the role of Grushenka, the 19th century Russian temptress in *The Brothers Karamazov*. But Fox wasn't interested in Monroe appearing in such serious melodrama. On June 16, 1957, Philip K. Scheuer of the *Los Angeles Times* ran the headline, "*The Brothers Karamazov* Rolling—Without Marilyn." Richard Brooks wrote and directed the film, and while he conceded that Monroe would have made a fine Grushenka and would have been "tremendous box office," her negotiations with the studio fell through "because of her contractual demands and personal troubles." Brooks went on to say that he told his producer that he didn't want to write the adaptation if he had to write it *for* Marilyn Monroe. His answer was, "I don't think you should try." By 1958, the film was released by MGM. Maria Schell got the longed-for role of Grushenka. While the feature film bypassed her, an August 8, 1955, headline in the *Los Angeles Times* announced "Marilyn Finally Gets Offer to Play in Russian Classic." Albert McCleery, executive producer of the new NBC drama series based on the classic novel, announced he would give Monroe a chance to prove she could do it in a three-part serialization of the Fyodor Dostoevsky novel.

The Blue Angel (1959)

For this remake of Marlene Dietrich's 1930 classic, Fox wanted Monroe to play the lead role of Lola-Lola. Now with her own production company, Monroe had script approval and she rejected this film. Swedish actress May Britt played the lead instead. It was a poor imitation of the original. Monroe was wise to reject the part. Author Lois Banner claims that Monroe was paid her $100,000 fee for the film, despite never shooting a scene. Fox breached their contract by not casting co-stars or a director in the time frame specified in Monroe's contract. For once the tables were turned; it was usually Monroe who was in breach of contract, not the studio (Banner, *MM; Personal: From the Private Archive of Marilyn Monroe*, p. 126).

Middle of the Night
(1959)

Monroe wanted to play the role of Betty Preisser in the film; however, it ended up being a Columbia production and Kim Novak got the part. The head of Columbia, Harry Cohn, was desperate to discover "another Marilyn," and Novak was thought to have been "It."

Time and Tide

A letter from Twentieth Century–Fox to Marilyn Monroe Productions (March 4, 1959) informs Monroe that as per their agreement, her services are required and she is to commence work on a new film on April 14, 1959, *Time and Tide*. Elia Kazan was slated to direct. It never happened. As per Monroe's Fox contract, if the studio didn't have another film lined up for her by April 14, 1959, they'd lose one of the four films agreed upon by both parties. While Monroe was usually the one causing production delays, this time it was Kazan causing the problems. He demanded extensive script rewrites so Monroe was told to stay in New York until she was needed. She would still be paid from the original start date. As weeks passed, Kazan felt that Lee Remick would be a better casting choice, but that was the least of the studio's problems. On June 25, 1959, Monroe's lawyer informed Fox that her contract stipulated that their client must start work within ten weeks of the official start date, and since the studio failed to ask for an extension, they were in breach of the contract. Although she didn't work a day on the film, she demanded her salary in full and to be released from the obligation of one of the owed films. Fox had been so distracted by Kazan's demands they failed to check the fine print on Monroe's contract, but it was airtight. Fox lost a film and were obligated to pay Monroe's salary in full.

1959

The Coshocton Tribune (November 3, 1959) reported that Fox was yearning to have Monroe play the daughter of Mae West in a film that was "currently being blueprinted," and that she was also slated to take on the lead role when *Goodbye Charlie*, the Broadway comedy starring Lauren Bacall, was made into a film. *Goodbye Charlie* wasn't released until late 1964; Tony Curtis, Debbie Reynolds and Pat Boone starred in the Fox production.

The Story on Page One
(1959)

Directed and written by Clifford Odets, the courtroom drama starred Rita Hayworth. Though Monroe was the original choice for Jo Morris, illness got in the way and she was forced to drop the project after Dr. Mortimer Rodgers, her New York gynecologist, operated to relieve her chronic symptoms of endometriosis.

The Apartment (1960)

Hot on the heels of the success of *Some Like It Hot,* this was Billy Wilder's next feature film. While Monroe was interested in playing Fran Kubelik, Wilder barely got through *Some Like It Hot* without having a nervous breakdown. Though he always knew the end result would be brilliant, he and Jack Lemmon couldn't imagine doing back-to-back films with Monroe, at least not without putting themselves into early graves. *The Apartment* went on to become a commercial and critical success, earning a multitude of Oscar nominations, including a win for Best Picture.

It's easy to see the direction that Monroe's career might have taken had she collaborated with Wilder a couple more times.

Can-Can (1960)

This Walter Lang–directed musical-comedy-romance starred Frank Sinatra, Maurice Chevalier, Louis Jourdan and Shirley MacLaine in the role of Simone Pistache, the part Monroe turned down.

1960–1961

When Marilyn Monroe turned down the role of Anna O. (pseudonym of real life patient Bertha Pappenheim) in the John Huston–directed *Freud* (1962), her decision was strongly influenced by Anna Freud's (Freud's youngest child) disapproval of the film, as well as her New York–based psychoanalyst Dr. Marianne Kris, whose father had been Freud's tarot partner (Roudinesco, *Philosophy in Turbulent Times*). In the John Huston papers at the Margaret Herrick Library, a handwritten letter from Monroe (November 5, 1960) states, "I wouldn't want to be part of it [*Freud*], first because of his [Freud's] great contribution to humanity and secondly, my personal regard for his work." The film was released in 1962, with Montgomery Clift playing the title role.

1961

George Axelrod was hired to loosely adapt Truman Capote's 1958 novella *Breakfast at Tiffany's* into the 1961 romantic comedy of the same name. Axelrod was originally told to write the screenplay with Monroe in mind for the female lead. Even this late into her career, Monroe had little faith in her own decisions. When her acting coaches Lee and Paula Strasberg advised her that playing the role of a call girl may taint her image, she dropped out of the production (Jorgensen, *Edith Head*, p. 278). While Capote was disappointed with the decision to cast Audrey Hepburn as Monroe's replacement, it is now hard to imagine anyone

Paris Blues (1961)

This Martin Ritt–directed film about jazz life, racism and the freedom a jazz musician was given in France (as opposed to the United States) eventually starred real-life husband and wife Paul Newman and Joanne Woodward, along with Sidney Poitier, Louis Armstrong and Diahann Carroll. Monroe was initially interested in playing Woodward's part of Lillian Corning.

Rain (TV, 1961)

In a 1961 letter to Marilyn, Somerset Maugham wrote, "I am so glad that you are going to play Sadie [Thompson] in the TV production of *Rain*. I am sure you will be splendid. I wish you the best of luck" (Banner, *MM; Personal*, p. 186). Initially, Monroe wanted her acting coach Lee Strasberg to direct the film, but NBC refused. Then when George Roy Hill was attached as director, Strasberg's constant interference caused Hill to threaten to quit. The most fascinating part of this lost project is that *Twilight Zone* creator and writer Rod Serling was hired for $25,000 to write the script. Serling met with Monroe (whose salary would have been $100,000) to discuss the project. After he turned in two drafts, NBC was silent. When he contacted the studio to find out why, he was told that Monroe preferred the original 1923 play *Rain: A Play in Three Acts* and she was rehearsing *that* version, not his. Serling was livid. NBC had specifically hired him to update the *Rain* story, which he did. The cracks were beginning to show long before filming would begin, so it's no surprise that filming didn't begin—at all. Following the filming of *The Misfits*, *The Windsor Star* (February 10, 1961) reported on Monroe's hospitalization and subsequent in-patient therapy being the cause of her missing the signing of the *Rain* contract with NBC. The network released a statement confirming that the role would still be hers, "if her health permits, but the presentation on TV may be delayed until next fall..." Then, on June 29, 1961, Monroe was hospitalized again, this time for emergency surgery and the removal of her gall bladder. Despite the delays, NBC remained confident the film would begin shooting and *Rain* was given a tentatively scheduled airdate for Sunday, October 29, 1961. NBC eventually wrote it off as a financial loss and nixed the project altogether.

August 7, 1961 (dated letter)

From Monroe's press agent Arthur P. Jacobs, written correspondence about her interest in a remake of *Of Human Bondage* as well as another film, *Celebration* with George Roy Hill as the suggested director. Jacobs goes on to say that he recalled that Hill held "no specific, inimitable interest for you and that it was my understanding that you were not interested in *Celebration* (Banner, *MM; Personal*, p. 155). *The Naked Truth* was a film project that Monroe discussed with producer Harold Mirisch in 1961, but it never eventuated due to her death.

August, 1962

Just days before her death, Monroe was in talks with songwriter Jule Styne about a possible musical remake of *A Tree Grows in Brooklyn* with Frank Sinatra. She agreed to fly to New York and had set up an August 9 meeting with Styne. She was also in talks to star in the comedy *I Love Louisa* with Dean Martin. After viewing some of his work, Monroe agreed on J. Lee Thompson as director for the film. Shooting of *I Love Louisa* was scheduled to begin in the early months of 1963. Styne had agreed to write new songs for Monroe to sing in the film. Martin was also interested in her co-starring in an untitled film project alongside him, Frank Sinatra, Sammy Davis, Jr., Joey Bishop and Peter Lawford, otherwise known as The Rat Pack. Additionally, around the same time, an Italian film company was courting her with a lucrative four-film deal (Smith, p. 15). At the time of Monroe's death, a typed letter from a representative of Anita Loos was found in her home. Letter writer Natalia Danesi Murray offered to send Monroe the script and the music, if she was interested, for the proposed film that was based on the French play *Gogo*. Monroe was to be the star of the film. (Riese and Hitchens, *The Unabridged Marilyn*, p. 278). Along with her renegotiations (including a second film deal worth $750,000) on *Something's Got to Give,* Monroe was busier and more in-demand than ever.

Irma La Douce
(1963)

Despite their tumultuous relationship, the combination of Monroe and Billy Wilder worked magically on film, and for that reason alone, Wilder seriously considered casting Monroe in the title role of the Parisian prostitute, Irma La Douce. Shirley MacLaine eventually played the part, even receiving a Best Actress Oscar for her work. Filming began in October 1962, a few months after Monroe's death.

The Stripper
(1963)

Monroe refused the role of a sexpot in this film; Joanne Woodward starred in it a year after Monroe's death. Written by William Inge (*Bus Stop*), *The Stripper* follows the life of a failed actress who turns to stripping for a living.

1964

Two years after Monroe's death, Shirley MacLaine played Louisa in the black comedy *What a Way to Go!* (1964), an all-star vehicle. Producer Arthur P. Jacobs had originally intended to cast Monroe in MacLaine's role (Jorgensen, *Edith Head*, p. 308).

Goodbye Charlie (1964)

According to author Lois Banner, this Fox movie was originally slated to be made in 1961 with Monroe starring, but Fox was unable to find co-stars and a director in the time frame specified in Monroe's contract. Fox had to pay her $100,000 anyway; Marilyn didn't have to shoot a single scene. It did nothing to help the tension between Monroe and the studio. Fox felt duped, but Monroe's contract was tight (Banner, p. 126). The film was later made with Tony Curtis, Pat Boone and Debbie Reynolds in the part originally slated for Monroe, that of a gangster who is killed and reincarnated as a blonde.

Of Human Bondage (1964)

Director Henry Hathaway had Monroe in mind for the role of Mildred Rogers from the outset, but she died before the film went into production. In August of 1961, Monroe was told that Marlon Brando might be her co-star; he became unavailable and Paul Scofield was suggested instead. José Ferrer was mentioned as a possible director. Kim Novak and Laurence Harvey eventually starred; Henry Hathaway directed initially but dropped out early. Screenwriter Bryan Forbes replaced him, albeit briefly, with the job eventually being completed by Kenneth Hughes (www.tcm.com).

[Marilyn Monroe] stood for life. She radiated life. In her smile hope was always present ... her death did not mar this final image. She had become a legend in her own time, and in her death, took her place among the myths of our century.

—John Kobal, in Riese and Hitchens, p. 345.

Bibliography

Books

Aggrawal, Anil. *Necrophilia: Forensic and Medico-Lethal Aspects.* Boca Raton: CRC Press, 2011.

Badman, Keith. *The Final Years of Marilyn Monroe: The Shocking True Story.* London: JR, 2010.

Bacall, Lauren. *By Myself and Then Some.* New York: HarperEntertainment, 2005.

Banner, Lois. *Marilyn: The Passion and the Paradox.* New York: Bloomsbury.

Banner, Lois, and Mark Anderson. *MM; Personal: From the Private Archive of Marilyn Monroe.* New York: Abrams, 2010.

Bergreen, Laurence. *As Thousands Cheer: The Life of Irving Berlin.* New York: Viking, 1990.

Bigsby, Christopher. *Arthur Miller: 1915–1962.* Cambridge: Harvard University Press, 2009.

Bosworth, Patricia. *Montgomery Clift: A Biography.* New York: Harcourt Brace Jovanovich, 1978.

Buskin, Richard. *Blonde Heat: The Sizzling Screen Career of Marilyn Monroe.* New York: Billboard, 2001.

Buskin, Richard. *The Films of Marilyn Monroe.* Lincolnwood, IL: Publications International, 1992.

Capua, Michaelangelo. *Montgomery Clift: A Biography.* Jefferson, N.C.: McFarland, 2002.

Channing, Carol. *Just Lucky I Guess: A Memory of Sorts.* New York: Simon & Schuster, 2002.

Coleman, Terry. *Olivier.* New York: H. Holt, 2005.

Conway, Michael, and Mark Ricci. *The Complete Films of Marilyn Monroe.* Secaucus, N.J.: Citadel Press, 1964.

Cotten, Joseph. *Vanity Will Get You Somewhere.* San Francisco: Mercury House, 1987.

Cramer, Richard Ben. *Joe DiMaggio: The Hero's Life.* New York: Simon & Schuster, 2000.

Curtis, Tony, and Barry Paris. *Tony Curtis: The Autobiography.* New York: Morrow, 1993.

Curtis, Tony, and Mark A. Vieira. *Some Like It Hot: Me, Marilyn and the Movie.* London: Virgin Books, 2009.

Eliot, Marc. *Cary Grant: A Biography.* New York: Harmony Books, 2004.

Engelberg, Morris, and Marv Schneider. *DiMaggio: Setting the Record Straight.* St. Paul: MBI, 2003.

Ferguson, Michael. *Idol Worship: A Shameless Celebration of Male Beauty in the Movies,* 2d ed. Sarasota: STARbooks Press, 2004.

Flinn, Caryl. *Brass Diva: The Life And Legends of Ethel Merman.* Berkeley: University of California Press, 2007.

Fujiwara, Chris. *The World and Its Double: The Life and Work of Otto Preminger.* New York: Faber and Faber, 2008.

Gottfried, Martin. *Arthur Miller: His Life and Work.* Cambridge: Da Capo Press, 2004.

Hansford, Andrew, and Karen Homer. *Dressing Marilyn: How a Hollywood Icon Was Styled by William Travilla.* Millers Point, N.S.W.: Murdoch, 2011.

Harris, Warren G. *Clark Gable: A Biography.* New York: Harmony, 2002.

Haspiel, James. *The Unpublished Marilyn.* Edinburgh: Mainstream, 2000.

Hirsch, Foster. *Otto Preminger: The Man Who Would Be King.* New York: A. Knopf, 2007.

Huston, John. *An Open Book.* New York: De Capo Press, 1994.

Hyams, Joe. "Marilyn Monroe Drops Walk to Become a 'Real Actress.' *Youngstown Vindicator,* November 28, 1955.

Jorgensen, Jay. *Edith Head: The Fifty Year Career of Hollywood's Greatest Costume Designer.* Philadelphia: Running Press, 2010.

Kanfer, Stefan. *Groucho: The Life and Times of Julius Henry Marx.* New York: Knopf, 2000.

Landis, Deborah Nadoolman. *Dressed: A Century of Hollywood Costume Design.* New York: Collins Design, 2007.

Lang, Fritz, and Barry Keith Grant. *Fritz Lang: Interviews.* Jackson: University Press of Mississippi, 2003.

Leaming, Barbara. *Marilyn Monroe.* New York: Crown, 1998, p.16.

MacCann, Graham. *Marilyn Monroe.* Cambridge: Polity Press, 1988, p. 45.

McCarthy, Todd. *Howard Hawks: The Grey Fox of Hollywood.* New York: Grove Press, 1997.

Miller, Arthur. *Timebends: A Life.* New York: Grove Press, 1987.

Miracle, Berniece Baker, and Mona Rae Miracle. *My Sister Marilyn: A Memoir of Marilyn Monroe.* Chapel Hill: Algonquin Books of Chapel Hill, 1994.

Mitchum, Robert, Charles Champlin, and Jerry Roberts. *Mitchum: In His Own Words.* New York: Limelight Editions, 2000.

Morgan, Michelle. *Marilyn Monroe: Private and Undisclosed (New Edition: Revised and Expanded).* London: Constable & Robinson, 2012.

Nelson, Nancy. *Evening with Cary Grant: Recollections in His Own Words and by Those Who Knew Him Best.* New York: W. Morrow, 1991.

Newton, Michael. *The Encyclopedia of Unsolved Crimes.* New York: Facts on File, 2009.

Nixon, Marni, with Stephen Cole and Marilyn Horne. *I Could Have Sung All Night: My Story.* New York: Billboard, 2007.

Olivier, Laurence. *Confessions of an Actor: An Autobiography.* New York: Simon & Schuster, 1982.

Playboy Magazine Price Guide Checklist. Playboy Magazine, 1996.

Quirk, Lawrence J., and William Schoell. *Joan Crawford: The Essential Biography.* Lexington: University Press of Kentucky, 2002, p. 166.

Riese, Randall, and Neal Hitchens. *The Unabridged Marilyn: Her Life from A to Z.* New York: Congdon & Weed, 1987.

Roudinesco, Elisabeth. *Philosophy in Turbulent Times: Canguilhem, Sartre, Foucault, Althusser, Deleuze, Derrida.* New York: Columbia University Press, 2008.

Sanders, George. *Memoirs of a Professional Cad.* New York: Putnam, 1960.

Schwarz, Ted. *Marilyn Revealed: The Ambitious Life of an American Icon.* Lanham, MD: Taylor Trade, 2009.

Server, Lee. *Robert Mitchum: "Baby, I Don't Care."* New York: St. Martin's Press, 2001.

Slatzer, Robert F. *The Life and Curious Death of Marilyn Monroe.* New York: Pinnacle House, 1974.

Smith, Ella. *Starring Miss Barbara Stanwyck.* New York: Crown, 1974.

Smith, Matthew. *Victim: The Secret Tapes of Marilyn Monroe.* London: Century, 2003.

Solomon, Aubrey. *Twentieth Century–Fox: A Corporate and Financial History.* Metuchen, NJ: Scarecrow Press, 1989.

Spoto, Donald. *Marilyn Monroe: The Biography.* New York: HarperCollins, 1993.

Staggs, Sam. *All About All About Eve.* New York: St. Martin's, 2001.

Summers, Anthony. *Goddess: The Secret Lives of Marilyn Monroe.* London: Guild, 1985.

Taraborrelli, Randy J. *The Secret Life of Marilyn Monroe.* New York: Grand Central, 2009.

Tosches, Nick. *Dino: Living High in the Dirty Business of Dreams.* New York: Delta Trade, 1991/1992.

Victor, Adam. *The Marilyn Encyclopedia.* Woodstock, NY: Overlook Press, 1999.

Wagner, Robert J., with Scott Eyman. *Pieces of My Heart: A Life.* New York: HarperEntertainment, 2008.

Walker, Alexander. *Elizabeth: The Life of Elizabeth Taylor.* New York: G. Weidenfeld, 1991.

Wallach, Eli. *The Good, the Bad, and Me: In My Anecdotage.* Orlando: Harcourt, 2005.

Wilder, Billy, and Robert Horton. *Billy Wilder: Interviews.* Jackson: University Press of Mississippi, 2002.

Yankee, Luke. *Just Outside the Spotlight: Growing Up with Eileen Heckart.* New York: Back Stage, 2006.

Magazines

Andrews, Suzanna. "Arthur Miller's Missing Act." *Vanity Fair*, September 2007.

Hall, James E. "Marilyn Monroe Was Murdered: An Eyewitness Account." *Hustler*, May 1986.

LOOK, November 3, 1960.

McIntyre, A. T. "Making *The Misfits* or Waiting for Monroe or Notes from Olympus." *Esquire*, March 1961.

Merryman, Richard. "A Last Long Talk with a Lonely Girl." *Life*, August 17, 1962.

"Monroe Felt Greene Was Assuming Too Much Control." *Sunday Times Magazine,* July 22, 2001.

Monthly Film Bulletin. Undated, 1953.

Redbook, 1952.

Stare, Vol. 1, #6, 1952.

Time, June 9, 1952.

Time, July 27, 1953.

Vanity Fair, November 2010.

Whitcomb, John. *Cosmopolitan*, December 1960.

Newspapers

"Actress Wins All Demands from Studio." *The Los Angeles Mirror News,* January 5, 1956.

"*All About Eve* (review)." *Daily Variety,* September 13, 1950.

"*All About Eve* (review)." *Hollywood Reporter,* September 13, 1950.

"*The Asphalt Jungle* (review)." *Daily Variety,* May 5, 1950.

"*The Asphalt Jungle* (review)." *Hollywood Reporter*, May 5, 1950.

Bacon, James. "What Hollywood Says About Marilyn Monroe." *Gadsden Times*, July 17, 1960.

Bean, Margaret. "'Let's Make It Legal' Rated as Only Fair." *The Spokesman-Review*, November 14, 1951.

Berg, Louis. "Marilyn Gets Her Medal." *Los Angeles Times*, April 28, 1957.

Bigsby, Christopher. "Marilyn Monroe and Arthur Miller: Extract from Christopher Bigsby's Biography." *The Telegraph*, November 16, 2008.

Cohen, Harold V. "Marilyn Monroe at the Fulton in 'Seven Year Itch.'" *Pittsburgh Post-Gazette*, June 23, 1955.

The Coshocton Tribune, November 3, 1959.

Crowther, Bosley. "'As Young as You Feel,' with Monty Woolley Leading the Way, Opens at Palace." *New York Times*, August 3, 1951.

Crowther, Bosley. "'Don't Bother to Knock,' Starring Marilyn Monroe and Richard Widmark, Opens at Globe." *New York Times*, July 19, 1952.

Crowther, Bosley. "Gable and Monroe Star in Script by Miller." *New York Times*, February 2, 1961.

Crowther, Bosley. "'Gentlemen Prefer Blondes' at Roxy, with Marilyn Monroe and Jane Russell." *New York Times*, July 16, 1953.

Crowther, Bosley. "Look at Marilyn! A Lot Is Seen of Miss Monroe (As a Symbol) in 'The Seven Year Itch.'" *New York Times*, June 12, 1955.

Crowther, Bosley. "Marilyn Monroe vs. Scenery at Roxy." *New York Times*, May 1, 1954.

Crowther, Bosley. "Milton Berle Steals Show in 'Let's Make Love.'" *New York Times*, September 9, 1960.

Crowther, Bosley. "'Monkey Business,' a 'Screwball Comedy' with a Chimpanzee, Starts Run at the Roxy." *New York Times,* September 6, 1952.

Crowther, Bosley. "Of Size and Scope: The Wide Screen Viewed in the Light of 'How to Marry a Millionaire.'" *New York Times,* November 15, 1953.

Crowther, Bosley. "The Proof of Marilyn: 'Bus Stop,' a Good Role and a Challenge Are Met by Miss Monroe." *New York Times*, September 9, 1956.

Crowther, Bosley. "The Screen: Marilyn Monroe Arrives." *New York Times*, September 1, 1956.

Crowther, Bosley. "Screen: Prince and Girl." *New York Times*, June 14, 1957.

Crowther, Bosley. "The Screen: Summer Bachelor's Itch." *New York Times*, June 4, 1955.

Crowther, Bosley. "Screen: 'There's No Business,' Etc." *New York Times*, December 17, 1954.

Crowther, Bosley. "The Screen: Trio of Stars in Cinemascope." *New York Times*, November 11, 1953.

Crowther, Bosley. "'We're Not Married,' Fox Farce by Nunnally Johnson, New Feature at Roxy Theatre." *New York Times*, July 12, 1952.

"DA Rules Out Murder Plot in Marilyn Monroe." *Dallas Morning News,* December 29, 1982.

The Daily Register, August 5, 1952.

Daily Variety, Thursday, September 5, 1946.

Daily Variety, April 1, 1951.

"*Dangerous Years* (review)." *Daily Variety,* December 12, 1947.

"*Dangerous Years* (review)." *Hollywood Reporter*, December 12, 1947.

"*The Fireball* (review)." *Daily Variety,* August 14, 1950.

"*The Fireball* (review)." *Hollywood Reporter,* August 14, 1950.

"French Star Distressed by Breakup." *Spokane Daily Chronicle*, November 14, 1960.

Gehman, Richard. "The Big M." *The Milwaukee Sentinel,* May 1, 1960.

"'Grubby' Marilyn Monroe Made Laurence Olivier 'Age Fifteen Years' During Filming." *The Telegraph,* January 24, 2013.

Hastings, Chris. "'Try to Be Sexy' [sic]: How Larry Olivier Set Out to Humiliate Monroe." *The Telegraph*, August 31, 2003.

Heffernan, Harold. *Dallas Morning News*, June 18, 1950.

Henry, O. "The Cop and the Anthem." *New York World,* December 4, 1904.

Hollywood Reporter, July 25, 1952.

Hollywood Reporter, December (no date), 1954.

Hollywood Reporter, May 4, 1955.

Hollywood Reporter, May 24, 1955.

"Hollywood Shocked by Marilyn's Death." *Plain Dealer*, August 6, 1962.

Hopper, Hedda. "Europeans Are Curious About Marilyn Monroe: Quiz Director." *Chicago Tribune,* Tuesday, October 9, 1962.

Hopper, Hedda. "Hollywood." *New York Daily News,* June 15, 1954.

Hyams, Joe. "Marilyn Is Back! She's the Same Old Marilyn—Tardy, Temperamental and Terrific." *Los Angeles Times*, October 5, 1958.

Johnson, Erskine, "Hollywood Today." *Ocala Star-Banner,* September 9, 1960.

Johnson, Erskine. "'Misfits' Stresses More Mood Than Thought." *Pittsburgh Press*, September 6, 1960.

Kelly, Herb. "Monroe Sings, Dances, Jokes—and Makes Love." *The Miami News*, August 25, 1960.

Kilgallen, Dorothy. *Salt Lake Tribune*, December 1, 1960.

King, Susan. "Marilyn Monroe's Last Film Work Resurrected for New Documentary." *Los Angeles Times*, May 28, 2001.

Kingsport Times, August 18, 1961.

"*Ladies of the Chorus* (review)." *Daily Variety,* December 3, 1948.

"*Ladies of the Chorus* (review)." *Hollywood Reporter*, December 3, 1948.

Lesner, Sam. "Joshua Logan Feels 'Camelot'" His Finest." *Toledo Blade*, September 24, 1967.

Levine, Debra. "Jack Cole Made Marilyn Monroe Move." *Los Angeles Times,* August 9, 2009.

Lindeman, Edith. "River Film Is Scenic Wonder." *Richmond Times Dispatch*, May 15, 1954.

"*Ladies of the Chorus* (review)." *Daily Variety,* December 3, 1948.

Los Angeles Herald-Examiner, April 1953.

Los Angeles Times, January 29, 1953.
Los Angeles Mirror, January 1956.
"*Love Happy* (review)." *Daily Variety,* September 21, 1949.
"*Love Happy* (review)." *Hollywood Reporter,* October 10, 1949.
Lyons, Leonard. *Advocate,* July 5, 1956.
"Marilyn a la Mack Sennett." *New York Times,* February 22, 1959.
"Marilyn Finally Gets Offer to Play in Russian Classic." *Los Angeles Times*, August 8, 1955.
"Marilyn Goes Swimming in Her 'Birthday' Suit." *The Press-Courier,* May 26, 1962.
"Marilyn Monroe Nearly Drowned." *Los Angeles Times*, August 14, 1953.
Martin, Edward. "'Don't Bother' Proves Monroe's Ability." *San Diego Union,* August 18, 1952.
"Martin Follows Marilyn Monroe In Film Walkout." *Lewiston Morning Tribune,* June 10, 1962.
The Miami News, July 9, 1950.
The Miami News, November 10, 1963.
Monahan, Kaspar. "Marilyn Monroe Ideally Cast in 'Let's Make Love.'" *Pittsburgh Press,* August 29, 1960.
Monahan, Kaspar. "'Monkey Business' at Harris: Cary and Ginger Cavort Like Kids." *Pittsburgh Press*, September 25, 1952.
"Monroe & Montand: Double Dynamite!" *The Southeast Missourian,* March 17, 1961.
"Montand Recalls His Hollywood Affair." *The Evening News,* July 24, 1987.
"Moods of an Idol." *Sydney Morning Herald,* May 25, 1980.
New York Daily News, January 1980.
New York Journal-American, November 14, 1960.
New York Times, November 25, 1951.
"Niagara Falls Vies with Marilyn Monroe." *New York Times*, January 22, 1953.
"Odets' 'Clash by Night' on Screen." *New York Times*, June 19, 1952.
The Oelwein Daily Register, March 1, 1948.
Parsons, Louella O. "Marilyn Monroe: From Orphanage to Stardom." *San Diego Union,* April 1, 1951.
Parsons, Louella O. "Marilyn Monroe Gets First Starring Role in 'Cold Shoulder.'" *The Deseret News,* July 19, 1950.
Parsons, Louella O. "Marilyn or Jayne to Star in 'Kind Sir.'" *Milwaukee Sentinel*, October 9, 1956.
Peel, John. "Durango's Brief Brush with Marilyn." *The Durango Herald,* January 15, 2012.
"Pink Tights Irk Marilyn." *Pittsburgh Post-Gazette*, January 26, 1954.
Pittsburgh-Post Gazette, March 31, 1964.
"Producer Can't Make 'Love' Until Marilyn Gets the Urge." *The Sun,* February 18, 1960.
Reno Evening Gazette, June 22, 1970.
Rosenfeld, Megan. "Joshua Logan Steps Into Another Role—As Teacher." *Sarasota Herald-Tribune,* August 11, 1981.
Ryan, Pat. "The Prince, the Showgirl, and the Stray Strap." *New York Times*, November 11, 2011.
Schallert, Edwin. "Barker as Musical Named For Monroe." *Los Angeles Times*, July 15, 1955.
Schallert, Edwin. "'Clash by Night' Proves Forceful, Provocative." *Los Angeles Times,* June 7, 1952.
Schallert, Edwin. "Marilyn Monroe Shows New Glow in 'Blondes.'" *Los Angeles Times*, August 1, 1953.
Scheuer, Philip K. "'Don't Bother to Knock' Self-Conscious Thriller." *Los Angeles Times,* July 31, 1952.
Scott, Vernon. "Sinatra, Marilyn Monroe May Co-Star." *The Press-Courier*, August 12, 1960.
Shearer, Lloyd. "Who Really Runs Hollywood?" *Advocate,* Baton Rouge, Louisiana, August 12, 1962.
"Some Concerned Over Marilyn: Nature of Her Illness Brings Conflicting Reports." *Lewiston Daily Sun*, February 10, 1961.
Some Like It Hot (review). *Variety,* February 24, 1959.
Springfield Sunday Republican, August 1, 1982
Springfield Union, September 20, 1954.
"Star Puts Over Theme Song, But Is Weak on Acting." *Springfield Union*, May 14, 1954.
Stars and Stripes, July 24, 1954.
Stars and Stripes, December 15, 1955.
Sullivan, Chris. "Jack Cardiff: Life Behind the Lens." *The Independent*, December 9, 2005.
"Sweatergirl Marilyn Monroe Admits 'Arty' Calendar Pose." *Stars and Stripes,* April 6, 1952.
Taubman, Harold. "A Cheer for Controversy." *New York Times*, February 2, 1964.
"Temperament Pays Off for Marilyn." *Daytona Beach Morning Journal*, July 17, 1960.
Thomas, Bob. "Billy Wilder Finds Marilyn Reports Fantastically Early." *Ocala Star-Banner*, August 15, 1958.
Thomas, Bob. "Marilyn Discusses Film," *Kentucky New Era*, May 16, 1960.
Thomas, Bob. "Marilyn Monroe Story Is Over, But There Are Fond Memories." *The Milwaukee Journal*, August 8, 1962.
Thomas, Bob. "Movie 'Let's Make Love' Has Its Grim Side." *Meridien-Journal*, May 26, 1960.
Tri City Herald, August 6, 1962.
Variety, February 1953.
Variety, August 17, 1955.
Variety, June 1956.
Weiler, A. H. "Screen: 2-Hour Comedy." *New York Times,* March 30, 1959.
We're Not Married (review). *Variety,* July 25, 1952.
Wilson, Earl. "Marilyn Monroe Gone Ten Years." *Plain Dealer,* August 6, 1972.
The Windsor Star, February 10, 1961.
Youngstown Vindicator, June 4, 1954.
Zolotow, Maurice. "The Mystery of Marilyn Monroe." *Milwaukee Sentinel,* October 16, 1955.

Special Collections and Miscellaneous

The Margaret Herrick Library (AMPAS Special Collections)

Billy Wilder papers.
Charles Brackett papers: 20th Century–Fox memorandums (1954).
George Cukor papers: *Let's Make Love* correspondence regarding Marilyn Monroe from Arthur Miller (April 30, 1960). Letter from Cukor regarding Monroe's firing from *Something's Got to Give* (July 3, 1962). Letter from Cukor regarding Monroe's death.
Hedda Hopper papers: Letter from Hopper (to John Knight) discussing Monroe's death and how the telephone company would not reveal who made third call to Monroe on August 15, 1962.
John Huston papers: *Freud* casting and handwritten letter from Monroe about why she decided not to pursue the project.
Lester Cowan papers (1949–1950).
Los Angeles (California) Orphans Home (files; 1935–1937).
Mary Pickford papers: Letter from Mary Pickford (July 20, 1949) requesting that her name be removed from *Love Happy* due to her dissatisfaction with the production.
Production Code Administration Papers, MPAA Collection (*Some Like It Hot* file), Margaret Herrick Library (*AMPAS Special Collections*), Fairbanks Center for Motion Picture Study.

University of California, Los Angeles (UCLA)

Darryl Zanuck memo to Nunnally Johnson (October 24, 1951).
Darryl Zanuck memos to Irving Berlin (December 13 and 17, 1952).
Twentieth Century–Fox Legal Records.
Twentieth Century–Fox Scripts Collection.

University of Southern California (USC)

Warner Bros. Archive (Jack L. Warner Collection).

National Library of Australia

Jocelyn Rickards papers.

Miscellaneous

Donald O'Connor interview, *Larry King Live*, 2001.
FBI public records (Marilyn Monroe file, reprocessed version, January 4, 2013).
Jack Benny Show—transcript of September 13, 1953, show.
Marilyn Monroe autopsy report.
Marilyn Monroe death certificate.
New York Times Archive.
Tommy Ewell interview 1987 (TV).

Correspondence with the author

November 22, 2011—E-mail from Harlan Boll (publicity for Carol Channing) in relation to her performance in Broadway's *Gentlemen Prefer Blondes* and Marilyn Monroe's month-long attendance as an audience member before reprising Channing's role of Lorelei Lee for the screen.
December 13, 18, 20, 2011—University of Southern California (USC), Cinema-Television Library material/special collections (e-mails from Ned Comstock), including trade paper reviews (1947–1950: *Daily Variety* and *Hollywood Reporter*), press book collection (various productions) and select material sourced from the 20th Century–Fox Collection (memos/letters/conference notes from Darryl Zanuck).
December 15, 2011—E-mail from Hal Schaefer regarding his musical collaborations with Marilyn Monroe.
January 27–March 24, 2011—E-mail communication with Luke Yankee, son of Academy Award-winning actress Eileen Heckart regarding his mother's admiration for Marilyn Monroe, as well as their working relationship on *Bus Stop* (1956).
May 24–August 5, 2012—E-mail correspondence with Lois Smith, Marilyn Monroe's New York publicist during the time she traveled east with Milton Greene, commenced work at the Actor's Studio, married Arthur Miller, left New York City for England and the duration of *The Prince and the Showgirl*. Smith said, "I was very fond of her, but I left for another job."
May 25–April 9, 2012—E-mail correspondence with Angela Allen, script supervisor on *The Misfits* (1961).
February 10, 2013—E-mail correspondence with Marian Collier Neuman, actress in *Some Like it Hot* (train berth scene; holding cocktail shaker and the hot water bottle, along with a scene featuring Marilyn Monroe and Tony Curtis in the toilet).
February 10–February 16, 2013—E-mail correspondence with world-renowned Marilyn Monroe collector and lecturer Greg Schreiner.
February 12–February 16, 2013—E-mail correspondence with world-renowned Marilyn Monroe collector and lecturer Scott Fortner.
February 14–February 19, 2013—E-mail correspondence with actor Christopher Riordan.
March 3–April 18, 2013—E-mail correspondence with Academy Award-winning actor/dancer George Chakiris.

Websites

Betts, Hannah. "Marilyn Monroe: The Star with Marbles in Her Bra." *The Telegraph*, March 13, 2012 (www.telegraph.co.uk).

Bigsby, Christopher. "Marilyn Monroe and Arthur Miller: Extract from Christopher Bigsby's Biography." *The Telegraph*, November 16, 2008 (www.telegraph.co.uk).

Burnside, Anna. "Monroe, Miller, Montand, Signoret: When Golden Couples Meet." *The Independent*, February 22, 2011 (www.independent.co.uk).

Finnigan, Kate. "Dressing Marilyn Monroe." *The Telegraph*, October 9, 2011 (http://fashion.telegraph.co.uk/).

Hyde, Theresa. "Conversation with the Devil: Interview with Tony Randall." *Houston Theatre*, March 11, 2000 (www.houstontheatre.com).

"Joe DiMaggio Died Convinced JFK Had Monroe Killed," *The Scotsman*, February 11, 2003 (www.scotsman.com).

Leigh, Wendy. "My Friend Marilyn Did Not Kill Herself." *Daily Mail*, March 3, 2007 (www.dailymail.co.uk).

Mondello, Bob. "Remembering Hollywood's Hays Code, 40 Years On." *National Public Radio*, August 8, 2008 (www.npr.org).

Rennel, Tony. "She Was a Sex Symbol and He Was an Aloof Intellectual. Why Did Marilyn Monroe Marry a Misfit?" *Daily Mail*, December 19, 2008 (www.dailymail.co.uk).

Taraborrelli, Randy J. "Joe DiMaggio Wanted Marilyn Monroe to Be His Demure Housewife So When She Posed for This Picture He Beat Her Up." *Daily Mail*, September 1, 2009 (www.dailymail.co.uk).

"The Lost Marilyn Monroe Nudes: Outtakes from Her Last On-Set Shoot Revealed in June's V.F." *Vanity Fair,* May 1, 2012 (www.vanityfair.com).

www.afi.com
www.ancestry.com
www.cursumperficio.net
www.dvdaust.com
www.dvdjournal.com
www.forbes.com
www.glbtq.com
www.ibdb.com
www.imdb.com
www.immortalmarilyn.com
www.lovingmarilyn.com
www.marilynmonroememories.co.uk
www.marilynmonroepages.com
www.mysterioustimes.net
www.newspaperarchive.com
www.oldmagazinearticles.com
www.tcm.com
www.trivia-library.com

Index

Numbers in **_bold italics_** indicate pages with photographs.

Aaker, Lee 76
Academy Awards 1, 43, 48, 95, 105, 108, 109, 121, 141, 143, 151, 168, 181, 191, 192, 193
Across the Wide Missouri 182
Actors Laboratory 31, 32, 53
Actors Studio 53, 113, 121, 122, 142, 188
Adair, Yvonne 87
Adams, Casey 121
Adamson, Harold 86
Addinsell, Richard 131
Adler, Buddy 120, 187
The Adventures of Don Juan 21
Advocate 4
The African Queen 100
After the Fall 170–171
"After You Get What You Want You Don't Want It" 105
Aguglia, Mimi 45
Ahern, Lloyd 60, 74
Ainsworth, Helen 29
"Ain't There Anyone Here for Love" 90
Albert, Eddie 182
Alberta, Canada 100
Alexander's Ragtime Band 106
"Alexander's Ragtime Band" 105
All About Eve 41, 45, 48, **_49_**, 181
Allan, Richard 81
Allan, Rupert 130
Allen, Fred 69, 76
Allen, Steve 171
Allyson, June 45, 46, 47
Alton, Robert 109, 110
Amagansett, Long Island, New York 141
American Film Institute 143, 147
anamorphic lens 95
Anderson, Daphne 131
Andes, Keith **_65_**, 66
Andrews Lake 182
Andriot, Lucien 49
Anna Christie 121
Annie Get Your Gun 107
"Anyone Can Tell I Love You" 35
"Anyone Here for Love?" 86
The Apartment 191
Arden, Eve 69, 70
Arlen, Harold 121
Armstrong, Charlotte 70

Armstrong, Louis 192
Arthur Miller: 1915–1962 58
Artist Alliance, Inc. 38
As Young as You Feel 51, **_52_**, 53–56, 59
The Asphalt Jungle 43, **_44_**, 45, 160, 181
Associated Press 156, 157
Atteridge, Harold 143
Australian tour 186
Autry, Gene 38, 180
Axelrod, George 112, 116, 120, 121, 188, 191

Baby Doll 188
Baby, I Don't Care 102
Baby Ruth candy bars 40
Bacall, Lauren 95, **_96_**, 97–98, 100, 190
Backus, Jim 70, 71
Bacon, Lloyd 180
Baden, Dr. Michael 167
Baker, Carroll 88
Baker, Gladys 183
Baker, Roy 70
Ball, Jane 19
Ballard, Lucien 62, 70, 74
Bancroft, Anne 70, 72, 73
Banff National Park 100
Banner, Lois 188, 189, 192, 193, 194
Bardot, Brigitte 139
The Barker 187
The Barkleys of Broadway 109
Barris, George 176
Barry, Dave 143
Barrymore, Lionel 45, 46
Barton, James 158
Bassler, Robert 41, 62
Bates, Barbara 48, 62, 63, 64
Baxter, Anne 41, 48, **_49_**, 60, 76, 83
Be Your Age 77
Beach, Wally 117
Bean, Margaret 64
Beckett, Scotty 29
Beddoe, Don 70, 72
Begley, Bert 47
Bel Air Hotel 33, 189
Belasco, Leon 38, 40
Belgard, Arnold 29
Bennett, Constance 51, 54
Benny, Jack 184, 185

Benoff, Mac 38
Benson, Sam 74
Berg, Louis 133
Bergen, Polly 178
Bergman, Ingrid 187
Berle, Milton 154
Berlin, Irving 105, 106, 107
Bernard, Butch 113
Bernie, Ben 143
Bernstein, Walter 171
Besser, Joe 151, 154
Betts, Hannah 33
Beverly Carlton Hotel 57
Beverly Hills Hotel 21, 151, 155
Bigsby, Christopher 53, 58
Bishop, Joey 193
Blaine, Vivian 186
Blaustein, Julian 70
Bliss-Hayden Miniature Theatre 31
Blonde Heat: The Sizzling Screen Career of Marilyn Monroe 41, 85, 120, 129, 157, 182
"Blondel" 93
Bloom, Rube 151
Blore, Eric 38
The Blue Angel 189
Blue Book Modeling Agency 19, 29
Blue Dragon Café 124, 125
The Bobby True Trio 35
Bogart, Humphrey 100
Bolenders, Ida and Albert 15–16, 18, 172
Boone, Pat 190, 194
Born Yesterday 181
Bosworth, Patricia 165, 167
Bouchey, Willis 70
Boyer, Charles 187
Boyle, Edward G. 143
Bracken, Eddie 69, 70
Brackett, Charles 81, 186
Brady, Scott 83
Brando, Marlon 194
Brascia, Johnny 109
Braus, Mortimer 62
Bray, Robert 121
Breakfast at Tiffany's 191
Breen, Richard L. 81
Breen Office 111, 115, 116
Brennan, Walter 32, 41, 70
Brentwood 178
Bridge, Al 69

203

British Academy of Television Arts and Sciences (BAFTA) 43, 95, 112, 121, 131, 143, 151
Britt, May 189
Brodine, Norbert 45
Brooks, Rand 35, 37
Brooks, Richard 189
The Brothers Karamazov 189
Brown, Barbara 50, 51
Brown, James 47
Brown, Joe E. 143, 144–145
Brown, Vanessa 117
Brown, Wally 51
Bryan, Dora 87
Bryant, Nana 35, 37
Brynner, Yul 151, 152
Buck, Jules 60
Bulova watches 40
Burnett, W.R. 43
Burns, David 151
Burns, Kevin 177–178
Burr, Raymond 38
Burton, Richard 174
Bus Stop 21, 120–121, **122**, **123**, 124–125, **126**, 127–131, 137, 147
"The Bus Stop Song" 121
Buskin, Richard 41, 85, 120, 129, 157, 182
By Myself and Then Some 97
"By the Beautiful Sea" 143
"Bye, Bye Baby" 87, 185

Cadillac 185
Cagney, Jeanne 70
Cahn, Sammy 151
Calgary, Canada 103–104
Calhern, Louis 43, 69
Calhoun, Rory 41, 95, 98, 100, 101, 103, 182
Cal-Neva Lodge 166
Cameron, James 49
Can-Can 191
Canadian Rockies 100
Capote, Truman 191
Cardiff, Jack 131, 135, 137
Carey, Macdonald 62, **63**, 64, 182
Carmichael, Hoagy 86
Carole, Joseph 34
Carroll, Diahann 192
Carroll, Harry 143
Carroll, John 32, 34
Caruso, Antony 43
Cary Grant: A Biography 80
Casey, Kenneth 143
Cashin, Bonnie 32
Castro, Fidel 8
Catholic League of Decency 116
Cedars of Lebanon Hospital 80
Celebration 192–193
Celli, Teresa 43, 45
Chakiris, George 1, 2, 91, 105, 108
Chamberlain, George Agnew 32
Chanel No. 5 84
Channing, Carol 87
Chapman, Marguerite 112
Charisse, Cyd 171, 172, 176
Chayefsky, Paddy 61
Cheesecake Queen of 1952 64
Chevalier, Maurice 191

Chicago, Illinois 40, 170
Chief Yowlachie 41
Chrétien, Henri 95
Christian Science 16
Christmas Day 1963 178
CIA 5, 7–8, 138
Cincinnati, Ohio 43
Cinemascope 95, 96–97, 100, 102, 105, 112, 121, 151, 185, 188
"The Clarion Call" 76
Clark, Colin 133
Clark, Fred 95
Clark Gable: A Biography 165
Clash by Night 56, 64, **65**, 66–67
Claude Productions 176
Clemmons, Jack 8, 10, 11
Cleopatra 171, 174
Cleveland, Ohio 40
Clift, Montgomery 147, 158, **159**, 160, 161, 165, 167–168, **169**, 191
Clyde McCoy and His Sugar Blues Orchestra 143
Coast Guard 83
Coates, Carroll 151
Coburn, Charles 77, 86, 87, 88, **89**, 91, 180
Coca-Cola 61
The Coconut Girl 133, 135
Cohen, Harold V. 117
Cohn, Harry 32, 36, 37–38, 181, 190
Colbert, Claudette 62, **63**
Cold Shoulder 48, 181
Cole, Jack 91–93, 109, 110
Collins, Joan 186
Collins, Russell 81
Columbia Studios 32–33, 34, 36, 37–38, 53, 87, 180, 181, 190
Columbia University Hospital 166
Comedy Theatre 138–139
Confessions of an Actor 141
Conklin, Chester 47
Connors, Chuck 178
Conover, David 18–19
Conreid, Hans 121
Consolidated Film Industries 18
Conte, Richard 181
Coogan, Jackie 98
Cook, Elisha, Jr. 70, 71
"Cool It, Baby" 151
Cooper, Gary 115, 116
Cooper, Melville 38
The Cop and the Anthem (1917 silent film) 77
The Cop and the Anthem (1954 Red Skelton Christmas Show) 77
Corbett, Glenn 47
Corbett, Scott 60
Corcoran, Donna 70, 71
Cornthwaite, Robert 77
Coshocton Tribune 190
Cosmopolitan magazine 158–159, 176
Cotten, Joseph 81, 83, 84, **85**, 86
Cowan, Jerome 29
Cowan, Lester 38, 39–40
Cox, Wally 171, 172, 175
Craft, Roy 80
Crain, Jeanne 60, 76, 83, 180

Crawford, Joan 23, 139
Creature from the Black Lagoon 114, 117
Crisp, Donald 50
Crosby, Bing 154–155
Crowther, Bosley 56, 91, 100, 104, 110, 117, 129, 140
The Crucible 170
"Cry" 110
Crystal Star Award 131, 141
Cuba 8, 138
Cukor, George 151, 153, 156, 157, 171, 172, 174, 175, 176, 177, 181
Cummins, Peggy 180
"La Cumparsita" 143
Cupidone 80
Curtis, Tony 120, 143, 144, **145**, 146, 147, 148, 149, 190, 194

Dahl, Arlene 139
Dailey, Dan 41, 105, 179, 180
Daily Register 33
Daily Variety 19, 50
Dale, Esther 77
Dalio, Marcel 86
Dallas 27
The Dallas Morning News 45
Dangerous Years 29, **30**, 31, 34, 50
Darby, Ken 100, 121
D'Arcy, Alex 95
Darling, I Am Growing Younger 77
Darvi, Bella 183
Darwell, Jane 69
David, Michael 151
David di Donatello Awards 131, 141
Davies, Marion 186
Davis, Bette 48, **49**
Davis, Drusilla 109
Davis, Sammy, Jr. 12, 193
Dawson, Beatrice 131
Day, Doris 178
Day, Vera 131, 134
Day-Lewis, Daniel 170
Dayton, Nevada 158
Dean, Loomis 180
DeCamp, Rosemary 29
De Chazza, Pepe 109
Dekker, Albert 51, 54
Denver, Colorado 41
Denver & Rio Grande Western Railroad 41
The Deseret News 181
Detroit, Michigan 40
Deutsch, Adolph 143
Deutsch, Armand 45
Diamond, I.A.L 60, 62, 77, 105, 143, 144–146
"Diamonds Are a Girl's Best Friend" 23, 24, 25, 86, 90, 91–93, 95; dress 24, 25
Dietrich, Marlene 189
DiMaggio, Joe 8–9, 11–**14**, 80, 107–108, 112, 116, 117, 118, 131, 166, 183
DiMaggio, Joe, Jr. 9, 12, 13, 14
DiMaggio: Getting the Record Straight 9
Directors Guild of America (DGA Awards) 43, 112, 121, 143, 158

Dodger Stadium 176
Don't Bother to Knock 21, 70, **71**, 72–74, 81
Dostoevsky, Fyodor 189
Dougherty, Ethel 18–19
Dougherty, Jim 12, 18–19, 29
Douglas, Paul 65, 66, 67, 69, 70
"Down Among the Sheltering Palms" 143
"Down, Boy" 88, 91
"Down in the Meadow" 100
Down Syndrome 168, 170
Dratler, Jay 68
Dressed: A Century of Hollywood Costume Design 91
Dumke, Ralph 47
Dunne, Irene 171
du Plessix Gray, Francine 168
Durango, Colorado 41, 182

Easter Parade 109
Eastham, Richard 105
Edgar Allan Poe Awards 43
Edith Head 194
Edwards, Stacy 118
The Egyptian 183
Ekberg, Anita 139
Eliot, Marc 80
Elizabeth: The Life of Elizabeth Taylor 168
Elizabeth II see Queen of England
Emerson, Hope 70
Empire Theatre 139
Engelberg, Dr. Hyman 7, 10
Ephron, Henry 105–106
Ephron, Phoebe 105–106
Esquire 33, 158
Esther the Chimp 77, 78
The Evening News 155
"Every Baby Needs a Da Da Daddy" 35
Ewell, Tom 112, 113, 115, 116–118, 120

Famous Artists Agency 56, 183
Fanfare d'Amour 144
Fanfaren der Liebe 144
Fapp, Daniel L. 153
"Fastest Rising Star of 1952" 21
Fay, Frank 60
FBI 7–8
Feldman, Charles K. 56, 112, 183
Felton, Verna 70, 72
Fenton, Frank 100, 104
Ferrer, Jose 194
Field, Betty 121
Fields, Joseph 86
The Films of Marilyn Monroe 73
Finishing the Picture 170, 171
The Fire Ball 47–48, 181
Fisher, Joan 63
Fisk Tires 40
Flavin, James 74
Fleischer, Richard 186
"flying red horse" see Mobil Oil
Flynn, Errol 21, 185
Forbes 11
Forbes, Bryan 194
Forbes, Louis 49

Ford, Tennessee Ernie 100
Form Divine 183
Forty Guns 188
Foulk, Robert 74
The Four Lads 121
The Four Million 76
Fox Film Corporation 32
Francis, Anne 83
Freddie the Freeloader 76
French, Hugh 56
Freud 164, 191
Freud, Anna 137, 191
Friedlob, Bert E. 47
Fuller, Samuel 188
Fulton Theatre 116
Furse, Roger 131, 133, 140

Gable, Clark 18, 158, 160, 161, 161, 165, 166, 167, **169**, 182, 187
Gable, John Clark 185
Gable, Kay 165, 166
Gabor, Zsa Zsa 69
Gadsden Times 157
Gaines, Richard 29
Gallaudet, John 45
Garland, Judy 13
Garner, James 178
Garnett, Tay 47
Garr, Eddie 35, 37
Gaynor, Mitzi 69, 70, 105, 106, 109, 111
Gehman, Richard 156, 157
General Brock Hotel 85
General Electric 40
Genesis Awards 158
Gentlemen Prefer Blondes 1, 11, 21, **23**, 24, **25**, 26, 86–87, **88–89**, 90–91, **92**, 93, **94**, 95, 100, 185, 186
George Washington Bridge 95
Geray, Steven 35, 86
Giancana, Sam 7, 8
Gibbs, A.H. 143
Gifford, C. Stanley 17–18
"The Gift of the Magi" 76
Gilchrist, Connie 41
Gillespie, Haven 81
The Girl in Pink Tights 183
The Girl in the Red Velvet Swing 186
"Give Me the Simple Life" 151
Glamour Preferred 31
Gleason, James 69
"God Bless America" 107
Goddard, Grace McKee 16, 18, 29
Gogo 193
"Golden Dreams" 24, 26
Golden Globes 1, 43, 77, 112, 117, 121, 143, 151, 158, 181
Golden Laurel Awards 131, 143, 151
Goldstein, Leonard 182
The Good, the Bad, and Me: In My Anecdotage 161
Goodbye, Charlie 190, 194
Goodman Theatre 170
Goodwin, Harold 131
Gordon, Bruce 38
Gordon, Lee 186
Gordon, Michael 178

Gottfried, Martin 151
Gould, Deborah 8
Goulding, Edmond 68, 179
Grable, Betty 29, 87, 95, **96**, 97, 98, 99, 100, 179, 182, 186
Grammy Awards 143
Grandison, Lionel 11
Granger, Farley 76, 186
Grant, Cary 77, 79, 80, 81, 144, 151, 152, 171, 187
Grauman's Chinese Theatre 93
Gray, Billy 143
The Greatest Show on Earth 81
Green Grass of Wyoming 180
Greene, Amy 141–142, 185
Greene, Milton 112, 120, 129, 131, 133, 137, 141, 142, 185
Greenson, Dr. Ralph 7, 9, 166
Greenway, Tom 74
Grey, Joe 143
Griffith, Richard 125
The Gun and the Cross 186
Gurdin, Dr. Michael 57
Guys and Dolls 186

Hagen, Earle 105, 151
Hagen, Jean 43
"Hair of Gold" 180
Hakim, Andre 74
Hal Roach Studios 49
Hale, Alan, Jr. 50, 51
Halop, William 29
"Happy Birthday, Mr. President" 174
Hardt, Eloise 171
Hardwick, Paul 131
Harline, Leigh 77
Harlow, Jean 33, 37, 187
Harrah's Club 164
Harrison, Doane 143
Hart, Anne 87
Harvey, Harry, Jr. 29
Harvey, Laurence 194
Hathaway, Henry 81, 83–84, 85, 194
Haver, June 32, 34, 60
Haworth, Ted 143
Hawks, Howard 76, 77, 79, 80, 81, 86, 93
Hawthorne, California 15
Hayden, Sterling 43
Hayes, Alfred 64
Haymes, Dick 179
Hays Code 91, 146, 147
Hayworth, Rita 57, 190
Head, Edith 48
"Heat Wave" 105, 107–109, 110, 112, 118
Hecht, Ben 77
Heckart, Eileen 121, **126**, 127–128, 147
Heffernan, Harold 45
Hefner, Hugh 26
Heilweil, Alexandra 171, 172
Henaghan, Jim 80
Henrikson, Bert 143
Henry, O. 74, 76, 77
Henson, Gladys 131
Hepburn, Audrey 191–192

Herbert, F. Hugh 32
Heston, Charlton 151, 152
"Hey You with the Crazy Eyes" 151
Hickman, Darryl 29
Hill, George Roy 192–193
Hitchcock, Alfred 147
Hodiak, John 182
Hoffa, Jimmy 7, 8
Hoffman, Kurt 144
Hogan, Mickey 182
Hogan, Tilford 17
Hohenberg, Margaret 137
Holden, William 115, 116
Holliday, Judy 29, 48, 86, 87, 181
Holliday, Marjorie 74
Holly Golightly 192
Hollywood Production Code 25
The Hollywood Reporter 70, 116, 186
Hollywood Studio Club 35
Holm, Celeste 48, 49
Holmes, Taylor 86, 87
Home Town Story 48, *49*, 50–51, 181
Homolka, Oscar 112, 114
Hopper, Hedda 108, 177
The Horn Blows at Midnight 184, 185
Hornblow, Arthur, Jr. 43
Hoshelle, Marjorie 37
Hotel del Coronado, Coronado, California 143
House Un-American Activities Committee 53
How to Be Very, Very Popular 98, 186
How to Marry a Millionaire 21, 86, 95, *96*, 97–100, 185
Hubert, Rene 41
Hudson, Rock 151, 153
Hudson River, New York 95
Hughes, Howard 29
Hughes, Kenneth 194
Hull, Henry 32
Hull, Josephine 48
Hunnicutt, Arthur 41
Hunter, Jeffrey 83, 183
Huston, John 43, 45, 124, 158, 160, 161, 162, 163, 164–165, **169**, 191
Hutton, Betty 57
Hutton, Marion 8, 40
Hyams, Joe 121, 147
Hyde, Johnny **55**, 57–58, 59
Hyde-White, Wilfrid 151, 154, 157

I Could Have Sung All Night 95
I Love Louisa 193
"I Wanna Be Loved by You" 143
"If You Believe" 105, 110
"I'm Gonna File My Claim" 100, 109
"I'm So Crazy for You" 35
"I'm Through with Love" 143
"Incurably Romantic" 151
Indiscreet 187
Inge, William 120, 121, 125, 193
Iowa 34
Irma La Douce 193

"I've Got My Love to Keep Me Warm" 105
Iver Heath, Buckinghamshire, England 131
Ives, Burl 180

The Jack Benny Show 184–185
Jackson, Harry 41
Jackson, Michael 11
Jacobs, Arthur P. 192–193, 194
Jaffe, Sam 43
James, Harry 98, 100
James, Lorenzo 167
Japan 109, 183
Jasper National Park 100
jazz 192
Jeakins, Dorothy 81, 153
Jean de Florette 155
The Jean Harlow Story 187
Jean Louis 158, 171, 173
Jenssen, Elois 68
Jergens, Adele 35, **36**, 37
Jewel of Bengai 186
Johnson, Erskine 80, 163
Johnson, Nunnally 68, 70, 95, 96, 171, 177
Jones, Carolyn 112
Jones, Harmon 51
Joslyn, Allyn 51, 179
Jourdan, Louis 83, 191
Joy, Leatrice 60
Judgment at Nuremberg 168
Just Lucky I Guess: A Memoir of Sorts 87
Just Outside the Spotlight: Growing Up with Eileen Heckart 127

Kahn, Gus 143
Kalmar, Bert 143
Kane, Hermett 187
Kanin, Garson 181
Kansas 34
Kanter, Hal 153
Kaplan, Sol 81
Karger, Anne 35
Karger, Fred 34–35
Karger, Mary 35
Karlan, Richard 74
Karlson, Phil 34
Karnes, Robert 32
Kaus, Gina 68
Kazan, Elia 53, 188, 190
Keating, Larry 77
Kelley, Barry 43, 45, 46
Kelley, Natalie 26
Kelley, Tom 24, 26, 65
Kelly, Gene 155, 183
Kemper, Charles 41, 179
Kennedy, John F. 7, 9, 14, 138, 173, 174
Kennedy, Robert F. 7–8, 9, 11
Kennedy Center 9
Kent, Jean 131, 136
Ketchum, Idaho 121
Keyes, Evelyn 112
Kind Sir 187
King, Dennis, Jr. 151
King, Henry 76, 102, 182
King, Larry 111

King, Louis 180
The Kingsport Times 23
"Kiss" 81, 84
Kline, Benjamin H. 29
Knight, Esmond 113
Knots Landing 27
Knotts, Don 178
Kobal, John 195
Kool cigarettes 40
Korea 183
Korean trip 183
Koster, Henry 75, 96
Krasna, Norman 153, 187
Krasner, Milton 48, 74, 77, 112, 121
Kris, Dr. Marianne 165, 166, 191
Kulky, Henry 60

Ladd, Alan 186
Ladies of the Chorus 34–35, **36**, 37–38
"Ladies of the Chorus" (song) 35
The Lady and the Lumberjack 186
The Lady or the Tiger 183
Lake Louise 100
Landau, Arthur 187
Lang, Charles, Jr. 143
Lang, Fritz 64, 66, 67
Lang, Walter 105, 111, 112, 179, 191
Lange, Hope 121, 125
Lantz, Louis 100
LaShelle, Joseph 100
"The Last Leaf" 76
"A Last Long Talk with a Lonely Girl" 95
Laughton, Charles 74
Lawford, Peter 7–8, 12, 27, 130, 178, 193
Lawrence, Marc 43
"Lazy" 105, 110, 111
Lederer, Charles 77, 86
Ledontal, Henri 77, 78
Lee, Lester 34–5
Leicester Square 139
Leigh, Vivien 134, 137, 138, 139, 140
Leigh, Wendy 11
LeJeune, C.A. 111
LeMaire, Charles 48, 62, 74, 95, 105
Lemmon, Jack 143, 144, **145**, 146, 148, 149, 150, 191
"Let's Have Another Cup o' Coffee" 105
Let's Make It Legal 62, **63**, 64
Let's Make Love 151, **152**, 153–157, 161, 166, 175
"Let's Make Love" (song) 151
Levant, Oscar 76
The Lewiston Daily Sun 165–166
Lewiston Morning Tribune 172
Lexington, Kentucky 43
Library of Congress 14, 43
Life 39, 80, 85, 176, 180
Lili 117
Lind, Carole 29
Lind, Jenny 30
Lindeman, Edith 104
Lipton, Harry 29, 57

"A Little Girl from Little Rock" 86
Little, Very Reverend Monsignor Thomas F. 146
"The Little White Cloud That Cried" 110
Livingston, Jay 143
Lloyd, Jimmy 180
Lockhart, Gene 179
Loeffler, Louis R. 104
Loew's State Theatre 112, 116
Logan, Joshua 120, 121, 124, 125, 126, 127, 128, 129, 132–133, 137
Logan, Michael 143, 144
Lombard, Carole 30
London, England 131, 137, 139, 140, 174
London Sunday Observer 111
Lonelyhearts 147
Long, Tamara 87
Look 45
Loos, Anita 86, 193
Loos, Mary 41
Lorelei 87
Lorelei Lee 1, 87, 95
Los Angeles, California 8, 112, 113, 158, 164, 167
Los Angeles Herald-Examiner 84
Los Angeles Mirror News 124
Los Angeles Orphans' Home 16, 80
Los Angeles Police Department 5, 8, 12
Los Angeles Times 31, 66, 74, 91, 103, 125, 133, 140, 182, 186, 187, 189
Love Happy 38, *39*, 40
Love Nest 34, 60, *61*, 62
Lower, Ana 18–19, 34
Luez, Laurette 180
Lundigan, William 60
Lyceum Theatre 87
Lynn, Jeffrey 49, 50–51
Lynn, Mara 151
Lyon, Ben 29, 30
Lytess, Natasha 34, 55–56, 57–59, 65, 67, *92*, 93, 97, 101, 102, 113, 181, 183

MacBride, Donald 112, 114
MacDonald, Joseph 51, 74, 81, 95
MacKenzie, Joyce 41
MacLaine, Shirley 128, 172, 191, 193, 194
Maddow, Ben 43
"Maf" 8
Mafia 7–8
Magnum Photo Agency 168
Malneck, Matty 143
"A Man Chases a Girl (Until She Catches Him)" 105
Mankiewicz, Joseph L. 48, 49
Mansfield, Jayne 174–175, 187, 188
Mantle, Mickey 9
Mapes Casino, Reno, Nevada 158
Maples Hotel 164
Margaret Herrick Library 186, 191
"Marie" 105
Marilyn Monroe and Arthur Miller: Extract from Christopher Bigsby's Biography 53
Marilyn Monroe Productions 11,
112, 120, 125, 131, 133, 141, 142, 172, 190
Marilyn Monroe: The Final Days 177
Marilyn: The Passion and the Paradox 188
Marilyn: The Untold Story 183
Marlowe, Hugh 48, 77, 78
Marshall, Marion 8
Martin, Dean 12, 131, 171, 172, 173, 174, 175, 176, 177, 193
Martin, Edwin 74
Martin, Ida 17
Martin, Mary 187
Marx, Chico 38, 40
Marx, Groucho 38, 39, 40
Marx, Harpo 38, 40
Marx Brothers 38, 40
Massey, Ilona 38, 40
Mather, Jack 74
Matos Rodriguez, Gerardo 143
Matthau, Walter 116
Mature, Victor 139, 181
Maugham, Somerset 192
Mayers, Bernard 105
MCA 113
McCallister, Lon 32
McCarthy, Sen. Joseph 53
McCarthy, Kevin 158, 161
McCleery, Albert 189
McCoy, Clyde 143
McCoy, Horace 47
McEvoy, Renny 50
McGiver, John 171
McHugh, Frank 105
McIntire, A.T. 33
McIntyre, John 43
McKinley Hotel 71
McLean, Barbara 182
medical examiner 167
Meet Me After the Show 182
Mellor, William C. 38
Melson, Inez 12, 81, 130
Memoirs of a Professional Cad 48
Memorial Day 175
Menjou, Adolphe 182
Merande, Doro 112
Mercer, Johnny 121, 171
Meridien-Journal 157
Merman, Ethel 105, 106, 107, 109, 111
Merrill, Gary 48
Merryman, Richard 95, 176
the "Method" 53, 121, 137
Metty, Russell 158
MGM 43, 45, 49, 182, 189
The Miami News 40
Middle of the Night 190
The Midwife of Pont Clary 189
Milestone, Kendall 130
Milestone, Lewis 130
Milland, Ray 186
Miller, Arthur 12, 53, 125, 129, 130, 131, 136, 137, 138, 139, 140, 141, 142, 148–149, 152, 153, 154, 158, 159–160, 161, 163, 164, 165, 167, 168, **169**, 170, 178, 187, 189; plays 132, 138–139, 170–171
Miller, Daniel 168, 170
Miller, David 38
Miller, Eve 105
Miller, Isidore 14
Miller, Jane 170
Miller, Morton 158
Miller, Rebecca 168, 170
Miller, Robert 170
Mills, Thomas R. 77
Milwaukee, Wisconsin 40
The Milwaukee Sentinel 156, 157, 187
Minciotti, Silvio 65
Miracle, Berniece 12
Mirisch, Harold 193
The Misfits 131, 154, 158, **159**, 160–171, 175, 192
Misfits Flat, Stagecoach, Nevada 158
Miss Cheesecake of the Year 64
Missing Persons' Bureau 17
Missouri 34
Mitchell, Cameron 95, 98
Mitchell, Millard 83
Mitchum, John 47
Mitchum, Robert 47, 100, **101**, 102, 103, 104
Mobil Oil 40
Mocambo 111
Mockridge, Cyril 32, 41, 51, 60, 62, 68, 95, 100, 120–121
Molas Lake, Colorado 41
Monahan, Kaspar 81
Monkey Business 21, 24, 77–81
Monroe, Della 16–17
Monroe, Jack 17
Monroe, Marilyn **22, 23, 25, 30, 33, 36, 42, 44, 46, 49, 52, 55, 61, 63, 65, 68, 75, 82, 85, 88–89, 92, 94, 96, 101, 106, 108, 119, 122, 145, 159, 169, 173**; addiction 9; anxiety 4, 9; autopsy 10–11; birth 15; death 3, 4, 5, 7–8, 10; depression 9; diary 8; divorces 11, 19; drug use 4, 7, 9; father 17–18; foster parents/guardians 15–17; funeral 12–13; health issues 4, 9; homes 8, 15, 16, 177; husbands 13; insecurity 3, 4; insomnia 9; Los Angeles Orphans' Home 16; Marilyn Monroe Productions 11; marriages 11, 13; miscarriages 9; model 1, 19; mother 15–18; murder 4–5, 7–8, 10; Norma Jeane 1, 13, 15–19, 29; overdose 7, 10; pets 8, 15; pregnancies 9; rape 17; relationship with Kennedys 7–8; sexual abuse 4; sexual molestation 17; suicide 10–11; tardiness 3, 9; therapy 7, 9; Twentieth Century-Fox 10, 19
Monroe, Marion Otis 17
Monroe, Otis 17
Montalban, Ricardo 45, 46–47, 81, 182
Montand, Yves 151, 153, 154, 155, 156, 157, 161
Montgomery Clift: A Bibliography 168

Montgomery Clift: A Biography 167
Monthly Film Bulletin 84
Moore, Dickie 29, 31
Moore, Victor 69, 112, 115
Morath, Inge 168, 170
Moriarty, Evelyn 175
Morley, Robert Christopher 171, 172
Morosco, Walter 32
Morrison, Charlie 111
Morrison, Marilyn 111
Mortenson, Gladys Baker 12, 15–18, 80–81
Mortenson, Martin Edward 17
Mother Wore Tights 29, 179
Move Over, Darling 178
MPAA 146
Mrs. Dewey 16
Murder by Strangulation 100
Murray, Christopher 125
Murray, Don 121, *122*, 124–125
Murray, Eunice 7–8
Murray, Natalia Danesi 193
Murray, Patricia 125
Murrow, Edwin R. 185
Musaraca, Nicholas 64
Muscular Dystrophy Association 176
My Favorite Wife 171
"My Heart Belongs to Daddy" 151, 154
My Mother-in-Law, Miriam 62
My Week with Marilyn 128, 133
The Mystery of Marilyn Monroe 67

Nadoolman, Deborah 91
Naish, J. Carroll 65, 66
The Naked Truth 193
National Board of Review 43, 131
National Catholic Legion of Decency 146
National Concert Artists Corporation 29
National Film Preservation Board 143
National Film Registry 43, 143
NBC 192
Nebraska 34
Negulesco, Jean 1, 71, 76, 95, 100, 104, 171, 177, 189
"A New Wrinkle" 24
New York City, New York 40, 53, 76, 112, 113, 116, 117, 118, 121, 122, 136, 137, 142, 165, 167, 170, 173, 179
New York Daily News 104
New York Hospital 166
New York Journal-American 155
New York Times 56, 69, 70, 84, 91, 100, 110, 117, 128, 129, 140, 146, 153, 170
New York World 76
New York Yankees 13
Newcomb, Pat 176
Newman, Alfred 48, 74, 95, 98, 105, 112, 121
Newman, Joseph 60
Newman, Lionel 70, 81, 84, 100, 105, 153

Newman, Paul 192
Niagara 33, 41, 81, *82*, 83–84, **85**, 86, 100
Niagara Falls, New York 83, 84
Nivea 34
Nixon, Marni 86, 95
Noguchi, Thomas 7, 11
Nolan, Lloyd 180
Noonan, Tommy 86, 87
North, Alex 158
North, Sheree 183, 186
North Fork Store, National Forest, Idaho 121
Norwalk State Hospital 16
Novak, Kim 172, 190, 194

O. Henry Award 77
O. Henry's Full House 41, 74, **75**, 76–77
O'Brian, Hugh 105
O'Brien, Pat 47–48, 143
Ocean's Eleven 130
O'Connell, Arthur 121, 128
O'Connor, Donald 105, *106*, 107, 111–112
O'Dea, Denis 81, 83
Odets, Clifford 64, 190
The Oelwein Daily Register 34
Of Human Bondage 192, 194
"Oh, What a Forward Young Man You Are" 41
O'Hara, Maureen 180
Okinawa 35
Olivier, Laurence 131, 132–133, 134, 135, 136, 137, 138, 139–140, 141
"One Silver Dollar" 100
12305 Fifth Helena Drive, Brentwood 177
An Open Book 165
Orry-Kelly 143, 179
Owen, Gillian 131

Paar, Jack 60, 62
Paget, Debra 183
Palace Theatre 87
Palmer, Ernest 32
Panavision 97
Pappenheim, Bertha 191
Paris Blues 192
"Park Avenue Fantasy (Stairway to the Stars)" 143
Parkside House 131
Parsons, Harriet 64, 66
Parsons, Louella A. 53, 165, 166, 181, 187
Patrick, Lee 105
Patterson, Elizabeth 179
Payne Whitney Psychiatric Hospital 165, 166
Peck, Gregory 151–152, 154, 156
People in the Wind 121
Perlberg, William 179
Pershoff, Nehemiah 143
Person to Person 185
Personal: From the Private Archive of Marilyn Monroe 189
Peters, Jean 51, 54, 76, 81, 83
Philosophy in Turbulent Times 191

Phoenix, Arizona 121, 124, 127–128
Photoplay 21, 142
Pickford, Mary 38, 40
Pieces of My Heart: A Life 64
Pierson, Arthur 29, 49, 50
Pinewood Studios 131
Pinkard, Maceo 143
Pittsburgh Post-Gazette 117, 156, 183
The Pittsburgh Press 81, 153
The Plain Dealer 160
Planer, Frank 171
Playboy 26
Playboy Magazine Price Guide Checklist 26
Plaza Hotel 133
Plowman, Melinda 50, 51
Poitier, Sidney 192
Porter, Cole 151
Powell, Dick 45, *46*, 47
Powell, William 95, 99
Power, Tyrone 182–183
Powers, Tom 45
Preminger, Otto 100, 101, 102, 103, 104, 147
Presidential Birthday Gala 14, 173
Presley, Elvis 11
The Press-Courier 153, 175
"A Pretty Girl Is Like a Melody" 105
The Prince and the Showgirl 113, 131, *132*, 133–142
Princess Margaret 139
Princess of the Nile 182–183
Producers Guild of America Awards (PGA) 143
Production Code Administration 80, 146
Promises! Promises! 175
Prunzik, Karen 87
Pyramid Lake, Nevada 158

Quail Canyon, Reno, Nevada 158
Queen of England 139; *see also* Elizabeth II

Radioplane Company 18–19
Raft, George 143, 144
Rain 192
Rain: A Play in Three Acts 192
Raintree County 167
Raksin, David 45, 179
Randall, Tony 151, 154, 156, 157, 188
"Randolph Street Rag" 143
"The Ransom of Red Chief" 76
Rat Pack 130, 193
Ratoff, Gregory 48, 76
Rattigan, Terence 131, 133
Ray, Johnnie 105, 110, 111
Ray Anthony and His Orchestra 171
Raymond, Robin 105
The Red Skelton Show 77
Redbook 80
Redman, Frank 34
Reid, Elliott 86, 87
Reisch, Walter 81

"Remember" 105
Remick, Lee 172, 190
Renie 51, 60, 62
Rennie, Michael 83, 183
Reno, Nevada 158, 161, 161, 162, 164, 170
Reno Evening Gazette 149
Rettig, Tommy 100, 101, 102, 103, 104
Revere, Anne 32, 179
The Revolt of Mamie Stover 188
Reynolds, Debbie 26, 119, 142, 190, 194
Reynolds, Marjorie 50
Richmond Times Dispatch 104
Rickards, Jocelyn 140
Riders of the Whistling Pines 38, 180
Right Cross 45, **46**, 47
Riordan, Christopher 129–131
Risdon, Elisabeth 179
Ritt, Martin 192
Ritter, Thelma 48, 49, 51, 53–54, 158, 161, 178
The River of No Return 21, 100, **101**, 102–105, 109
"River of No Return" (song) 100, 104
RKO 64, 65
Robbins, Jerome 92
The Robe 96
Robert Meltzer Award 43
Robert Mitchum: Baby I Don't Care 102
Roberts, Allan 34–35
Roberts, Roy 179
Robertson, Dale 76
Robin, Leo 86
Rockhaven Sanatarium 81
Rockwood, Colorado 41
Rodgers, Dr. Mortimer 190
Rodman, Tori 177
Rogers, Ginger 68, 77, 78, 87
Rome, Italy 174
Romm, Harry A. 34
Ronell, Ann 38
Rooney, Mickey 47–48
Rose, Helen 45
Rosson, Harold 43
Rosten, Hedda 131
Roudinesco 191
Roxy Theatre 95
Royal Film Performance 139
Royal Triton Gasoline 181
Rozsa, Miklos 43
Rubin, Stanley 100, 102, 104
Ruby, Harry 143, 151
Rudolph the Chimp 77
"Runnin' Wild" 143
Russell, Jane 11, 86, 87, 90, 91, 93, **94**, 95, 186, 188
Ryan, Robert 65, 66
Ryman, Lucille 32, 34

Sacks, Patti 35
"A Sailor's Not a Sailor ('Til a Sailor's Been Tattooed)" 105
Sale, Richard 41, 62, 182
San Diego, California 149

San Diego Union 74
Sanders, George 48, **49**
Sauber, Harry 34
Schaefer, Hal 105, 110
Schallert, Edwin 66, 91, 187
Schell, Maria 189
Schenck, Joseph 32, 45
Scheuer, Philip K. 74, 140, 189
Schiller, Lawrence 174, 175
Schnee, Charles 45
Schreiner, Greg 93, 166, 175
Schwab's Drug Store 110
Scofield, Paul 194
Scott, Randolph 171
Scott, Zachary 62, **63**
Screen Actors Guild (SAG) 117, 155, 161
screen test 181
Scudda-Hoo! Scudda-Hay! 31, 32, **33**, 34
Seaton, George 179
Segall, Harry 77
Sen Yung, Victor 41
Sergeant York 95
Serling, Rod 192
Server, Lee 102
Seven Arts Productions 158
The Seven Year Itch 13, 21, 26, 112–118, **119**, 120, 150
Shamroy, Leon 105, 179
Sharaff, Irene 91
Shaw, Anabel 29
Shawlee, Joan 143
Shayer Detective Service 17
Shields, Arthur 179
The Shocking Miss Pilgrim 179
Show Boat 106
Showalter, Max aka Casey Adams 81, 83, 85–86
Shurlock, Geoffrey 146
Sidney, George 187
Siegel, Sol C. 77, 86, 105, 106
Signorelli, Frank 143
Signoret, Simone 151, 155, 157
Silvers, Phil 171
Silverton, Colorado 41
"Simple Melody" 105
Sinatra, Frank 8, 12, 131, 166, 171, 183, 191, 193
"Sing Me the Song That Sells" 151
Sitting Pretty 180
Skelton, Red 77
Skolsky, Sidney 84, 187
Skouras, Spyros 56
Slatzer, Robert 13
The Sleeping Prince 133
The Smiling Rebel 187
Smith, Barbara 41
Smith, Constance 83
Snively, Emmeline 19, 29
Snyder, Allan ("Whitey") 12, 30–31, 32, 129
Some Like It Hot 21, 113, 142, 143–144, **145**, 146–150, 153, 191
"Some Like It Hot" (song) 143
Some Like It Hot: Me, Marilyn and the Movie 120, 146, 148, 149
Something's Got to Give 4, 10, 21, 56, 161, 171–172, **173**, 174–178, 193

Something's Gotta Give (song) 171
"Somewhere Over the Rainbow" 13
The Southeast Missourian 153
Special Olympics 170
"Specialization" 151
Spencer, Douglas 77, 100
Spencer, Herbert W. 105
Spenser, Jeremy 131, 136
Spewack, Bella 171
Spewack, Sam 171
The Spokane Daily Chronicle 155
The Spokesman Review 64
Springfield Union 117
Stage Door 32
Stahl, John M. 179
Stanley, Ralph 29
Stanwyck, Barbara 65, 66, 67, 188
Stapleton, Maureen 83, 121, 147
Stare 21
Starring Miss Barbara Stanwyck 188
Stars and Stripes 26, 64, 188
Steinbeck, John 74
Stern, Bert 176
Stevenson, Edward 74
Stewart, Jimmy 115, 151, 153
Stewart, Marianne 45
Stewart, Paul 69, 70
Stone, George E. 143
Stone, Milburn 47
The Story on Page One 190
Strasberg, Lee 13, 113, 121, 122, 124, 125, 137, 166, 170, 191, 192
Strasberg, Paula 67, 113, 121, 125, 131, 132, 136, 137, 140, 162, 163, 166, 170, 177, 191
Strauss, Robert 112, 114
The Stripper 21, 193
Sturges, John 45
Styne, Jule 86, 193
"subway dress" 26, 117–119
"Sugar Blues" 143
Sullivan, KT 87
The Sun 155
Sun Valley, Idaho 95, 121, 125
Sunday Times Magazine 142
Sundberg, Clinton 51
Susie-Q Ranch 124
Sutton, Grady 171
"Sweet Georgia Brown" 143
Sydney Morning Herald 138

Tamblyn, Russ 51
Taradash, Daniel 70
Tashlin, Frank 38
Taubman, Howard 170
Taylor, Dwight 68
Taylor, Elizabeth 128, 167–168, 174
Taylor, Frank E. 158, 164
Technicolor 21, 41, 81, 83, 85, 90, 95, 100, 131, 179, 183
The Telegraph 33, 136
"That Old Black Magic" 121, 129
There's No Business Like Show Business 1, 21, 105, **106**, 107, **108**, 109–112
"There's No Business Like Show Business" (song) 105, 107
36 Sutton Place South, Sutton Place, Manhattan 95

www.ingramcontent.com/pod-product-compliance
Ingram Content Group UK Ltd.
Pitfield, Milton Keynes, MK11 3LW, UK
UKHW050509130925
2927IPUK00016B/80